TASCHEN

KÖLN LONDON MADRID NEW YORK PARIS TOKYO

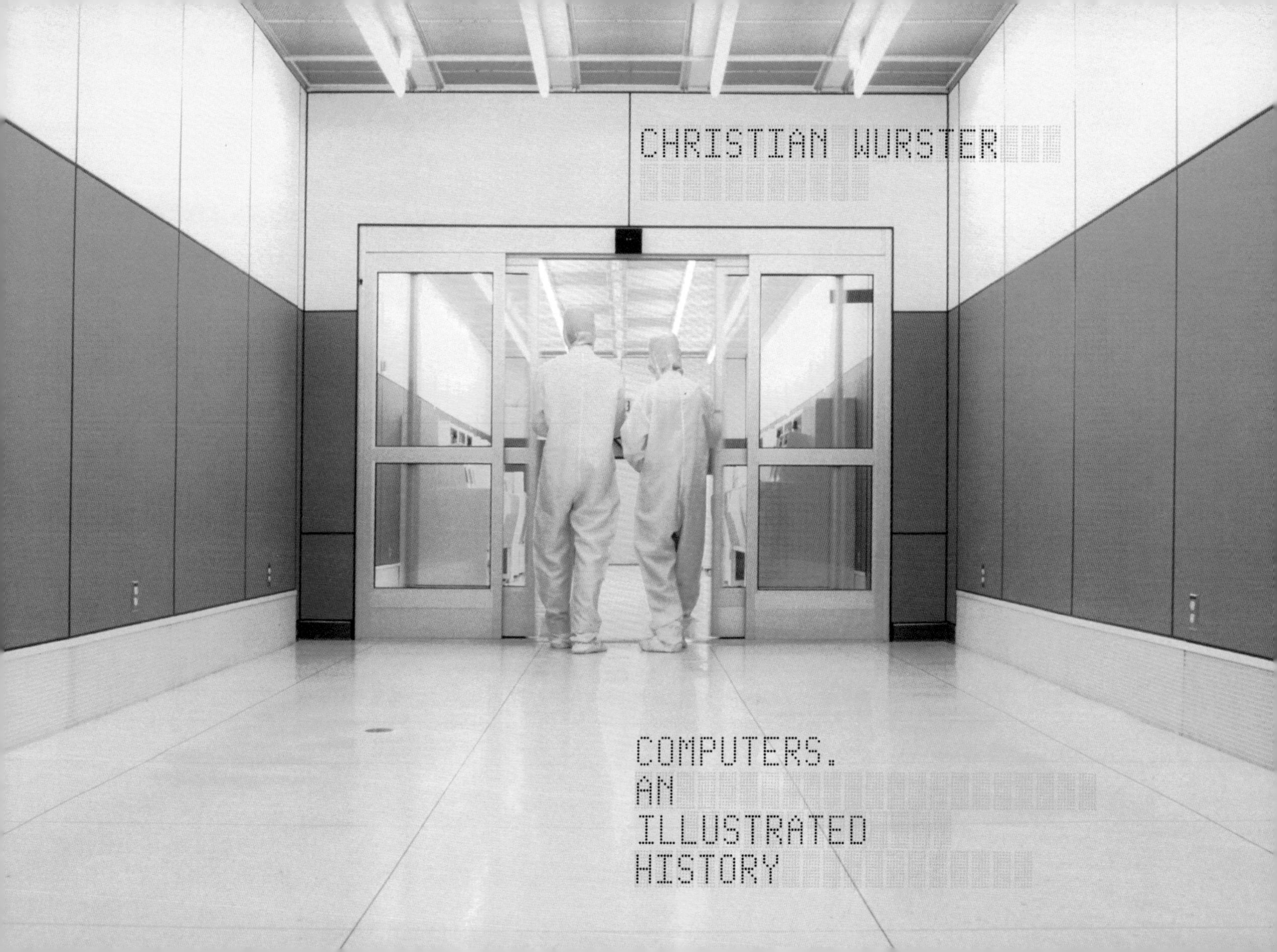

CHRISTIAN WURSTER

COMPUTERS. AN ILLUSTRATED HISTORY

CONTENTS

0.0 MAN / MACHINE / INTERFACE 006

1.0 THE SCIENTIFIC AND MILITARY COMPUTERS 016
2.0 THE MAINFRAME COMPUTER 042
3.0 THE MINICOMPUTER 104
4.0 THE MICROCOMPUTER 130
5.0 THE DESKTOP COMPUTER 222
6.0 CONVERGENCE AND VOLATILISATION 272

I PERSONS / COMPANIES / COMPUTERS 298
II BIBLIOGRAPHY 324
III PHOTO CREDITS 325
IV INDEX 326

0.0

MAN / MACHINE / INTERFACE

P. 1: ILLUSTRATION FROM AN ADVERTISEMENT FOR REMINGTON RAND & UNIVAC. **1955**
P. 2: HEWLETT PACKARD'S FIRST HEADQUARTERS: A GARAGE IN PALO ALTO, CALIFORNIA
P. 3: HIGH-TECH WORKERS ENTERING A CLEAN ROOM
P. 4: THE MATRIX. **ANDY** AND **LARRY WACHOWSKI** USA **1999**

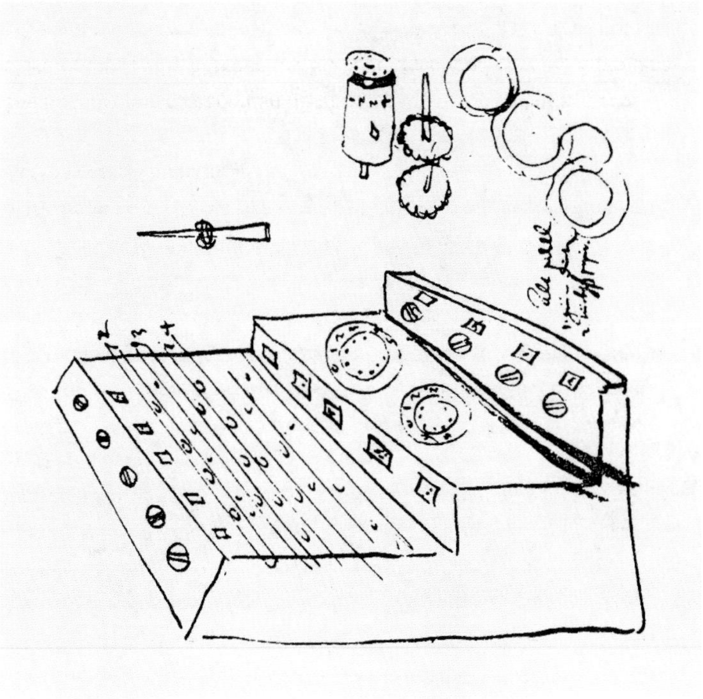

SCHICKARD'S SKETCH FOR A CALCULATING MACHINE. **1623**

0.1 THE PRE-HISTORY OF COMPUTERS

The term computer – from Latin *computare*, to calculate – is first recorded in 1646, used by Sir Thomas Browne to mean someone who performs the calculations needed to draw up a calendar. That is the meaning it retained until well into the 1930s: a person with mathematical training who was employed by an engineering firm or observatory to perform calculations with the aid of tables, had the title "the computer".

In 1820 the English inventor and mathematician Charles Babbage designed his Difference Engine to calculate mathematical functions and print them in the form of tables. This new technology was intended to replace the manually prepared tables, which were an important aid for scientists and engineers but suffered from numerous calculation and typesetting errors – the number only increasing as they were copied and reprinted.

In 1834 Babbage had the idea for a programmable calculating machine, which he named the Analytical Engine. For input and output of data, he made use of the perforated cards invented by the French engineer Jacques de Vaucanson. The prototypes included a 'mill' (arithmetic unit) and a 100-digit store for intermediate values. Even though Babbage never completed his machine, partly because of the difficulty of financing the work but mainly because he kept changing the design to incorporate new ideas, his theoretical approach possessed all the main elements of present-day computers. The Analytical Engine can therefore be seen as the first-ever design for a digital calculator and the forerunner of the computer.

Any attempt to define the starting point in the history of the computer is bound to be a controversial matter. On the one hand there are different ways of defining a computer. On the other hand we cannot escape the fact that inventions are cumulative: the individual contributions of many different people came together in the course of the development of the computer. Nevertheless, the successive steps from the abstract to the concrete, carried out by Leibniz, Babbage, Turing, Zuse, and von Neumann, were preceded by fundamental intellectual and technical developments, which have probably been best expressed by Zimmerli and Wolf as three parallel threads: formalisation, 'mathematisation', and mechanisation.

The origin of formalisation can be seen as the philosophical approach of formal logic, in particular the branch known as Aristotelian syllogistics. In the fourth century BC, Aristotle formulated various rules of logical combination by which two premisses that are related in a certain way lead to a formally correct conclusion – regardless of the content of the statements themselves. If the premisses are true, then the conclusion must also be true.

The history of calculation can be traced back to the writings of Herodotus in the fifth century BC, who described how the Egyptians added numbers by means of pebbles. The word *calculus* (Latin for pebble) is used to mean any system for obtaining particular figures

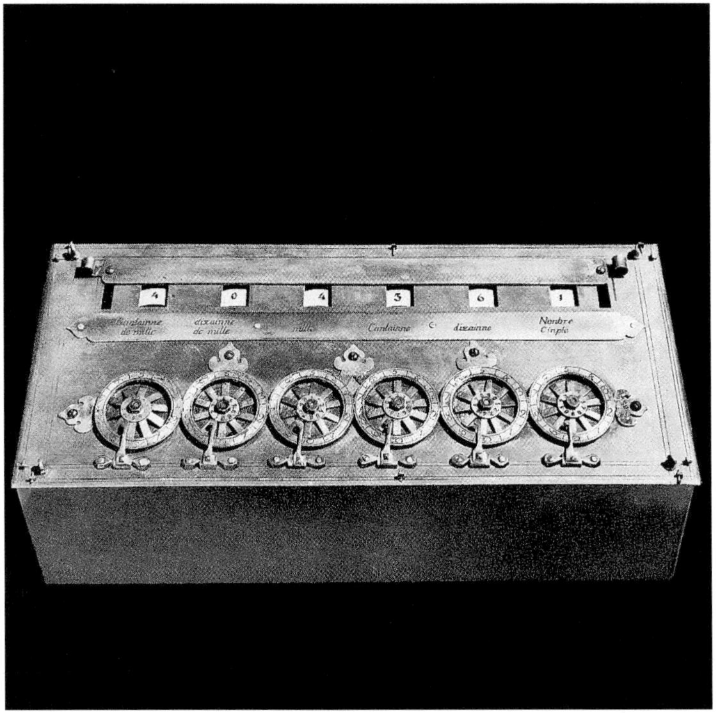

BLAISE PASCAL'S CALCULATOR, THE 'PASCALINE'. **1642**

THE 'DIFFERENCE ENGINE' BY CHARLES BABBAGE. **1820**

from other figures by applying particular rules. Again it is the form of the figures that counts, not their meaning. Calculating with numbers – and as a later refinement the use of algorithms – was thus the first calculus, or 'mathematisation', in this sense. In this context we should also mention the abacus, probably the first calculating machine ever.

The origins of complex mechanical developments can also be traced back to Herodotus, who reported on the engines of war known by the Romans as *mechanai*. Mechanisation means nothing more than replacing or magnifying muscle power (human or animal) by mechanical power of any kind. The wheel, the lever, and the pulley are classic examples of the mechanical principles involved. Though they were suitable for various tasks, the modus operandi of these early "machines" was clearly delimited; it is obvious at a glance how they are operated.

Mechanisation took a major leap when people succeeded in building machines which made muscle power superfluous, or which derived their own power from natural sources. Examples of that are the first water-wheels, windmills, and simple steam-powered machines.

But the final triumphal march did not come until the advent of the craft of precision mechanics in the 17th century. Outstanding examples of its ascendancy are the highly complicated French clocks and watches, or automata of the same period made by de Vaucanson and others. The watchmaker's craft provided the basis for the calculating machines which soon followed. The computer's earliest recognizable forerunners were, for example, the calculating machine made by the mathematician and astronomer Wilhelm Schickard of Tübingen in 1623, the 'Pascaline' by Blaise Pascal in 1642, or the stepped cylinder devised in 1673 by the German universal genius Gottfried Wilhelm von Leibniz – his was the first machine that could multiply and divide as well as add and subtract. Leibniz saw routine calculations as "undignified", and wished for a "living abacus", which he then set about to implement in the form of this and later machines.

James Watt's improved steam engine of 1769 is an important milestone in the history of mechanisation, and at the same time represents the birth of automation: its far-reaching effects marked the start of the Industrial Revolution and a new chapter in the history of mankind. Although the technical basis had existed for several hundred years, the quantum leap came with the automation that made the operator redundant. Watt's invention within an invention was the centrifugal or "flying-ball" governor, which increased or reduced the amount of steam entering the cylinder, depending on the power required. This was the first time that a machine was able to control itself.

The idea of a programmable machine that can carry out not just one task, but a whole sequence of instructions, goes back to Joseph-Marie Jacquard's automatic loom from 1805. This machine was able to weave the most complicated patterns from a large number of different coloured yarns.

IN 1886 THE 26-YEAR-OLD HERMANN HOLLERITH INVENTED A MACHINE THAT COULD COUNT OVER TWICE AS FAST AS A HUMAN: IT OPERATED ELECTROMECHANICALLY WITH THE AID OF PUNCHED CARDS. THIS ILLUSTRATION SHOWS THE BOOKKEEPING DEPARTMENT OF A LARGE BERLIN COMPANY USING HOLLERITH PUNCHED CARDS. **1928**

To control the sheds and shuttles, Jacquard made use of an earlier invention by his countryman Jacques de Vaucanson: the perforated card. This machine was able to read the pattern from the two states 'hole' and 'not hole' in the succession of cards, and to reproduce that pattern of colours of its own accord. In a sense, Jacquard's loom was a kind of early digital graphics computer. Instead of the need for a person to operate various knobs, handles, and cranks in a particular sequence, a mechanism had now been created that made it possible for the machine, in effect, to operate the controls itself. It no longer had to wait for a human to give the next command. By creating a 'program' in

DATA TYPISTS. CIRCA **1920**

EMPLOYEES IN A PUNCHED-CARD RECORDS OFFICE. CIRCA **1925**

AN OFFICE IN THE EARLY 20TH CENTURY

advance, the human formulated complex tasks for the machine as a succession of simple steps. That also made it possible to adapt the same machine to different tasks.

The real achievement of de Vaucanson and Jacquard was therefore a successful implementation of the idea of being able to interact with a machine by means of an early form of machine language. The punched card later achieved its breakthrough when Hermann Hollerith, a German émigré to the USA, used electricity to analyse the data contained in the cards. This was applied with pioneering success to the US census of 1890.

The idea of a freely programmable machine took shape with Charles Babbage. His Analytical Engine (of which the 'mill' was finally completed by his son in 1906), also used punched cards to feed different calculation programs into the machine. The Analytical Engine thus combined, for the first time, the concepts of mathematisation and automation – a combination that was to have enhanced possibilities.

Every further development in the field of mechanisation and automation also increased the complexity of the machines; control and monitoring devices were thus required to use the improved performance and options to best advantage. The designers were also faced with the need

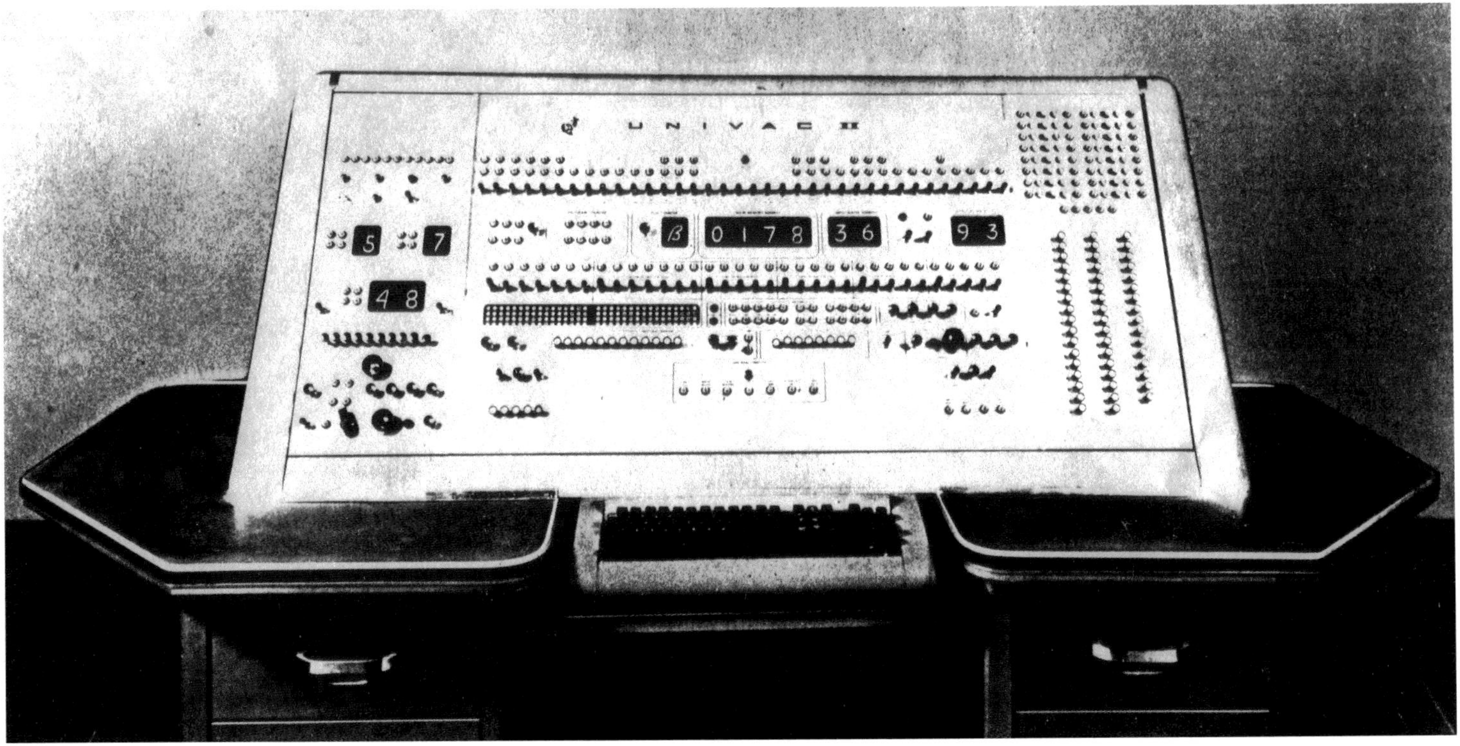

ALL THE IMPORTANT FUNCTIONS OF THE COMPUTER WERE COLLECTED TOGETHER ON THE OPERATOR CONSOLE OF THIS UNIVAC. THE UNIVAC, BUILT BY REMINGTON RAND, WAS THE FIRST SERIES-PRODUCED COMPUTER. **1951**

to arrange the growing number of levers, switches, knobs, and indicators sensibly, and above all, clearly. The purposeful relationship of controls and indicators to one another was the start of what we now call a user interface.

Of course, the physical interface between man and machine had always existed implicitly – for example, the handle of a hammer – but its explicit design now became an important criterion for the quality of the increasingly complicated tools.

Like all other mechanical aids devised by man, the computer is a tool intended to make life easier and more worth living. Unlike most tools, however, it is not designed for just one purpose or a few related purposes, but is a machine that, in Alan Turing's words, "is capable of simulating any other machine". Computers are thus universal machines, in the sense that they can do anything which can be described in mathematical terms.

This explains why the user interface, the meeting point between the human and the computer, is so important. As the point of access to the hardware, the operating system, and the applications software, the interface fulfils two fundamental roles: it makes it possible to specify tasks that the computer is to perform, and it allows us to receive the computer's solutions and results. It is therefore a basic function of the interface to allow interaction: to set up a means of communication between the machine and its user.

In line with continually changing technology, and the computer's altering roles and tasks, the interface has also had to change its nature over the years; the story of the interface can therefore be told only in conjunction with the history of the computer. For that reason, this book takes a special look at the machines which shaped each phase of development; also at the question of what tasks could be solved by which groups of users with what technical means and ideas.

1.0 THE SCIENTIFIC AND MILITARY COMPUTERS

"EVERYTHING THAT CAN BE INVENTED HAS BEEN INVENTED."

CHARLES DUELL, U.S. OFFICE OF PATENTS, 1899

1.1 THE Z3

The inspiration to build a computer came to Konrad Zuse of Berlin when he found himself faced with repetitive calculations in the course of his work as a civil engineer. He had the choice of spending hours on the tedious statics calculations or contracting out the work to one of the many calculation bureaus that could be found in any large city in those days. In 1934 he started on the design of a calculating machine that he

CABLES CONNECTING THE CONTACTS IN THE STORE OF A RECONSTRUCTED Z3

hoped later to produce in large numbers and sell to other consulting engineers. By 1938 he had constructed the first prototype, which he called the V1 (V for Versuch = experimental) but later renamed the Z1. Although it was primarily intended for calculations, there were indications that he was already thinking of other kinds of data processing. In the very first paragraph of his patent application we read: “In the present invention these switching elements are combined to form a storage device in which any desired data, for example numbers, can be held. [...] They can also be used to store other data, e. g. instructions for other machines (switching commands), combinations of letters (e. g. telegraph messages), decoded letters (cipher machine), or similar.”

In 1941 Zuse then completed his Z3, now considered the first fully-functional, program-controlled, and freely programmable computer anywhere in the world. The arithmetic unit and store were constructed from 2,200 telephone relays, which the inventor’s years of experiments had shown to be particularly reliable. The Z3 read its instructions – the program – from holes punched into 35-mm film, while the data were entered on a numeric keypad. The results could then be read out on a row of tiny lamps.

1.2 THE HARVARD MARK I

Three years later, on the other side of the Atlantic, scientists at Harvard University switched on their five-ton monster, 17 metres long, the Automatic Sequence-Controlled Calculator, otherwise known as the Harvard Mark I. Although it needed almost a second for a simple addition, and twelve times as long for a division, in America it was hailed as a triumphal success and the first computer.

The Mark I consisted of 750,000 electromechanical parts and was equipped with several devices for input and output of data. The values to be worked on were read in by a punched-card reader, and the results put out on a card punch. The computer was programmed by inserting wire links in a plugboard: the instructions were thus ‘written’ straight into the store in machine code. Machine code is the oldest means of interaction between man and computer: thus the point of contact – the interface with the user – was originally right inside the computer and on the computer’s own terms.

1.3 THE ENIAC AND EDVAC

Two publications dating from 1945 have made computer history, one from a technological point of view, the other conceptual.

In his paper *First draft of a report on the EDVAC*, the American mathematician John von Neumann formulated the structure of future computers by means of their functional components: arithmetic unit, control unit, store ('memory'), and input/output units. The layout became known as von-Neumann architecture, and has remained valid until this day.

Vannevar Bush, who had directed and coordinated all American research activities during the war, predicted a great future for the computer in his article *As we may think*: "Machines with interchangeable parts can now be constructed with great economy of effort. In spite of much complexity, they perform reliably. Witness the humble typewriter, or the movie camera, or the automobile. Electrical contacts have ceased to stick when thoroughly understood. Note the automatic telephone exchange, which has hundreds of thousands of such contacts, and yet is reliable. A spider web of metal, sealed in a thin glass container, a wire heated to a brilliant glow, in short, the thermionic tube of radio sets, is made by the hundred million, tossed about in packages, plugged into sockets – and it works! Its gossamer parts, the precise location and alignment involved in its construction, would have occupied a master craftsman of the guild for months; now it is built for thirty cents. The world has arrived at an age of cheap complex devices of great reliability; and something is bound to come of it."

THE HARVARD MARK I WAS THE FIRST COMPUTER IN NORTH AMERICA. CONSISTING OF SOME 750,000 ELECTROMECHANICAL PARTS, IT REQUIRED ROUGHLY A SECOND FOR A SIMPLE ADDITION. **1949**

The American government quickly recognised the enormous possibilities of computer technology, and commissioned a new digital computer with the name Electronic Numerical Integrator and Calculator, or ENIAC for short. This machine was intended to carry out ballistic calculations for

CABINETS AND PUNCHED-TAPE READER OF THE HARVARD MARK I. **IBM** USA **1944**

the US Army and work out the optimum configuration for bombing missions.

The ENIAC was completed in 1946 by the scientists Presper Eckert and John Mauchly; it was the first computer to use the improved vacuum tubes rather than electromechanical relays. Its signals took the form of pulses, making it roughly 1000 times faster than the Mark I. However, it stood nearly three metres high, occupied a room about 300 square metres in size, and needed frequent maintenance: the vacuum tubes were still very prone to failure and had to be replaced every two or three days.

The programs were entered in segments by means of plugboards and banks of switches. Each of the 6,000 switches was set by the 'ENIAC girls'; the machine calculated for a while and then came to a halt. Then the next segment of program was entered and the ENIAC continued operating on the intermediate results it had stored.

John von Neumann, who was in charge of building a hydrogen bomb for the US government in New Mexico, decided to check the feasibility of such a bomb on a modified ENIAC. The EDVAC (Electronic Discrete-Variable Automatic Computer) was the first in America in which the program could be read in from previously punched cards, one card for each instruction. This finally put an end to the time-consuming and error-

THE WHIRLWIND COMPUTER ASSISTED THE US MILITARY IN ITS SURVEILLANCE OF AMERICAN AIRSPACE: ALL THE RADAR STATIONS WERE CONTROLLED BY IT. IT WAS THE FIRST COMPUTER TO POSSESS A GRAPHICS INPUT/OUTPUT UNIT IN THE FORM OF A CIRCULAR CRT SCREEN AND A LIGHT PEN. **1952**

prone replugging and setting of switches that were needed for the Mark I and the ENIAC.

Von Neumann's calculations required a million punched cards, each card (data record) representing a single point mass in the bomb. The output records occupied a further million punched cards.

The work of entering individual computer 'words' in machine code had previously involved the physical act of inserting a plug or setting a switch; with the punched card, programming a computer now acquired a new dimension and a new interface by means of which the user could interact with the calculation – though still with a time delay.

1.4 THE WHIRLWIND

In 1951 a team of scientists at the Lincoln Laboratory in Cambridge, Massachusetts, completed the Whirlwind computer with a completely new and pioneering operator concept. The Lincoln Laboratory was the successor to the Radar Laboratory, a top secret American military research establishment from the days of the Second World War; as part of the SAGE project, up to 4,000 people were employed there on new technologies for displaying information and on human factors within the 'man/machine system'.

The objective of SAGE (Semi-Automatic Ground Environment) was to link together all the radar stations around the USA, analyse their signals, and if necessary guide fighter aircraft or missiles to intercept intruders. It was designed as a closed system in which the human components were fully integrated in the mechanised cycle of detection, decision and reaction.

The Whirlwind was the first computer with a graphics interface – albeit a very primitive one. Data output took place on a round cathode ray tube similar to that of a radar screen. With the aid of a light pen, developed at the Lincoln Laboratory in 1949, it was possible to point to symbols displayed on the screen and thus enter them in the computer.

A VIEW OF THE LARGE CABINETS OF THE WHIRLWIND COMPUTER. THE STORE USED MAGNETIC CORES, WHICH HAD PROVED CONSIDERABLY MORE RELIABLE THAN VACUUM TUBES OR MERCURY DELAY LINES. **1952**

In order to be able to display the movements of a possible opponent in a sensible way, the scientists had developed not only their own hardware but also – and almost as a by-product – a computer graphics system. The Whirlwind CRTs displayed the first-ever graphical symbols on a screen: the letters T for target and F for fighter. If a T symbol was selected on the screen with the light pen, the computer-controlled radar system started tracking the aircraft with a view to interception. SAGE, which was to remain in use until the mid-1980s, was therefore the first historic example of an interface in which the user interacts with a computer in real time by means of graphics.

In those days computers were so rare and so expensive that it seemed highly unlikely that they could bring about any economic impetus, still less social changes. Above all, it was the US military, the customer with the greatest funds at its disposal, that encouraged the development of computers with its huge demand for computing power. However, it was to be many years before the forward-looking operating principles and technologies resulting from military research were to become real products that shaped the relationship between humans and computers.

The only people with access to a computer were highly specialised mathematicians and scientists who designed programs and entered them on the plugboards, prepared the data, monitored the computing process, and then analysed the results of the calculations.

1.5 PLUGGING, SWITCHING, PUNCHING

The interface between the user and their computer consisted of numerous physical connections that had to be altered each time a new program was run. The interface was inside the computer; in effect, it was the computer. Soon toggle switches replaced the tangle of wires on the plugboard, which greatly simplified the job of entering programs. The interface for data input consisted of punched cards or paper tape, the same media often being used for output after the (possibly lengthy) calculation. Cards and paper tape were later used for the programs as well.

Plugging, switching, and punching were the physical modes of interaction of the early hardware-oriented man/machine interfaces. Furthermore, the human had to adapt himself to the needs and quirks of the machine.

THE ELECTRONIC NUMERICAL INTEGRATOR AND COMPUTER (ENIAC) COULD MULTIPLY 2000 TIMES FASTER THAN THE MARK I, BUT TOOK UP 140 SQUARE METRES OF FLOOR SPACE. THIS ILLUSTRATION SHOWS IT BEING PROGRAMMED IN 'BANKS': EACH CONNECTION HAD TO BE SET UP MANUALLY, USING SWITCHES OR PLUGBOARDS. USA **1946**

REPLUGGING THE CONNECTIONS ON THE ENIAC. USA **1946**

CONTROL DESK AND PLUGBOARDS OF THE BRITISH 'COLOSSUS' COMPUTER, WHICH WAS USED TO CRACK THE GERMAN 'ENIGMA' ENCRYPTION MACHINES IN THE SECOND WORLD WAR. THE COLOSSUS CONTAINED 2500 VACUUM TUBES AND COULD PROCESS UP TO 5000 CHARACTERS A SECOND. HOWEVER, IT WAS NOT FREELY PROGRAMMABLE, SINCE THE DECRYPTION ALGORITHM WAS HARD-WIRED INTO IT; IT WAS THEREFORE A SPECIAL-PURPOSE COMPUTER. **1944**

EMPLOYEES OF THE US BUREAU OF STANDARDS COMPARING THE PRINTOUTS AND SWITCH SETTINGS OF THEIR 'HIGH-SPEED' COMPUTER. **1950**

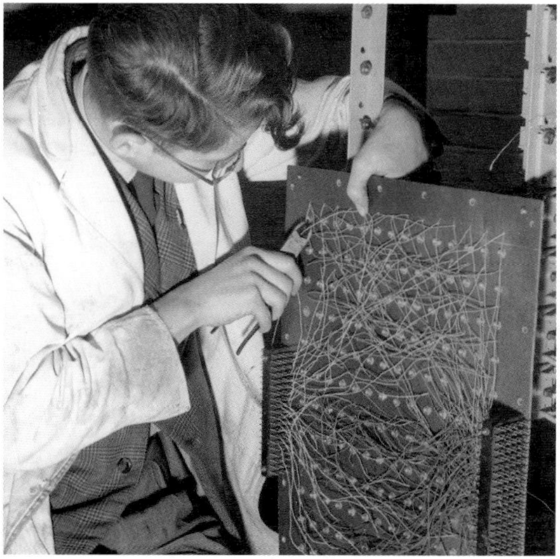

A SCIENTIST MODIFYING THE CABLE CONNECTIONS IN THE MULTIPLICATION UNIT OF THE AMERICAN ACE COMPUTER, SO AS TO FORMULATE A NEW CALCULATION. **1946**

A SWISS SCIENTIST ENTERING MATHEMATICAL EQUATIONS ON THE OPERATING CONSOLE OF HIS COMPUTER. **1949**

OPERATING CONSOLE AND FRONT PANEL OF A SCIENTIFIC COMPUTER IN THE UKRAINE. **1958**

REPLUGGING THE STORE CONNECTIONS OF A CHINESE SCIENTIFIC COMPUTER. **1949**

A FEW MEMBERS OF THE 4000-MAN SAGE TEAM WATCHING OVER AMERICAN AIRSPACE ON THEIR CRT SCREENS AND ANALYSING ALL THE SIGNALS IN ORDER TO BE ABLE TO DIRECT DEFENCE WEAPONS AGAINST AN ENEMY INTRUDER. **1955**

A MEMBER OF THE SAGE PROGRAMME IDENTIFYING AN AIRCRAFT ON HIS SCREEN WITH THE AID OF THE LIGHT PEN. **1955**

ZUSE Z4

EMIL ZOPFI

PROGRESS LAY DORMANT IN A SHED IN SOUTHERN BAVARIA. ITS CREATOR KEPT HIMSELF AND HIS YOUNG FAMILY ALIVE WITH ODD JOBS, PAINTED PICTURES OF CHAMOIS ON PIECES OF WOOD AS SOUVENIRS FOR THE AMERICAN TROOPS, AND IN BETWEEN DEVELOPED A LANGUAGE FOR PROGRAMMING AUTOMATIC CALCULATORS. THE WAR WAS OVER, GERMANY WAS IN RUINS, BUT KONRAD ZUSE'S Z4 HAD SURVIVED TO RISE LIKE A PHOENIX FROM THE ASHES. THE HISTORY OF THIS MACHINE IS MORE EXCITING THAN ANY ADVENTURE STORY.

IT STARTS IN BERLIN IN THE MID-1930S; THE PROTAGONIST IS A YOUNG CIVIL ENGINEER WHO HAS TAKEN IT INTO HIS HEAD TO BUILD "PROGRAM-CONTROLLED CALCULATING MACHINES" BECAUSE AS HE LATER SAID HE WAS "TOO LAZY TO KEEP MAKING ALL THOSE STATICS CALCULATIONS". WHILE STILL LIVING WITH HIS PARENTS HE CONSTRUCTED THE Z1, A MECHANICAL CONTRAPTION THAT NEVER WORKED RELIABLY. A FEW YEARS LATER HE WAS ABLE TO DEMONSTRATE THE Z3 TO A HANDFUL OF PEOPLE AT THE GERMAN AVIATION RESEARCH ESTABLISHMENT. THIS WAS AN ELECTROMECHANICAL MACHINE SOLDERED TOGETHER FROM SCRAP RELAYS AND TELEPHONE UNISELECTORS; THE PROGRAM WAS PUNCHED IN ROLLS OF USED 35-MM FILM. THE DATE, 12 MAY 1941, COUNTS AS THE BIRTH OF THE COMPUTER; ITS FATHER WAS KONRAD ZUSE. OFFICIALLY, HE WAS STILL EMPLOYED AS AN ENGINEER AT THE HENSCHEL AIRCRAFT WORKS, BUT ON THE SIDE HE WAS IN THE PROCESS OF SETTING UP HIS OWN COMPANY: ZUSE ENGINEERING WORKS AND CONSULTANCY, BERLIN.

FROM 1942 ON, ZUSE DEVELOPED THE Z4, A SYNTHESIS OF THE Z1 AND THE Z3. IT WAS ELECTROMECHANICAL, WITH THE FOUR BASIC OPERATIONS HARD-WIRED, AS WERE SQUARES AND SQUARE ROOTS, ALL USING 32-BIT BINARY FLOATING-POINT ARITHMETIC. AN ADDITION TOOK HALF A SECOND. ZUSE'S PROCESSOR ARCHITECTURE WAS YEARS AHEAD OF INTERNATIONAL DEVELOPMENTS, ALTHOUGH OF COURSE DURING THE WAR HE HAD NO CONTACT WITH OTHER COUNTRIES. HIS MECHANICAL STORE FOR 64 32-BIT

NUMBERS WAS A MASTERPIECE OF CRAFTSMANSHIP, WITH EACH OF THE 2048 BITS REPRESENTED BY A TINY PIN AND LATCH. PROGRAM CONTROL WAS BY MEANS OF TWO PUNCHED-TAPE READERS, ONE FOR THE MAIN PROGRAM AND THE OTHER FOR SUBROUTINES; LATER HE INCORPORATED CONDITIONAL JUMPS. FOR THE OPERATOR, THERE WAS A CONSOLE WITH NUMEROUS SWITCHES AND LAMPS.

THEN BOMBS FELL ON BERLIN; THE Z1 AND Z3 WERE BURIED UNDER THE RUBBLE. IN A BASEMENT ROOM, ZUSE AND ABOUT 20 ASSISTANTS DOGGEDLY CONTINUED WORKING ON THE Z4. IN THE LAST FEW DAYS BEFORE THE CITY FELL TO THE RUSSIANS, ZUSE MANAGED TO LOAD THE MACHINE ONTO A RAILWAY TRUCK AND ESCAPE TO THE SOUTH WITH HIS WIFE AND EMPLOYEES. FOR THE TIME BEING, NOBODY WAS INTERESTED IN THE MASS OF WIRES AND SWITCHES AND SURPLUS TELEPHONE RELAYS IN THE GARDEN SHED. IN HOPFERAU, NEAR FÜSSEN, WHERE ZUSE AND HIS FAMILY MOVED TO IN 1946, HE DEMONSTRATED THE Z4 TO THE ASTONISHED VILLAGERS. THE "COMPUTER CENTRE" WAS AT THE BACK OF A FORMER HITLER YOUTH BUILDING. "WE FOUND THE WHOLE THING TOTALLY CONFUSING", A NEIGHBOUR LATER RECALLED; "BUT ZUSE WAS CONVINCED THAT THE MACHINE WOULD ONE DAY CALCULATE ANYTHING YOU COULD POSSIBLY WANT IT TO."

ONE DAY IN 1949 A SMART CAR WITH SWISS NUMBER PLATES DROVE UP, AND A GENTLEMAN CLIMBED OUT. PROFESSOR EDUARD STIEFEL WAS THE HEAD OF THE NEWLY FOUNDED FACULTY OF APPLIED MATHEMATICS AT THE SWISS POLYTECHNIC (ETH) IN ZURICH, AND HAD GOT WIND OF THE CALCULATING MACHINE. HE DICTATED A DIFFERENTIAL EQUATION. ZUSE PUNCHED A PROGRAM IN A ROLL OF FILM AND PLACED IT IN THE READER; THE Z4 CLATTERED AWAY FOR A WHILE, AND CAME UP WITH THE RIGHT ANSWER. PROGRESS AGAIN SAW THE LIGHT OF DAY.

THE ETH OFFERED TO LEASE THE MACHINE FOR FIVE YEARS AT A PRICE OF 30,000 SWISS FRANCS. ZUSE FOUND PREMISES FOR HIS COMPANY IN NEUKIRCHEN, NEAR KASSEL, AND COMPLETELY OVERHAULED THE Z4; SIX MONTHS LATER IT TRAVELLED TO ZURICH. A HUNDRED GUESTS HAD ASSEMBLED FOR THE INAUGURAL CEREMONY, BUT SHORTLY BEFORE THE DEMONSTRATION, THE Z4 REBELLED: SPARKS FLEW, AND THERE WAS A

SMELL OF BURNING. THIS WAS THE INVENTOR´S GREAT MOMENT! ZUSE HAD ALWAYS BEEN A PRACTICAL MAN; HE ROLLED UP HIS SLEEVES AND SET TO WITH THE SOLDERING IRON. THE DEMONSTRATION WAS A SUCCESS.

MANY A NIGHT HE SPENT UNDER THE DOMED ROOF OF THE ETH LISTENING TO THE FAMILIAR CLATTER FROM HIS COMPUTER. THE Z4 WORKED RELIABLY IN ZURICH, CALCULATING THE FLUTTER OF JET AIRCRAFT WINGS, THE GRAND DIXENCE DAM, CRITICAL TURBINE SPEEDS, PROBLEMS IN OPTICS, AND MUCH MORE BESIDES. ZUSE, WITH A TYPICAL BERLIN SENSE OF HUMOUR, WROTE IN HIS MEMOIRS: "SO SLEEPY ZURICH FINALLY ACQUIRED A NIGHT LIFE, ALBEIT A MODEST ONE, IN THE FORM OF THE CLATTERING Z4".

AMBROS SPEISER, A YOUNG ELECTRICAL ENGINEER, WAS RESPONSIBLE FOR OPERATING THE COMPUTER. AS HE RECALLS, "THE Z4 WAS INTERACTIVE IN THE FULL SENSE OF THE WORD. THE MATHEMATICIANS COULD SEE THE INTERMEDIATE RESULTS; YOU COULD HEAR THE CALCULATION PROCEEDING IN THE RELAY CABINETS, SO YOU KNEW HOW IT WAS GETTING ALONG AND COULD INTERVENE IF NECESSARY."

THE Z4 NOW STANDS IN THE DEUTSCHES MUSEUM IN MUNICH. THE 2200 RELAYS AND 21 STEPPER SWITCHES, THE MECHANICAL SWITCHING DEVICES, THE TAPE READERS AND THE ELECTRIC TYPEWRITER ARE NOW QUIET, YET STILL THEY TELL THE STORY OF A GREAT IDEA.

2.0 THE MAINFRAME COMPUTER

"I THINK THERE IS A WOLRD MARKET
FOR MAYBE 5 COMPUTERS."

THOMAS WATSON, CHAIRMAN OF IBM, 1943

THE UNIVAC 1 WAS THE FIRST COMPUTER PRODUCED IN SUFFICIENT NUMBERS THAT IT COULD BE BOUGHT BY COMPANIES AND NON-GOVERNMENT INSTITUTIONS. THIS ILLUSTRATION SHOWS ITS OPERATING CONSOLE WITH CABINETS IN THE BACKGROUND AND SEVERAL MAGNETIC TAPE UNITS. **REMINGTON RAND** USA **1957**

2.1 THE UNIVAC

In the early 1950s the mainframe computer took its first slow and ponderous steps on the road to success. The new vacuum tubes that were now used instead of relays were not only many times faster than electromagnetic components but also lighter and more compact. As a result, the size and price of digital computers could be reduced significantly; all these factors had a favourable effect on the numbers of computers produced in the years that followed.

The market for these monsters – for that is what they were – was still very small in those days. By 1951 J. Presper Eckert and John W. Mauchly, who a few years earlier had designed the Mark I, were with the Remington Rand company and brought out the first commercial computer in America, the UNIVAC whose name stood for Universal Automatic Computer.

Some of the UNIVAC's design features seem strange from a present-day point of view. The storage system, which could hold 1000 words of 12 alphanumeric symbols, consisted of vacuum tubes and acoustic delay lines: each contained a tube of mercury with a piezo-electric crystal at each end. When a voltage was applied to one of the crystals it sent out mechanical oscillations which travelled the length of the tube before being converted back into an electrical signal by the crystal at the other end.

The UNIVAC had a front panel on which electrical connections could be made by means of a plugboard, and several magnetic tape units representing a new data storage system. Its price was considerable: half a million US dollars for the basic version, with a further $185,000 for the "high-speed" printer. The first computer was supplied to the US Census Bureau.

For many years the UNIVAC shaped the public image of what a computer should look like and how it should function. It acquired its fame not least through a spectacular television appearance in the 1952 presidential election. CBS used it to predict the winner from a sample of votes cast, broadcasting the results live on election day. When the computer forecast a landslide victory for Eisenhower, even though his rival Stevenson had led in all the polls, CBS got cold feet and manipulated the results, saying Eisenhower was expected to win by a close margin. In fact the UNIVAC turned out to be right, and Eisenhower had a clear lead. CBS later admitted that they should have placed more trust in the computer, which, of course, was excellent publicity for the UNIVAC.

OPERATING THE UNIVAC 1. **REMINGTON RAND** USA **1952**

IBM'S FIRST COMMERCIAL MAINFRAME COMPUTER: THE MODEL 701. **IBM** USA **1952**

2.2 IBM ENTERS THE ARENA

IBM (International Business Machines) announced its first commercial vacuum-tube computer in 1952: the Model 701, otherwise known as the Defense Calculator. IBM was then the world's largest manufacturer of Hollerith punched-card equipment for bookkeeping applications; though the company had been involved in developing the Harvard Mark I, it started building its own computers relatively late because it felt they posed a threat to its main line of business.

The 701 could execute 17,000 instructions per second, a remarkable speed for those days. The first customers were the US Government and several major research establishments that wished to automate their calculations. But soon the large corporations were also starting to order computers to replace the labour-intensive punched-card equipment they had been using for their accounts and payroll calculations.

The first commercial application programs were installed in the early 1950s in the customers' newly set-up computer centres, by an army of specialists sent out into the field by the few computer manufacturers then in existence. The programs were tailor-made for each company, the instructions entered line by line on punched cards. In the early years IBM derived considerable benefit from its leading position in the punched-card business. For a start it was familiar to every large American corporation; as the founder of mechanised data processing it also possessed know-how that stood the company in good stead when it entered the computer business. By 1956, 76 IBM Model 701 mainframe computers had been installed in North America, compared to 46 of the competitor UNIVAC.

That year IBM announced RAMAC (random-access method of accounting and control), the first magnetic disk system for computers, which played a pioneer role in data storage. The system could rapidly read or write any desired record on any of its 50 rotating disks representing a total capacity of five megabytes. It thus replaced the awkward punched cards and paper tape; and John von Neumann's principle of data and programs held in the computer could now become practical reality.

A year later, in 1957, IBM brought out FORTRAN (short for Formula Translator), a programming language based on algebraic expressions and mathematical formulae. Thanks to its simple structure, FORTRAN soon became the most popular language for mathematical and technical applications.

OPERATING CONSOLE OF THE IBM MODEL 704. **IBM** USA **1955**

OPERATING CONSOLE OF THE IBM MODEL 702. **IBM** USA **1953**

THE IBM 705 WAS SPECIALLY DESIGNED FOR COMMERCIAL APPLICATIONS, AND INCLUDED VARIOUS INPUT AND OUTPUT DEVICES AS WELL AS A LINE PRINTER. VISIBLE IN THE BACKGROUND ARE NUMEROUS MAGNETIC TAPE STORAGE UNITS, WHICH WERE SOON TO BE REPLACED BY THE NEW RAMAC TECHNOLOGY

2.3 ASCII

Until the early 1960s there was no sign of any uniform standards in computing; besides IBM and Remington Rand, manufacturers in Britain, France, Germany, and the Netherlands were selling vacuum-tube computers of all performance categories. Mainframe computers were complete solutions, and static in the sense that after being installed at the customer's premises they could be neither modified nor significantly extended. Each model represented its own standard. Software and operating systems that could be 'ported' to other machines did not exist.

Each type of computer also had its own format for data storage and transmission, making communication between different models practically impossible. In 1963 the American Standard Code for Information Exchange (ASCII) was introduced, so as to enable exchange of data between computers of different manufacturers. In the ASCII standard all the digits, upper-case and lower-case letters, and various symbols and control codes are assigned numerical values between 0 and 127 (later extended to 255), each with a fixed meaning.

In 1964 IBM revolutionised the computer market with its System/360, consisting of six processing units of differing performance and 40 associated peripheral units. This was the first computer 'family' and became a world-wide standard for mainframe computers, largely on account of the 'unbundling' strategy.

By unbundling, IBM meant its completely new policy of selling computers and peripherals separately. At the same time, the units could be connected together in any desired configuration: they were 'intercompatible'. The flexibility of this modular system allowed IBM to gain long-term customer loyalty: for example, the processor unit could simply be replaced if more computing power was needed.

The high development costs of about 5 billion dollars soon paid off, when the number of orders rose to over a thousand a month. System/360 was so successful that other manufacturers started building computers and peripherals to the same standard (IBM was again able to set industry standards some twenty years later when it entered the PC market). System/360 was to dominate electronic data processing well into the 1970s.

In this chapter of computer history the mainframe computer was used largely for scientific research and large-scale industrial applications. But computers also started to take over calculation and control functions in space exploration, atomic power stations, and major airports. Banks installed them, and they were used in industry to automate business applications that had traditionally been carried out with the aid of punched-card technology: stock control, bookkeeping, invoicing, and order processing. Soon one could detect signs of a slow penetration of society by the computer.

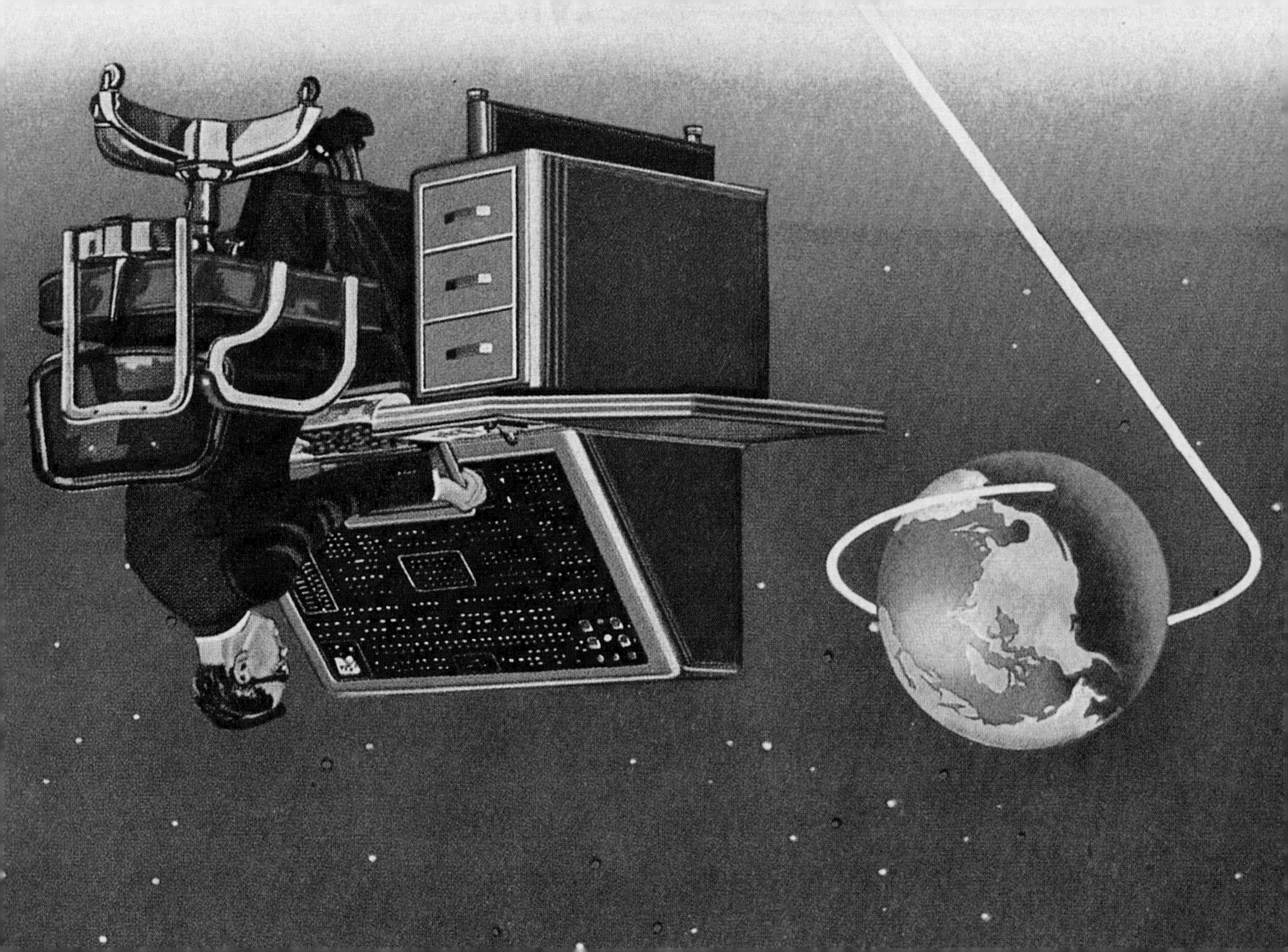

Remington Rand
Univac Electronic Computer

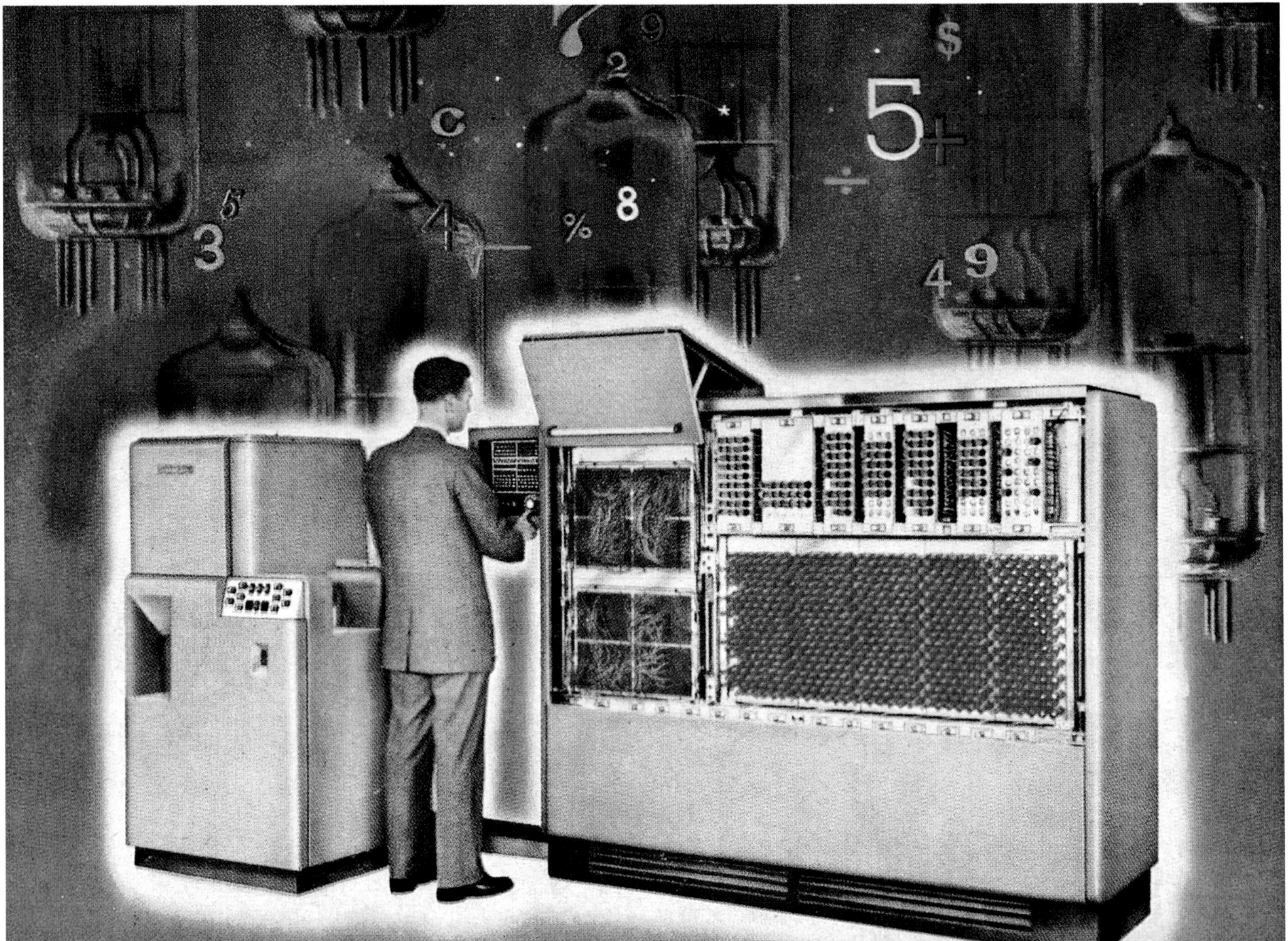

ILLUSTRATION FROM AN ADVERTISEMENT FOR REMINGTON RAND & UNIVAC. **1955**

<< ILLUSTRATION FROM AN ADVERTISEMENT FOR STEEL & UNIVAC. **1950s**
<<< CBS NEWSREADER WALTER CRONKITE COVERING THE US PRESIDENTIAL ELECTION IN 1952. THE UNIVAC THAT WAS ANALYSING THE RESULTS PREDICTED EISENHOWER'S VICTORY, TO EVERYONE'S SURPRISE AND CONTRARY TO ALL FORECASTS BASED ON OPINION POLLS. **1952**

IBM HARDDRIVE SYSTEM RAMAC. **1952**

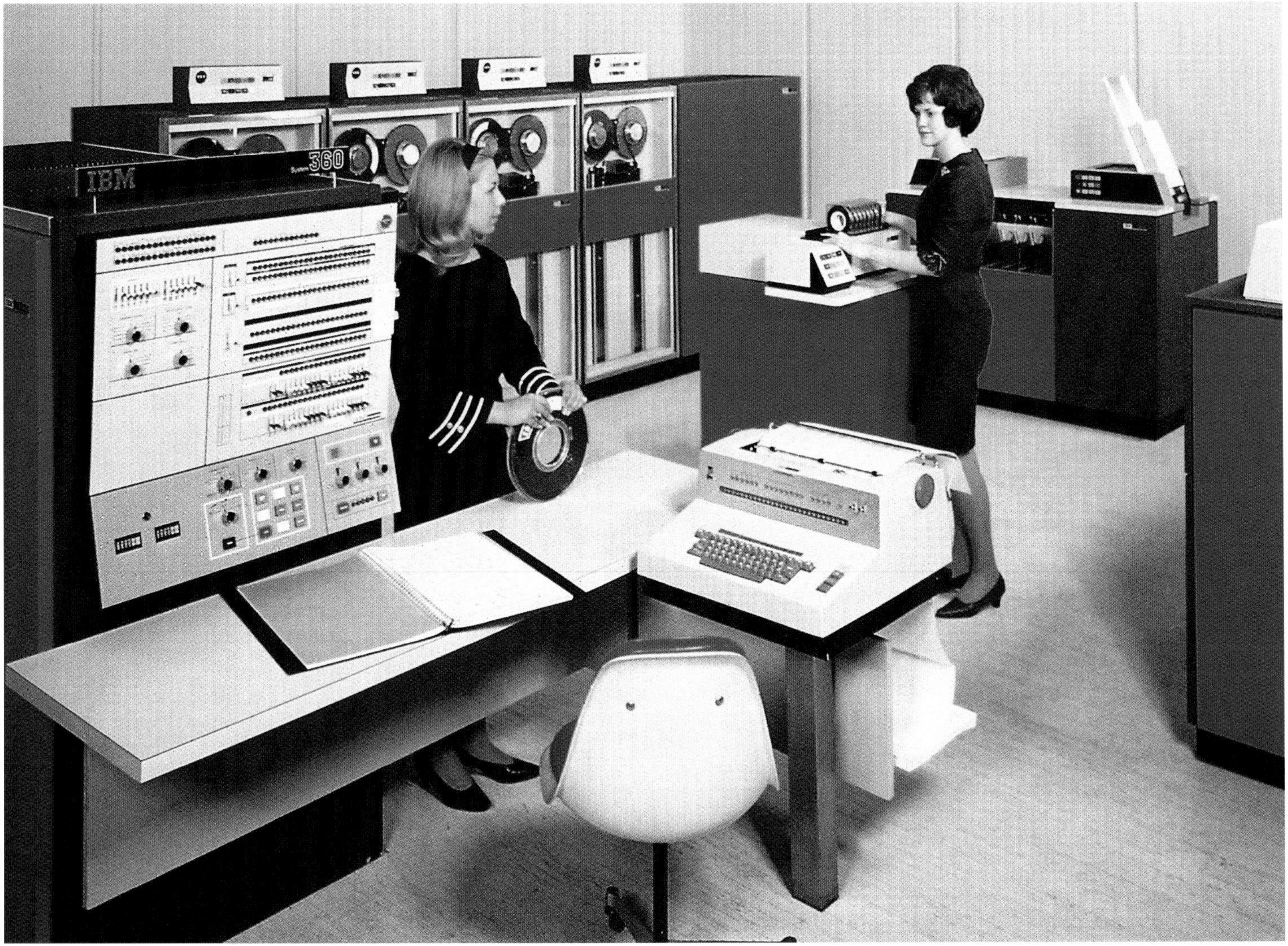
IBM
System 360

These systems were still far removed from the desk-top computer we have come to take for granted. Computers were physically separated from the offices of the people who used their services. In effect, they had a place of work of their own, in the form of a sterile air-conditioned computer centre. However, the front panel, as the interface between the computer and its operators, now developed into a rather more clearly laid-out console. This control desk, often several metres away from the computer cabinets themselves, contained all the input/output devices – switches and push-buttons, tape punch and teletypewriter – making the console the first universal man/machine interface.

Private, or personal computing, was still undreamed-of in the 1950s and 1960s, even if Vannevar Bush had described – as early as 1945 – a device that understood and typed spoken words. His special utopian vision was that one day the computer would act as a kind of mechanical extension to the human brain and its ability to make associations.

In spite of its limitations, the mainframe showed promise for further development. In 1964, Martin Greenberger posed the question of the future of the computer in the magazine *Atlantic Monthly*, stating almost clairvoyantly, "By achieving reliability along with capability, computers have won broad commercial acceptance. But what of the future? What can we expect as computers enter their third decade? Some conservatives have been predicting a deceleration of computer growth for at least five years now. Is there a plateau just over the horizon? Not if a recent turn in computer research is as significant as many of us believe it to be. General economic and political conditions permitting, this work will nourish a new wave of computer expansion. Computing services and establishments will begin to spread throughout every sector of American life, reaching into homes, offices, classrooms, laboratories, factories, and businesses of all kinds."

THE IBM STRETCH, THE DIRECT COMPETITOR OF THE UNIVAC LARC, SET NEW STANDARDS FOR PROCESSOR SPEED. SPECIALLY DESIGNED FOR SCIENTIFIC CALCULATIONS IN THE FIELD OF NUCLEAR PHYSICS, IT WAS ABOUT 100 TIMES FASTER THAN THE MODEL 704. THIS ILLUSTRATION SHOWS AN INSTALLATION AT THE RESEARCH LABORATORY OF THE ATOMIC ENERGY AUTHORITY IN LOS ALAMOS, NEW MEXICO. **IBM** USA **1961**

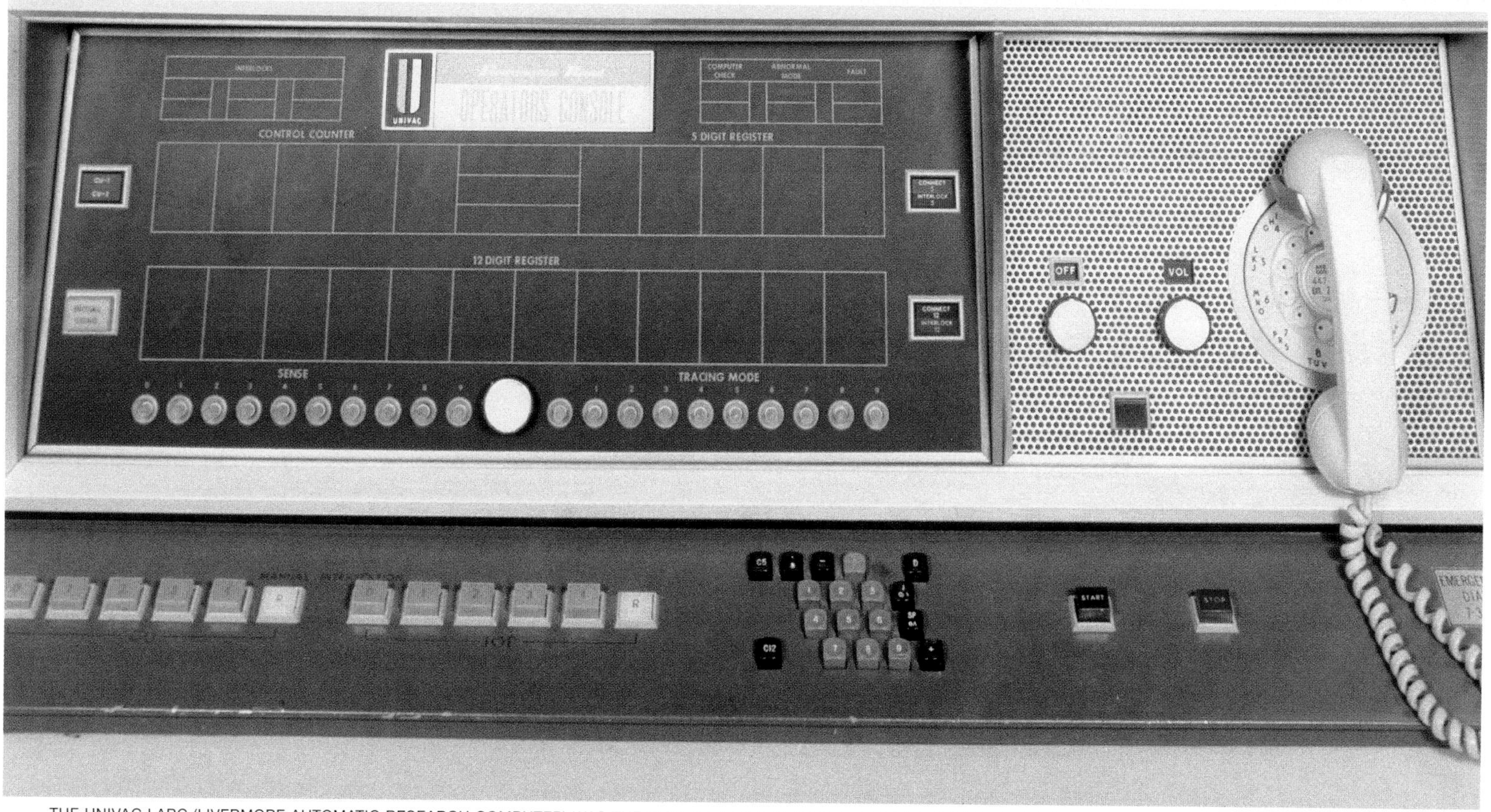

THE UNIVAC LARC (LIVERMORE AUTOMATIC RESEARCH COMPUTER) WAS THE WORLD'S FIRST MULTIPROCESSOR COMPUTER. ALONGSIDE THE IBM STRETCH, IT CAN BE REGARDED AS THE PROTOTYPE FOR THE LATER SUPERCOMPUTERS. IT ACQUIRED ITS NAME FROM THE FIRST CUSTOMER, THE LAWRENCE LIVERMORE LABORATORY IN CALIFORNIA, WHICH TOGETHER WITH LOS ALAMOS WAS CARRYING OUT RESEARCH INTO ATOMIC WEAPONS AND ENERGY. **REMINGTON RAND** USA **1960**

‹‹ THE SYSTEM/360 WAS NOT SIMPLY A COMPUTER BUT A WHOLE FAMILY OF COMPUTERS. IT PERMITTED ALMOST ANY IMAGINABLE CONFIGURATION, AND SO USHERED IN A NEW ERA IN COMPUTER HISTORY, DURING WHICH IBM ROSE TO BECOME THE ABSOLUTE MARKET LEADER. **IBM** USA **1964**

COMPUTER CENTRE WITH A UNIVAC 490 INSTALLATION. **REMINGTON RAND** USA **1961**

COMPUTER CENTRE WITH A UNIVAC III INSTALLATION. **REMINGTON RAND** USA **1962**

MICHAEL CAINE IN THE THRILLER “BILLION DOLLAR BRAIN” BY **KEN RUSSELL** GREAT BRITAIN **1967**

DORIS DAY AND RAY WALSTON IN THE COMEDY "CAPRICE" BY **FRANK TASHLIN** USA **1967**

YURI YARVET IN THE SCIENCE FICTION FILM "SOLARIS" BY **ANDREJ TARKOVSKY** USSR **1972**

THIS SYSTEM/360 MODEL 75, SHOWN AT THE APOLLO GROUND STATION IN GREENBELT, MARYLAND, CONTROLLED THE COURSE AND LUNAR ORBIT OF THE APOLLO 12 SPACECRAFT. IT HAD A CONSTANT NETWORK CONNECTION TO FIVE ADDITIONAL COMPUTERS LOCATED AT THE JOHNSON SPACE CENTER IN HOUSTON, TEXAS, AND WAS USED TO CALCULATE THE EFFECTS OF POSSIBLE COURSE CHANGES. **IBM** USA **1969**

THE MODEL 91 WAS THE MOST HIGHLY DEVELOPED COMPUTER OF THE SYSTEM/360 FAMILY, AND WAS EMPLOYED TO TACKLE THE MOST CHALLENGING SCIENTIFIC CALCULATIONS IN SPACE AND AVIATION, PLASMA PHYSICS, AND CHEMISTRY. **IBM** USA **1967**

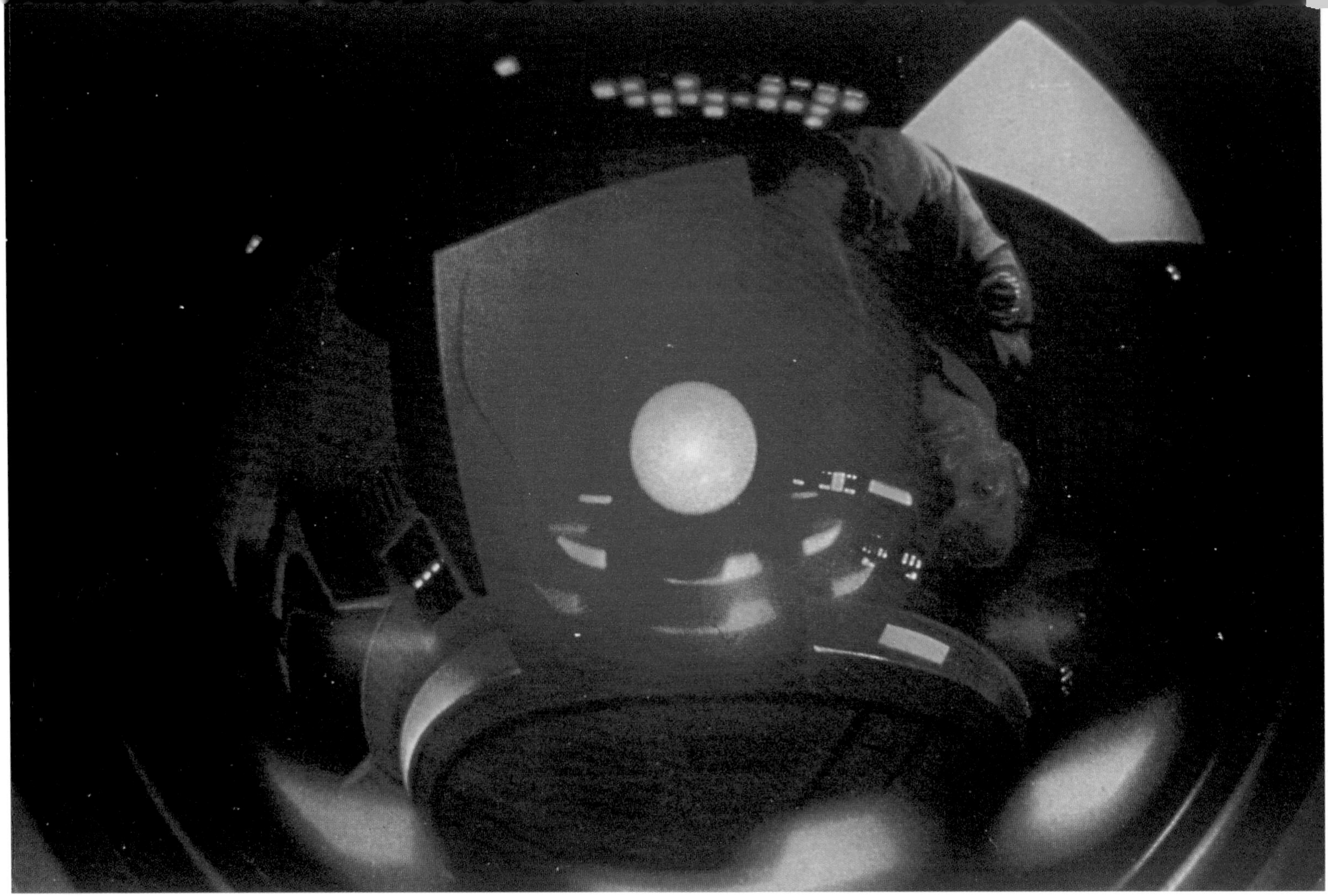

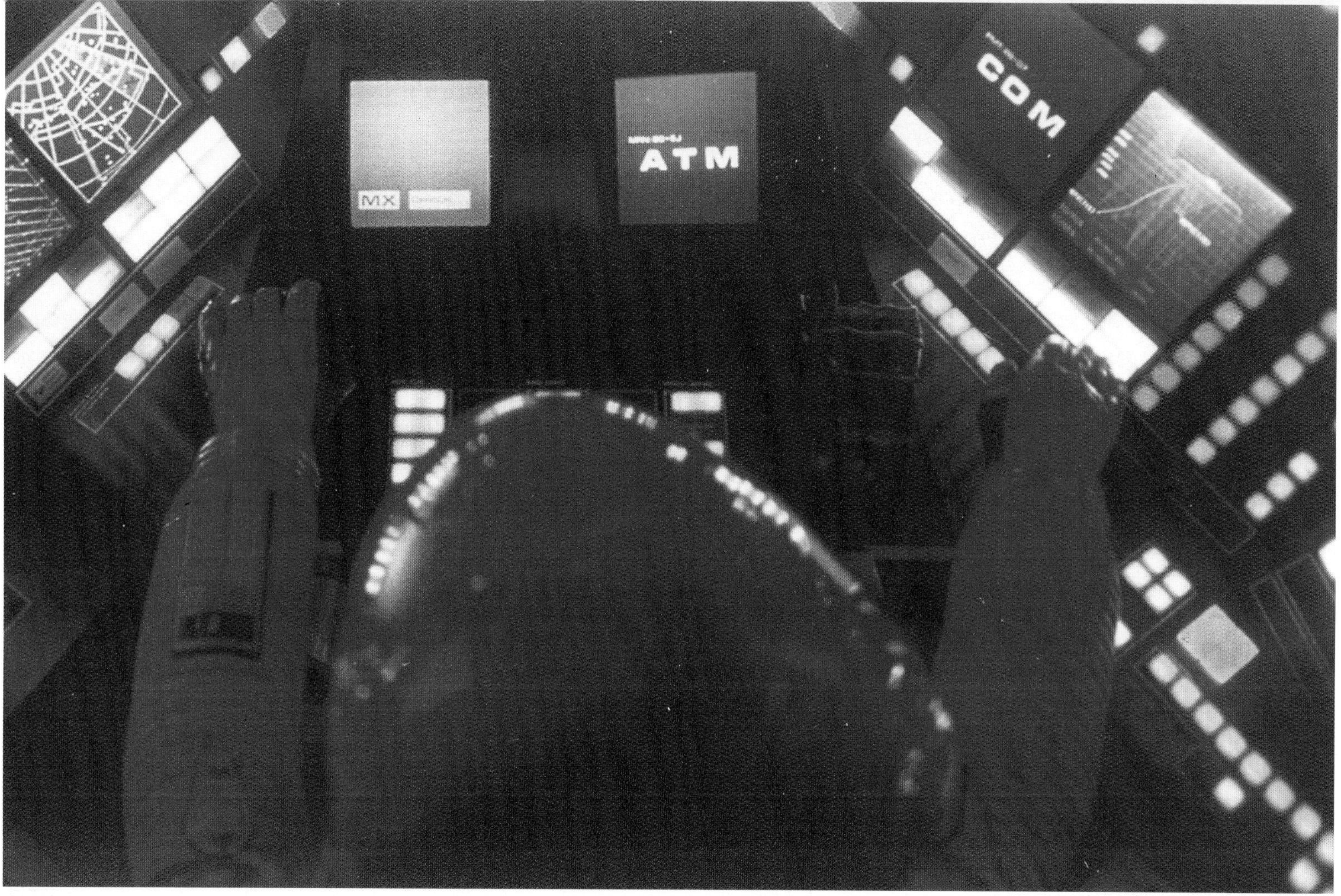

"EYE" (ABOVE) AND REMOTE CONTROL DEVICE (BOTTOM) OF THE HAL 9000, THE ON-BOARD COMPUTER FROM THE FILM "2001 – A SPACE ODYSSEE". COINCIDENCE? THE LETTERS H-A-L COME RIGHT BEFORE I-B-M IN THE ALPHABET, BUT HEURISTIC ALGORITHMIC IS A PROGRAMMING METHOD. **STANLEY KUBRICK** GREAT BRITAIN/USA **1968**

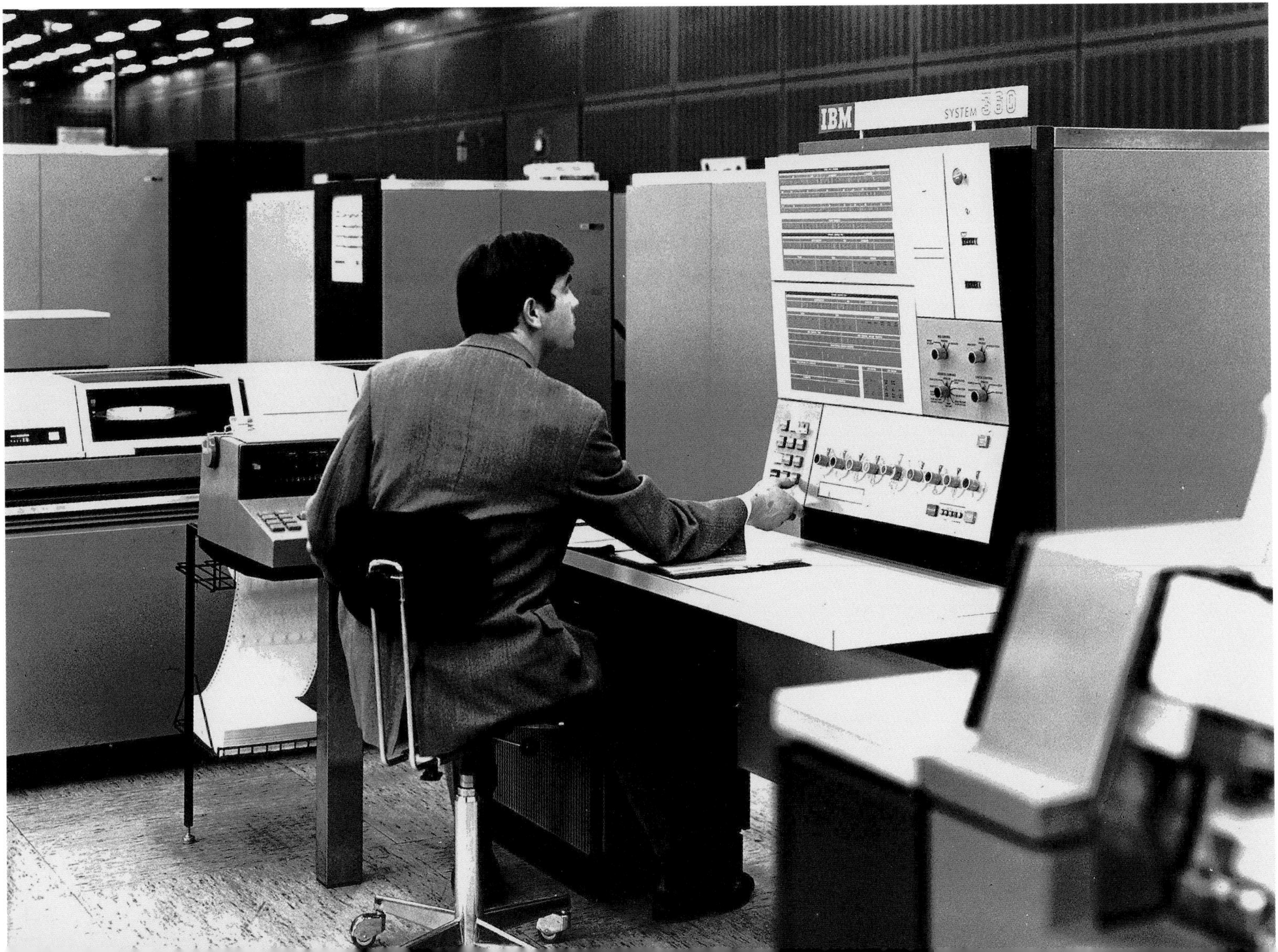
IBM
SYSTEM 360

IBM/360

EMIL ZOPFI

IT WAS LIKE RUNNING UP A POWER STATION. THE FALSE FLOOR OF THE COMPUTER CENTRE SHOOK, FANS HUMMED AND CHURNED UP THE AIR, MAGNETIC DISKS SANG OUT A TOP C. I PRESSED A BUTTON MARKED IPL: INITIAL PROGRAM LOAD. THE OPERATING SYSTEM LIFTED OFF, MYRIADS OF LITTLE LIGHTS DANCED, AND THE CONSOLE TYPEWRITER RATTLED OUT A CRYPTIC CODE. HASTILY I PILED THE PUNCHED CARDS ONTO THE RAILS OF THE HOPPER, AND THEY DISAPPEARED WITH A RATTER-TATTER INTO THE BOWELS OF THE BLUE METAL CASE, TO BE SPEWED OUT SHORTLY AFTERWARDS INTO THE STACKER. I FOLLOWED THEM WITH OTHER DECKS OF CARDS, RED, GREEN, AND BLUE: JOB-CONTROL LANGUAGE, PROGRAM, DATA. WHEN THE LINE PRINTER BEGAN HAMMERING OUT A PROGRAM LISTING AND ANY ERROR MESSAGES ON THE ZEBRA-STRIPED FAN-FOLD PAPER, WITH ITS CHARACTERISTIC VIBRATO SCREECH, I SANK BACK EXHAUSTED INTO A CHAIR. AN HOUR OF COMPUTER TIME ON THE IBM/360, NOW THAT WAS REAL COMPUTING!

IBM HAD ANNOUNCED ITS SYSTEM/360 ON 7 APRIL 1964, WORLD-WIDE, SIX DIFFERENT MODELS WITH DIFFERING PERFORMANCE, FROM THE 360-30 WITH 64 KILOBYTES OF MAIN STORE AND A CLOCK FREQUENCY OF NEARLY A MEGAHERTZ, ALL THE WAY TO THE 360-75 WITH 512 KILOBYTES AND 5 MEGAHERTZ. IT WAS THE BIRTH OF THE 8-BIT BYTE: THE PROCESSOR AND STORAGE MODULES WERE STRUCTURED THAT WAY, WHICH WAS EQUALLY SUITABLE FOR CHARACTERS, DECIMAL ARITHMETIC, BINARY, OR FLOATING-POINT CALCULATIONS. IT WAS POSSIBLE TO ADDRESS THE STUPENDOUS AMOUNT OF 24 MEGABYTES - THOUGH ONLY IN THEORY, BECAUSE THE MAXIMUM AVAILABLE AMOUNT OF MAGNETIC CORE STORE WAS 512 KILOBYTES.

"THE EVENT MARKED THE END OF THE PIONEER DAYS OF ELECTRONIC DATA PROCESSING", WROTE A FORMER EMPLOYEE OF IBM GERMANY IN AN APPRECIATION ON THE OCCASION OF THE 25TH ANNIVERSARY OF THE /360. BEFORE THAT, EVERY SYSTEM HAD BEEN A NEW CREATION WITH ITS OWN SYSTEM STRUCTURE, PERIPHERALS, AND SOFTWARE. IBM ALONE MAINTAINED SIX DIFFERENT PRODUCT FAMILIES; THE APPLICATIONS HAD TO BE REPROGRAMMED IF A CUSTOMER CHANGED SYSTEMS. NOW AN END WAS TO BE PUT TO THIS CONFUSION.

IBM DOMINATED 65% OF THE MARKET, AND WITH THE SYSTEM/360 ARCHITECTURE IT DICTATED AN INDUSTRIAL STANDARD THAT WAS FOLLOWED BY 80 TO 90% OF ALL MANUFACTURERS. IBM'S CLAIM TO BE ABLE TO SOLVE EVERY IMAGINABLE COMPUTING TASK WITH JUST ONE ARCHITECTURE WAS EXPRESSED BY THE LOGO, A COMPASS CARD. THE MAGIC NUMBER 360 STOOD FOR THE DEGREES IN A FULL CIRCLE.

THE TERM „ARCHITECTURE" WAS A NEW ONE IN THE COMPUTER BUSINESS. IT WAS UNDERSTOOD TO MEAN A FUNCTIONAL SPECIFICATION, RELEVANT TO ALL APPLICATIONS, THAT THE USER COULD CONSIDER FIXED, WHILE „DESIGN" AND „TECHNICAL IMPLEMENTATION" COULD BE MATCHED TO CURRENT TECHNOLOGY. THE GOAL WAS A CLEAR DISTINCTION BETWEEN LOGICAL AND PHYSICAL STRUCTURE. SYSTEM/360 WAS NOT YET BASED ON ICS, BUT USED HYBRID CIRCUITRY: TRANSISTORS, DIODES, RESISTORS AND CAPACITORS WERE GLUED TO CERAMIC SUBSTRATES AND CONNECTED USING THICK-FILM TECHNOLOGY.

FROM 1961 ONWARD TOM WATSON JUNIOR, THE CHAIRMAN OF IBM AND SON OF THE FOUNDER, HAD SPURRED HIS „LAME DUCKS", AS HE CALLED HIS CONSERVATIVE DEVELOPMENT ENGINEERS, TO A MAJOR EFFORT UNDER THE CODE NAME 'SPREAD'. BY THE END, THE LARGEST INDUSTRIAL DEVELOPMENT PROJECT IN HISTORY HAD COST TWICE AS MUCH AS THE MANHATTAN PROJECT FOR BUILDING THE ATOMIC BOMB. SIX FACTORIES WERE BUILT SPECIALLY, INCLUDING ONE EACH IN GERMANY AND FRANCE, AND 50,000 PEOPLE WERE EMPLOYED TO BUILD COMPUTERS ON PRODUCTION LINES FOR THE FIRST TIME. THE BUSINESS MAGAZINE *FORTUNE* DESCRIBED THE PROJECT AS „IBM'S FIVE BILLION DOLLAR GAMBLE", FOR THAT WAS THE STAKE: 5 BILLION DOLLARS.

THEY WERE PLAYING WITH MARKED CARDS, TOO. WHEN THE TIME CAME FOR ANNOUNCING THE /360, IT WAS BY NO MEANS READY. BUT WATSON HAD GOT WIND OF THE FACT THAT THE LITTLE CONTROL DATA CORPORATION HAD DEVELOPED ITS CDC 6600, THE LARGEST AND FASTEST COMPUTER IN THE WORLD, AND THAT WITH A TEAM OF ONLY 34 PEOPLE. THE COMPUTER WAS IN DIRECT COMPETITION TO THE TOP MODEL IN THE /360 RANGE, WHICH AS YET EXISTED ONLY ON PAPER.

THE IBM PROPAGANDA MACHINE WENT INTO ACTION, AND THE CUSTOMERS PUT THEIR FAITH IN IT AND THE COMPANY'S AURA. CDC SUFFERED BADLY, AND SUED IBM FOR UNFAIR BUSINESS PRACTICES IN ANNOUNCING "PHANTOM" COMPUTERS. THE CASE WAS SETTLED OUT OF COURT IN 1973: IBM CEDED TO CDC A SUBSIDIARY THAT OPERATED COMPUTING BUREAUS, AND MADE A FURTHER CASH PAYMENT OF $100 MILLION. PEANUTS FOR THE GIANT IBM, WHICH BY THEN WAS ALREADY PRODUCING THE FOLLOW-ON SYSTEM/370.

PARADOXICALLY, IBM'S SUCCESS WAS ALMOST ITS UNDOING, FOR IT EMBODIED THE CLASSIC CONCEPT OF CENTRALISED DATA PROCESSING. DURING THE 1980S THE USERS SWITCHED MORE AND MORE TO DISTRIBUTED SYSTEMS: PERSONAL COMPUTERS AND NETWORKED COMPUTING. AS IS NOW COMMON KNOWLEDGE, IBM SUCCEEDED IN ENTERING THIS MARKET JUST IN TIME, WITH A GOOD DEAL OF HELP FROM MICROSOFT.

WE CAN STILL REMEMBER THE SOLIDUS OR SLASH, THE "MARK OF NOBILITY" AS THE IBM HISTORIAN STEPHANIE SAND CALLED IT. IT CAN BE FOUND, FOR EXAMPLE, IN THE NAME OF THE OS/2 OPERATING SYSTEM FOR PCS. ITS ANCESTOR FROM THE 1960S, OS/360, WAS THEN THE MOST COMPLEX SOFTWARE EVER WRITTEN, WITH A MILLION LINES OF PROGRAM CODE. IT WAS RUMOURED THAT IT ALSO CONTAINED A STEADY THOUSAND PROGRAMMING FAULTS: FOR EVERY "BUG" THAT WAS FIXED, A NEW ONE WAS INCORPORATED OR CAME TO LIGHT. THE IBM/360 HELD A FURTHER SECRET. BESIDES THE MANY LAMPS AND SWITCHES AND BUTTONS, ON THE FRONT PANEL WAS A RED MUSHROOM THAT NOBODY COULD FAIL TO NOTICE. IT BORE THE LEGEND EMERGENCY SWITCH, BUT IT WAS DRUMMED INTO US ON THE TRAINING COURSE THAT IT WAS TO BE USED ONLY IN AN EXTREME EMERGENCY, FOR EXAMPLE WHEN SMOKE WAS ALREADY BILLOWING FROM THE CABINETS. NOBODY EVER FOUND OUT WHAT HAPPENED IF THIS PANIC BRAKE WAS ACTIVATED.

WIPING THE SWEAT FROM MY BROW, RELIEVED, I PILED MY BOXES OF PUNCHED CARDS, PACKET OF FAN-FOLD PAPER, DISK PACK AND MAGNETIC TAPES ONTO A TROLLEY AT THE END OF MY FIRST SESSION WITH THE /360. I STRAIGHTENED MY TIE; EVERYTHING HAD GONE ACCORDING TO PLAN, AND THE MACHINE HAD NOT GONE UP IN FLAMES. MY INITIATION CEREMONY OVER, I WAS NOW PART OF THE FAMILY.

FASHION SHOTS BY THE GERMAN CLOTHING COMPANY BLEYLE IN FRONT OF A SYSTEM/360. **IBM** GERMANY **1965**

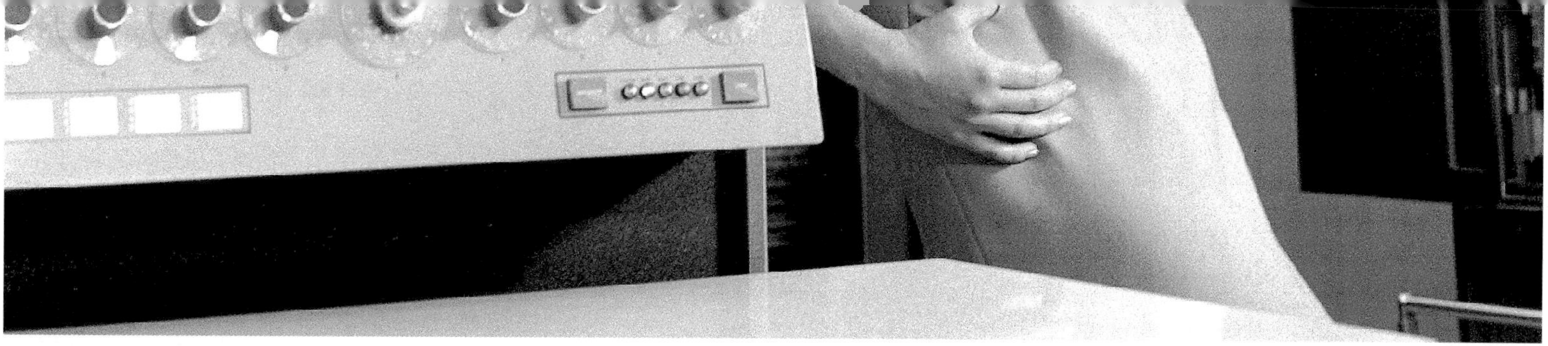

SYSTEM

360

SYSTEM/370 (SUCCESSORS TO THE SUCCESSFUL SYSTEM/360) MODEL 135. **IBM** GERMANY **1971**

SYSTEM/370 MODEL 148. **IBM** GERMANY **1973**

Burroughs
JENNY"B"

ILLUSTRATIONS FROM VARIOUS COMPUTER ADVERTISEMENTS BY BURROUGHS, WHICH MERGED WITH SPERRY RAND TO FORM UNISYS IN 1986. **BURROUGHS** USA **1964**

6
IBM 729
2
Umformer B

ABOVE AND PREVIOUS PAGES: VIEW INSIDE THE COMPUTER CENTRE OF THE GERMAN CHEMICAL GIANT BASF. **BASF** GERMANY **1965**

AS A RESULT OF NUMEROUS TECHNOLOGY EMBARGOES BY THE WEST, THE COMMUNIST BLOC IN EASTERN EUROPE WAS FORCED TO DEVELOP ITS OWN COMPUTER TECHNOLOGY. IT IS NOT HARD TO SEE THAT THIS EAST GERMAN EC 2640 MAINFRAME COMPUTER WAS A STRAIGHT COPY OF THE IBM SYSTEM/360, WHICH IT WAS ALSO COMPATIBLE WITH. **ROBOTRON** EAST GERMANY **1964**

SYSTEM/370 MODEL 115 (ABOVE) AND A COMPLETE MODEL 168 INSTALLATION (BELOW). **IBM** GERMANY **1973**

IT WAS THE WORLD'S FIRST SUPERCOMPUTER: THE CDC 6600, DESIGNED BY SEYMOUR CRAY. THE PLAN VIEW WAS IN THE SHAPE OF A CROSS, EACH ARM WITH ITS OWN COOLING CIRCUIT. THE VAST AMOUNT OF HEAT GENERATED COULD BE USED TO HEAT THE BUILDING IN WINTER. **CONTROL DATA CORPORATION** USA **1964**

THE IBM 3031 HAD ROUGHLY TWICE THE COMPUTING POWER OF THE FASTEST MODEL IN THE SYSTEM/370 RANGE, AND WAS AVAILABLE WITH A MAIN STORE OF 2, 3, 4, 5, OR 6 MEGABYTES. **IBM** FRANCE **1975**

THE UNIVAC 1100 SERIES WAS INTENDED TO BREAK THE DOMINANCE OF IBM'S SYSTEM/360; ABOVE ALL IT WAS IN DEMAND BY US GOVERNMENT AUTHORITIES AND THE MILITARY. SHOWN HERE IS A COMPUTER CENTRE WITH AN INSTALLATION OF THE TOP-OF-THE-RANGE MODEL. **REMINGTON RAND** USA **1972**

A SUPERCOMPUTER FROM THE HR-70 SERIES. **CONTROL DATA CORPORATION** USA **1974**

IN 1970 GENE AMDAHL, WHO HAD PLAYED A SIGNIFICANT PART IN DESIGNING THE SYSTEM/360, LEFT IBM TO BUILD SUPERCOMPUTERS. HE WAS SUCCESSFUL: THE AMDAHL 470 V/6 WITH UP TO 4 MEGABYTES OF MAIN STORE WAS NINE TIMES AS FAST AS THE FASTEST IBM MAINFRAME OF ITS DAY, AT A BASIC PRICE OF 2 MILLION DOLLARS. **AMDAHL** USA **1975**

THE 4341 MAINFRAME COMPUTER, INTRODUCED IN THE LATE 1970s, PROVIDED HIGH PERFORMANCE AT A FAVOURABLE PRICE. **IBM** GERMANY **1979**

CONTROL DATA
7600

THE COMPUTER CENTRE AT THE LAWRENCE LIVERMORE RESEARCH LABORATORY IN THE MID-70s WITH AN INSTALLATION OF THE 5-MILLION-DOLLAR CDC 7600 SUPERCOMPUTER. **CONTROL DATA CORPORATION** USA **1978**

COMPUTER CENTRE OF THE GERMAN RESEARCH ASSOCIATION IN MUNICH, WITH AN INSTALLATION CONTAINING TWO CRAY X-MP COMPUTERS. **CRAY** USA **1988**

THE CRAY-2, THE EPITOME OF THE SUPERCOMPUTER. **CRAY** USA **1985** >>

WHEN TOLD THAT APPLE WAS
BUYING A CRAY TO DESIGN THE
NEW MAC, SEYMOUR CRAY
REPLIED WRYLY THAT HE HAD
JUST BOUGHT A MAC IN ORDER
TO DESIGN THE NEXT CRAY.

3422 MAGNETIC TAPE SYSTEM. **IBM** GERMANY **1986**

THE JAPANESE FACOM VP 100 WAS ONE OF THE FIRST SUPERCOMPUTERS PRODUCED OUTSIDE NORTH AMERICA. **FUJITSU** JAPAN **1982**

THE FACOM M-320 (LEFT) AND V-870.
FUJITSU JAPAN **1982**

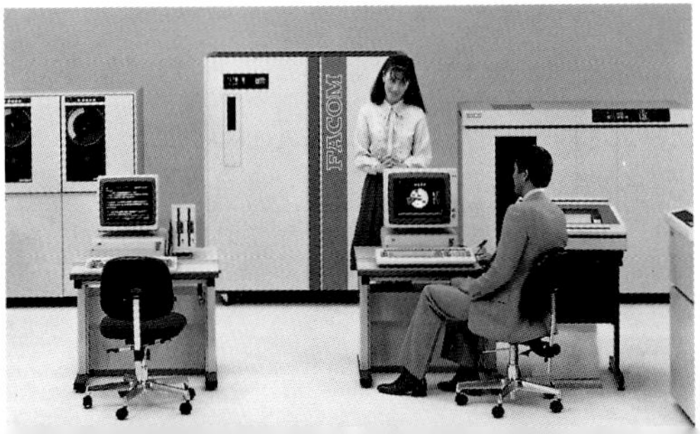

FACOM M-340. **FUJITSU** JAPAN **1981**

FACOM M-340 (LEFT) AND M-380 (ABOVE).
FUJITSU JAPAN **1981**

PANORAMIC VIEW OF A CONNECTION MACHINE 2 CLUSTER. **THINKING MACHINES** USA **1987**

THE FLICKERING ROWS OF LIGHTS INDICATE THAT THE SUPERCOMPUTER IS 'THINKING'. THE CONNECTION MACHINE 1, DESIGNED BY DANNY HILLIS, CONSISTED OF 65 536 1-BIT PROCESSORS. **THINKING MACHINES** USA **1986**

THE CONNECTION MACHINE 5, TALLER THAN A MAN, WAS THE FASTEST AND ALSO THE LAST SUPERCOMPUTER BY DANNY HILLIS, WHO FOLLOWED IN SEYMOUR CRAY'S FOOTSTEPS IN THE LATE 1980S, ADOPTING AN EXTRAVAGANT COMPUTER ARCHITECTURE FOR HIS CONNECTION MACHINES. **THINKING MACHINES** USA **1991**

THE JAPANESE SUPERCOMPUTER MP 6000 (TOP) AND THE GS 8900 MAINFRAME COMPUTER (BOTTOM). **HITACHI** JAPAN **1997** >>

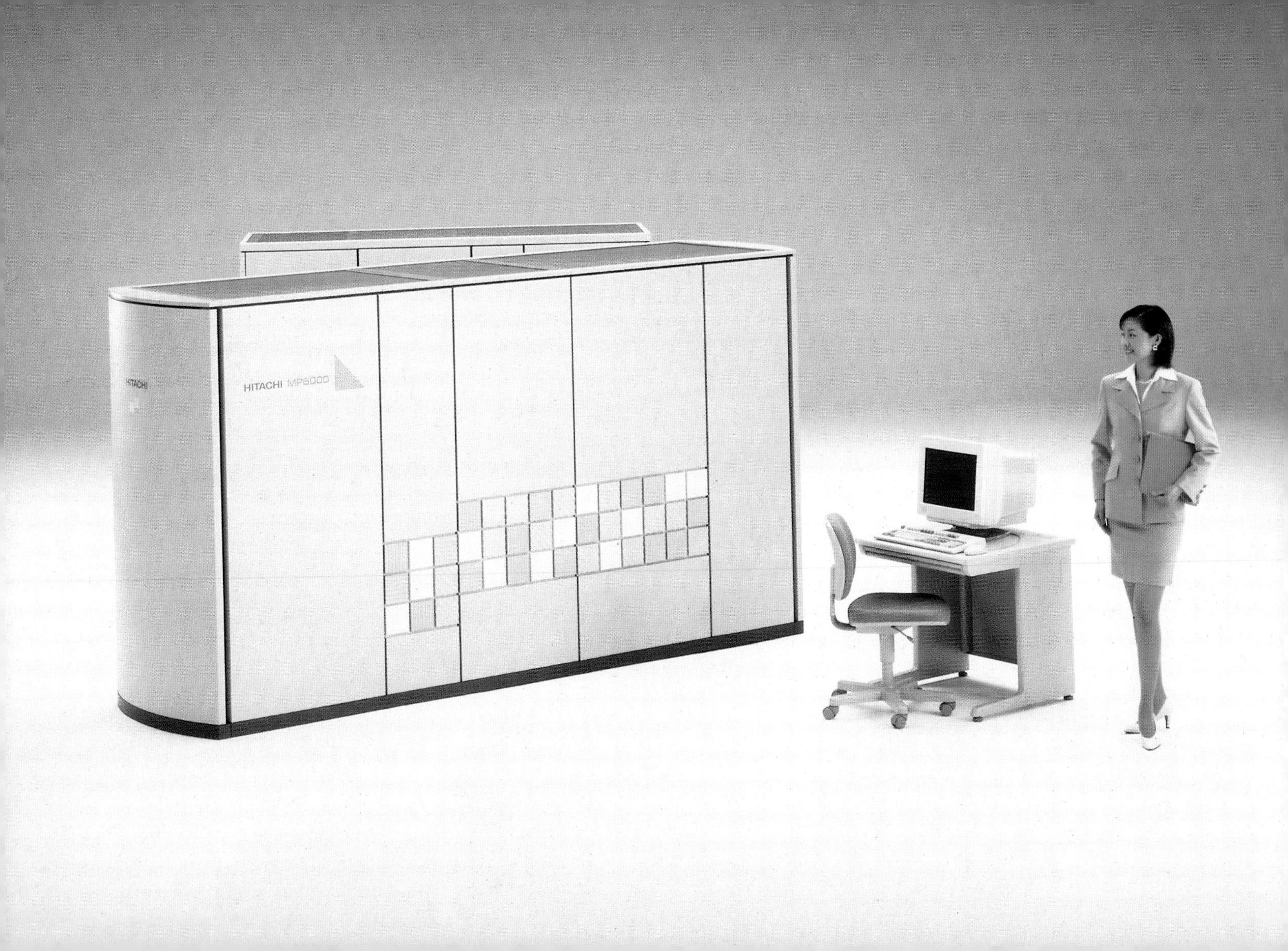
HITACHI
HITACHI MP6000

FUJITSU
GS8900

3.0 THE MINICOMPUTER

"COMPUTERS IN THE FUTURE MAY WEIGH NO MORE THAN 1.5 TONS."

POPULAR MECHANICS, 1949

<< THE "KITCHEN COMPUTER" IN VARIOUS GUISES. **HONEYWELL** USA **1968**

THE PDP-8i. **DIGITAL EQUIPMENT CORPORATION** USA **1960**

3.1 THE PDP-1

Years ahead of its time was the PDP-1 (Programmed Data Processor), the first computer made by Digital Equipment Corporation (DEC) in 1960. Its circuits were based on the transistor, which had been invented by William Shockley and others as far back as 1947 but first found application in other fields – the most famous example being the portable radio. The transistor represented a dramatic innovation in computer hardware: it was considerably smaller, faster, more reliable, and after a while, cheaper than the vacuum tube. In the transition phase to the minicomputer, the PDP-1 was the first general-purpose computer that could be used in real time. In contrast to all previous computers – and many that came later – the user could feed in his own program at any time, and data could be entered and printed out on a teletypewriter. For data output it was also possible to attach a circular monitor, still looking very much like a radar screen but allowing a row of up to twelve characters to be displayed.

Together with the light pen and other I/O components, the PDP-1 represented a very unusual computer system for its time, with extensive user interfaces. It had some remarkable similarities with the Whirlwind military computer of 1951, even though that was a highly specialised machine built for a specific task. The teletypewriter could also send data via the telephone lines to other computers at a distant location. This networking technology allowed universities and colleges to hire expensive computer time by the minute, which in the early 1960s came to be known as time-sharing operation. With the time-sharing concept, networking a central mainframe computer to several terminals – the ideal of a strictly hierarchical top-down architecture – became a new paragon for data processing at that time, and also had a lasting effect on the public image of a computer.

Time-sharing formed the basis for automation in banking, including the introduction of cashless payments, and also the first airline booking networks. The computer terminals in banks and airports were the first sign of a gradual computerisation of society; they were the first and closest contact that most people had with a digital computer. As long ago as the early 1960s, the pioneers of time-sharing took the stand that networking was the direction that computers would take. In view of the new options this technology opened up, Martin Greenberger, professor at the Massachusetts Institute of Technology, postulated in 1964: “Barring unforeseen obstacles, an on-line interactive computer service, provided commercially by an information utility, may be as commonplace by 2000 AD as the telephone service is today. By 2000 AD man should have a much better comprehension of himself and his system, not because he will be innately any smarter than he is today, but because he will have learned to use imaginatively the most powerful amplifier of intelligence yet devised.”

A COMPUTER-READABLE SCHOOL TEST BEING ANALYSED AUTOMATICALLY

3.2 THE PDP-8

The next chapter of computer history was ushered in by a technical innovation that allowed a dramatic miniaturisation of switching devices and thus of the entire computer. In 1958–59, Robert Noyce of Fairchild Semiconductors (later a cofounder of Intel) and Jack Kilby of Texas Instruments developed the integrated circuit independently of each other. In this new technology, transistors and their wiring (in the form of aluminium conductors) were vacuum-deposited on a layer of germanium – or later silicon – mounted on a substrate. The IC was not only faster, smaller, and more reliable than discrete transistors, but also much cheaper, once the production methods became reliable and therefore economically feasible.

"DOES NOT COMPUTE" ERROR MESSAGE FROM THE TELETYPE 33 ASR

Digital Equipment Corporation (DEC) was thus able to bring out the first minicomputer in the spring of 1965, the PDP-8, at a price of only $18,000. The PDP-8 revolutionised the way computers were used: the new circuits produced so little heat in operation that the machine no longer had to be housed in an air-conditioned room of its own. Its relatively compact dimensions also meant that it could be set up where it was needed. The close proximity to the computer, and the feel for its capabilities and limitations which the user soon acquired through 'interaction' with it, quickly made this minicomputer an indispensable assistant for scientists and engineers, who were the main users of the new class of computer.

Although its operation (like that of its predecessor the PDP-1) was a clear break with the methods used in mainframe computers, from the present-day point of view it was cumbersome. The user interface was

COMPUTERS IN A NORTH AMERICAN CLASSROOM IN THE MID-60s

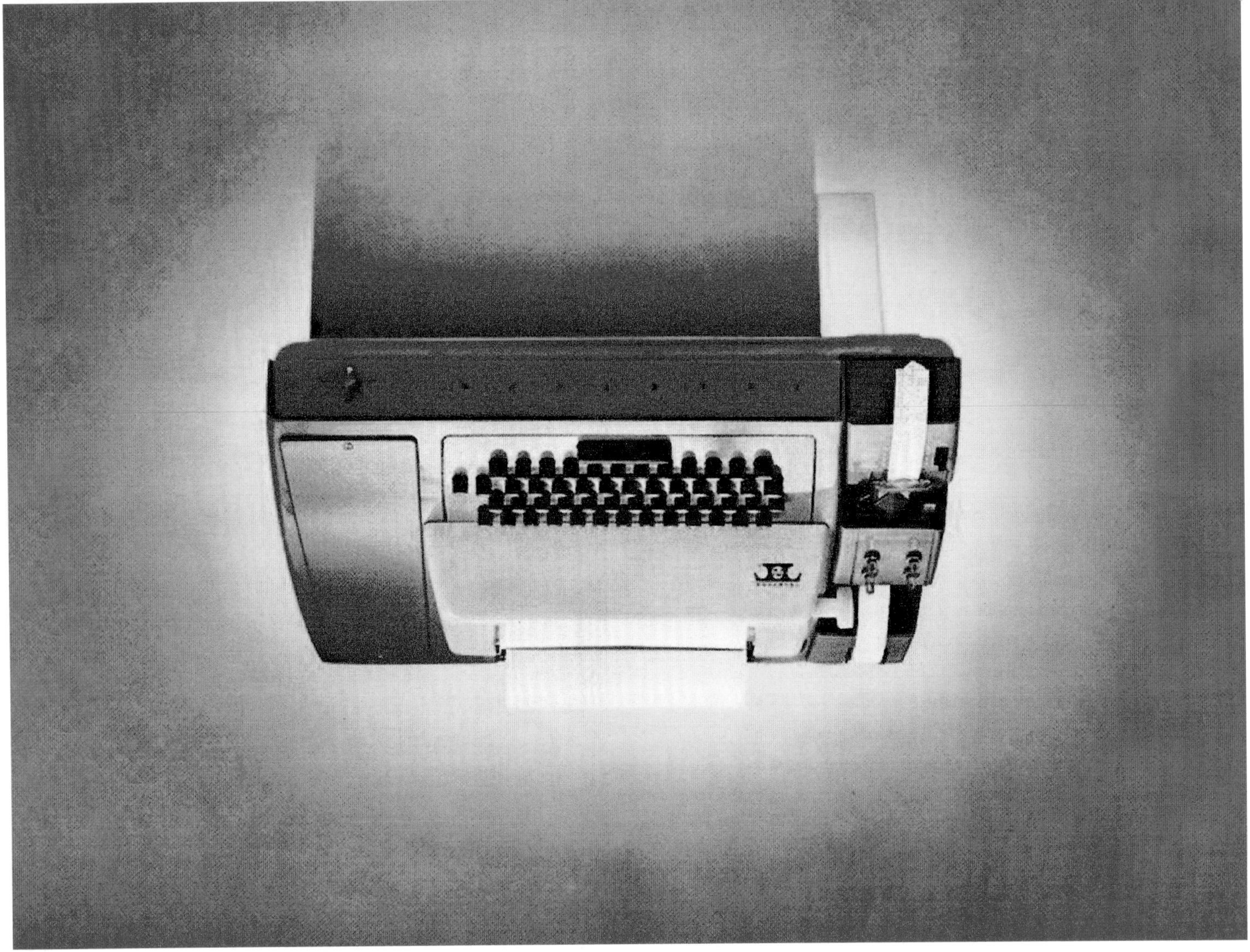

THE TELETYPE ASR 33 TELETYPEWRITER ACTED AS A UNIVERSAL INTERFACE TO THE COMPUTER. BY MEANS OF IT, PROGRAMS AND DATA WERE TYPED OR READ INTO THE COMPUTER, AND THE RESULTS OF THE CALCULATIONS PRINTED OR PUNCHED OUT. **TELETYPE** USA **1965**

PROGRAMMING LESSONS ON A TELETYPE IN THE SCHOOL, CONNECTED TO A CENTRAL COMPUTER VIA A TELEPHONE LINE. **TELETYPE** USA **1970**

also meagre: it consisted of rows of switches and lamps on the front panel, plus a separate teletypewriter, the Teletype 33 ASR. In order to run a program, the user had to load the paper tape in the teletypewriter and operate various switches on the PDP-8. The tape was now drawn through in staccato fashion before the computer started to execute the program – flickering lights indicated that the circuits were busy. The teletypewriter then noisily spewed out the results of the calculation, or, as frequently happened, the unhelpful message “does not compute”. In that case the programmer had to search for errors until finally the program ran to completion.

The Teletype itself, otherwise known as a universal input/output station, was outwardly very similar to the electric typewriter used by DEC for the PDP-1. It could print results on a roll of continuous paper or punch a tape. A fundamental difference was that it used the new ASCII standard, so it could communicate with most other computers. and had had a speed of up to 10 characters per second.

The keyboard used the standard QWERTY layout that had been devised by Christopher Sholes in the second half of the 19th century, after first experimenting with keys in purely alphabetic order.

The mechanism of the early typewriters was far from perfect, and the type bars tended to jam if one typed too fast. Sholes therefore deliberately changed the order so that letters which frequently occurred in sequence were not too close to each other on the keyboard; the levers were then less likely to get in each others’ way. His experiments led to the familiar layout with the top row starting QWERTY, which has remained the standard to this day in spite of many attempts to rationalise it (there are national variants; for example Germany uses QWERTZ, France AZERTY).

With the technological progress of the 1960s, computers experienced an enormous growth. As Gordon Moore, the president of the chip manufacturer Intel, stated in a lecture in 1965, the complexity of integrated circuits was doubling roughly every 18 to 24 months. Years later, his statement was applied to the increasing complexity of microprocessors and the resulting exponential rise in computing power, and became famous as Moore’s Law.

Meanwhile, IBM’s control of the mainframe market was so unmistakable that in the 1970s alone the corporation had to face over twenty ‘anti-trust’ lawsuits instituted by competitors.

Whereas IBM increasingly dominated the computer market in the 1960s and early 1970s, and the computer centre correspondingly symbolised the central power of mainframe data processing, the minicomputer was starting to provide more direct and personal contact with the user. Its era was marked by the image of the more compact computer for laboratories, factories, and offices, that could be set up where there were problems to be solved and could also be operated by just one person.

The advance of mainframes and minicomputers in the 1970s, and their increasing impact on working life, set off a continuing public debate – in Europe, at least – on the risks of the new technology and the 'rationalisation' of jobs. The opposing argument, put forward with equal vehemence, is that computers are able to free people from drudgery.

Their lower prices meant that computers now became affordable for smaller companies and offices; as a result of the advent of standard software, a move largely brought about by IBM, they could also be used by engineers, researchers, businessmen and others to solve a wide variety of problems.

Although one could not yet speak of real-time operation of these computers in the present sense of the word, at least they were now in the same room as the people using them. In the tradition of the console, the teletypewriter had become the universal input/output station, at which the program was read into the computer on paper tape, data could be typed in, and the results could be printed out after a delay. It combined a programming interface with a keyboard and a printer, to make a new and relatively compact universal interface.

However, the interactive options with this man/machine interface were still very limited and in principle one-sided. Output in the form of printed or punched data was not a very highly developed form of feedback from the computer to its user.

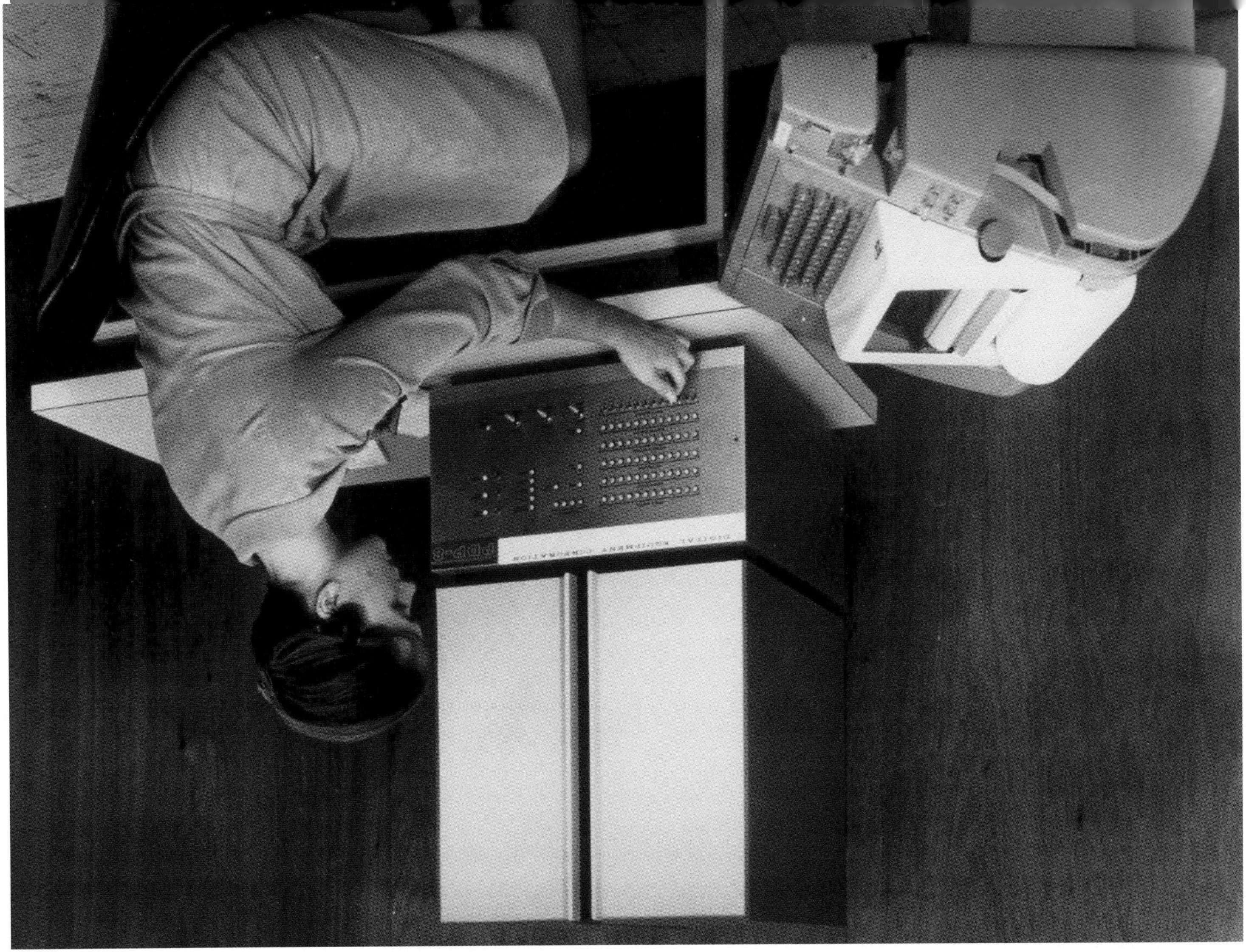
PDP-8
DIGITAL EQUIPMENT CORPORATION

DEC PDP-8i

EMIL ZOPFI

THE REVOLUTION REACHED ME IN 1968. IT TRUNDLED INTO THE LAB ONE MORNING IN THE FORM OF A BLACK CABINET. ON THE FRONT OF THE MYSTERIOUS BOX WAS A ROW OF TWELVE SWITCHES, WITH THE SAME NUMBER OF LAMPS ABOVE. BEHIND IT, PUSHED ALONG BY THE CARETAKER, CAME A TELEX MACHINE.

THE FLOWER-POWER GIRLS DOWN BY THE RIVER WERE WEARING MINISKIRTS THAT SUMMER, AND THE MACHINE BORE A SIMILAR NAME: MINICOMPUTER. OUR PROFESSOR HAD ORDERED THE PDP-8I DURING A TOUR OF THE USA, BECAUSE THERE, HE EXPLAINED, SUCH MACHINES WERE ALREADY BEING USED BY THE DOZEN FOR RESEARCH. THE LITTLE "I" STOOD FOR THE INTEGRATED CIRCUITS THAT THE LATEST MODEL WAS EQUIPPED WITH. THE CABINET STOOD MORE THAN MAN-HIGH, THOUGH THE COMPUTER ITSELF TOOK UP PERHAPS HALF THE AVAILABLE SPACE INSIDE. WE PULLED OUT A DRAWER AND WERE MET WITH THE SIGHT OF A TANGLE OF WIRES INSTEAD OF NEAT CABLES AND HARNESSES. I IMMEDIATELY ORDERED A WIRE-WRAP TOOL. I KNEW A BIT ABOUT ELECTRONICS, BUT NOTHING ABOUT COMPUTERS. THERE WAS NO SUPPORT IN SIGHT: THE NEAREST BRANCH OFFICE OF THE DIGITAL EQUIPMENT CORPORATION WAS IN PARIS, HEADQUARTERS IN MAYNARD, MASSACHUSETTS. KENNETH H. OLSEN HAD FOUNDED DEC IN 1957 WITH A DISUSED COTTON MILL AS HIS WAREHOUSE. ONCE WE WERE VISITED BY A NERVOUS CHAIN-SMOKING REPRESENTATIVE; HE GAVE A TALK THAT CONFUSED US MORE THAN IT EXPLAINED ANYTHING.

ON LOOKING BACK, I REALISE THAT THE REVOLUTION INVOLVED NOT JUST THE "MINI" SIZE OF THE COMPUTER "IT WAS STILL A GIANT BY TODAY'S STANDARDS" BUT ALSO THE FREE HAND THAT THE MANUFACTURER GAVE THE USERS. HAD TO, IN EFFECT, BECAUSE DEC POSSESSED NO AFTER-SALES SERVICE NETWORK. A SERIES OF BOOKLETS DESCRIBED THE CONCEPT AND THE FUNCTION, THE SOFTWARE AND THE HARDWARE DOWN TO THE LAST WIRE. DO-IT-YOURSELF WAS NOT ONLY ALLOWED BUT ACTIVELY ENCOURAGED. IN OUR CASE IT WAS ESSENTIAL, BECAUSE THE PROFESSOR HAD VISIONARY PLANS TO AUTOMATE

OUR PHYSICAL CHEMISTRY EXPERIMENTS, COLLECT ALL THE DATA AUTOMATICALLY, AND THEN ANALYSE IT. THE MAGIC WORDS WERE "DIRECT DIGITAL CONTROL".

THE CHALLENGE WAS GREAT, THE MACHINE WAS MINI, AND ITS PERFORMANCE NO GREATER THAN A PRESENT-DAY POCKET CALCULATOR. IT HAD COME ON THE MARKET IN THE SPRING OF 1965. "THE PDP-8 PUSHED THROUGH THE IDEA OF THE MINICOMPUTER", AS THE AMERICAN JOURNALIST TRACY KIDDER WROTE IN RETROSPECT; "THE MACHINE CAUGHT ON AND BROUGHT DEC ITS FIRST BIG MONEY".

I CONTRIBUTED ABOUT $5,000 TO THE TURNOVER. THAT WAS THE COST OF THE INTERFACE BOARDS I ORDERED FROM PARIS, SO THAT I COULD BUILD A CONTROLLER FOR STEPPER MOTORS. IT WAS A WHILE BEFORE WE COULD MAKE THEM TURN PRECISELY IN BOTH DIRECTIONS BY PROGRAM CONTROL "FOR A SINGLE TEST RUN TOOK UP ABOUT HALF A DAY".

THE "BOOTSTRAP LOADER" HAD TO BE ENTERED ON THE HANDSWITCHES: SEVERAL COMMANDS OF 12 BITS EACH, THE WORD LENGTH WITH THIS MACHINE. THEN THE TELEX MACHINE READ IN A TAPE CONTAINING THE BINARY LOADER, FOLLOWED BY THE PROGRAM EDITOR. THE RATTLE OF THE TAPE READER, THIRTY CHARACTERS A SECOND, PERVADED THE LAB FROM MORNING TILL EVENING AND MADE IT HARD TO THINK; OUR COFFEE CONSUMPTION ROSE APPRECIABLY. PUNCHING SOURCE CODE, READING IN THE ASSEMBLER, THREE PASSES OF THE SOURCE CODE BEFORE IT WAS ASSEMBLED, PRINTING OUT A LISTING, PUNCHING THE PROGRAM, READING IT IN, RUNNING IT "PROGRAMMING WAS BRAINWORK AND MANUAL WORK IN ONE. WE COULDN'T AFFORD TO MAKE MISTAKES, BECAUSE THAT MEANT ANOTHER HALF DAY OF MANIPULATING AND RATTER-TATTER. MANY PEOPLE HAVE REALISED, AFTER BUYING A COMPUTER, THAT THE MOST IMPORTANT THINGS ARE MISSING; WE MADE THAT DISCOVERY BACK IN 1968. A TAPE READER WITH TEN TIMES THE SPEED OF THE TELEX MADE LIFE MUCH EASIER.

WE PROGRAMMED IN ASSEMBLER, ONE LINE FOR EACH MACHINE-CODE INSTRUCTION. THE STORE WAS A GIGANTIC 4,096 WORDS, AND THE ARITHMETIC UNIT HAD AN ACCUMULATOR OF 12 BITS PLUS A CARRY

BIT, THE "LINK". IT WAS HIGHLY EDUCATIONAL: TWO'S COMPLEMENT ARITHMETIC BECAME SECOND NATURE TO ME. I'LL ALWAYS REMEMBER ONE COMMAND, CIA (COMPLEMENT AND INCREMENT ACCUMULATOR), WHICH WAS USED FOR SUBTRACTION. THERE WERE THE INEVITABLE FREQUENT JOKES ABOUT A CERTAIN ORGANISATION OF THE SAME NAME.

I HAVE GOOD MEMORIES OF THE PDP-8'S TRANSPARENCY. SO MUCH WAS VISIBLE THAT NOW COMES INTEGRATED, MEANING CONCEALED IN THE HARDWARE AND SOFTWARE. "A NICE LITTLE MACHINE, BUT IT COULD DO A LOT" RECALLED TED HOFF WHO AT THE TIME WAS DEVELOPING INTEGRATED CIRCUITS AT INTEL AND HAD A PDP-8 NEXT TO HIS DESK. IT GAVE HIM THE IDEA OF PUTTING AN ENTIRE COMPUTER ON ONE CHIP, SO THE PDP-8 COULD BE CONSIDERED THE ORIGINAL ANCESTOR OF ALL MICROPROCESSORS.

YEARS LATER, I AGAIN HAD A CHANCE TO PROGRAM A PDP-8. I WAS PLEASED TO DISCOVER THAT I COULD REMEMBER ALL THE COMMANDS. IF I HAD TO, I COULD PROBABLY STILL WRITE ASSEMBLER NOW, QUARTER OF A CENTURY LATER. A FEELING OF NOSTALGIA COMES OVER ME WHEN I THINK OF THE OLD MACHINES AND THEIR TECHNOLOGY: THEY REPRESENTED CRAFTSMANSHIP, EXPERIENCE, A SLICE OF LIFE AT THE PEAK OF A TECHNICAL REVOLUTION; A PART OF HISTORY, NOW MUSEUM PIECES.

ITS NOVEL CONCEPT MADE IT ONE OF THE MOST INFLUENTIAL COMPUTERS OF ALL: THE PDP-1. IN THE PICTURE CAN BE SEEN (FROM LEFT TO RIGHT) ITS OPERATING PANEL WITH A BUILT-IN MAGNETIC TAPE UNIT, A GRAPHICS CRT SCREEN WITH LIGHT PEN (SEE BELOW), AND THE TELETYPEWRITER FOR OPERATING THE COMPUTER. **DIGITAL EQUIPMENT CORPORATION** USA **1960**

THE PDP-8E, AN EVEN MORE COMPACT SUCCESSOR TO THE PDP-8. **DIGITAL EQUIPMENT CORPORATION** USA **1972**

digital
pdp8/e
digital equipment corporation · maynard, massachusetts
EMA
MEMORY ADDRESS
RUN
STATE
STATUS
AC
MD
MQ
BUS
SWITCH REGISTER
OFF
POWER
PANEL LOCK
ADDR LOAD
EXTD ADDR LOAD
START
CLEAR
CONT
EXAM
HALT
SING STEP
DEP

ILLUSTRATIONS FROM THE *SMALL COMPUTER HANDBOOK* SUPPLIED WITH THE PDP-8E.
DIGITAL EQUIPMENT CORPORATION USA **1972**

PDP-8E WITH A TELETYPE AS INPUT CONSOLE

PDP-8E WITH TAPE DRIVES, LINE PRINTER, AND INPUT TERMINAL

PAPER TAPE READER FOR THE PDP-8E

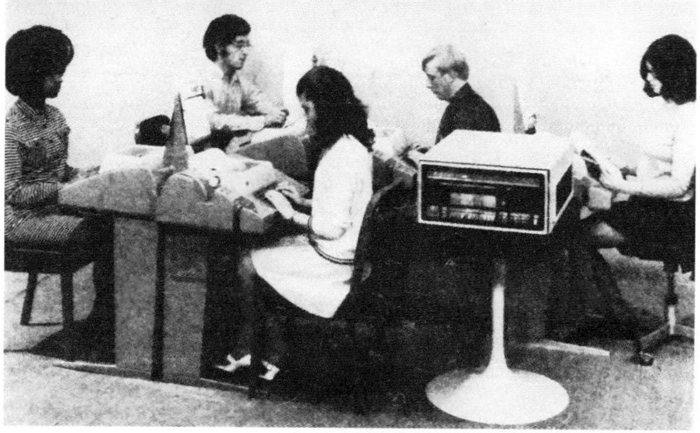

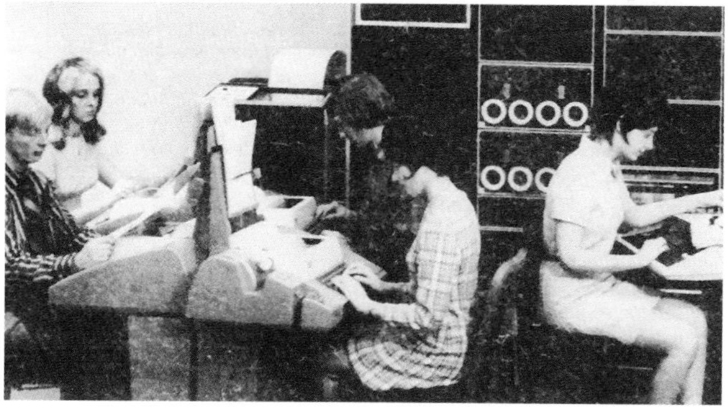

SEVERAL OPERATING CONSOLES NETWORKED TO A PDP-8E

316

THE H316 MINICOMPUTER WAS THE CIVILIAN VERSION OF THE "KITCHEN COMPUTER" WHICH WAS ABLE TO STORE RECIPES AND CALCULATE QUANTITIES OF ALL THE NECESSARY INGREDIENTS. AT A PRICE OF $10,000, THE AMERICAN DEPARTMENT STORE NEIMAN MARCUS DID NOT SELL A SINGLE ONE. **HONEYWELL** USA **1965**

There's a little bit of chicken in all of us.
One big trouble with being chicken is that you can wind up with nothing much to crow about.
Consider, for example, the job of picking a computer.
If you back off from the computer you honestly think is best and pick another one just because it's "safe", you're not doing yourself (or us) any good.
So get plenty of facts, then base your decision on them.
Find out which new-generation computers have been selling and why . . . and if you now have an older computer, which new models make conversion easiest.
Find out who has the best record for delivering both software and hardware on time.
Find out who has the widest choice of rental and purchase plans, and how this can save you money.
Find out who is best equipped to provide computer speed and capacity for both today's needs . . . and tomorrow's.
Get all the facts, then be hard-nosed about your decision.
Don't be chicken . . . be right.
Honeywell
ELECTRONIC DATA PROCESSING

"DON'T BE CHICKEN ... BE RIGHT." FROM AN ADVERTISEMENT FOR THE NEW MINI-COMPUTERS, WITH A GENTLE SIDESWIPE AT IBM. **HONEYWELL** USA **1967**

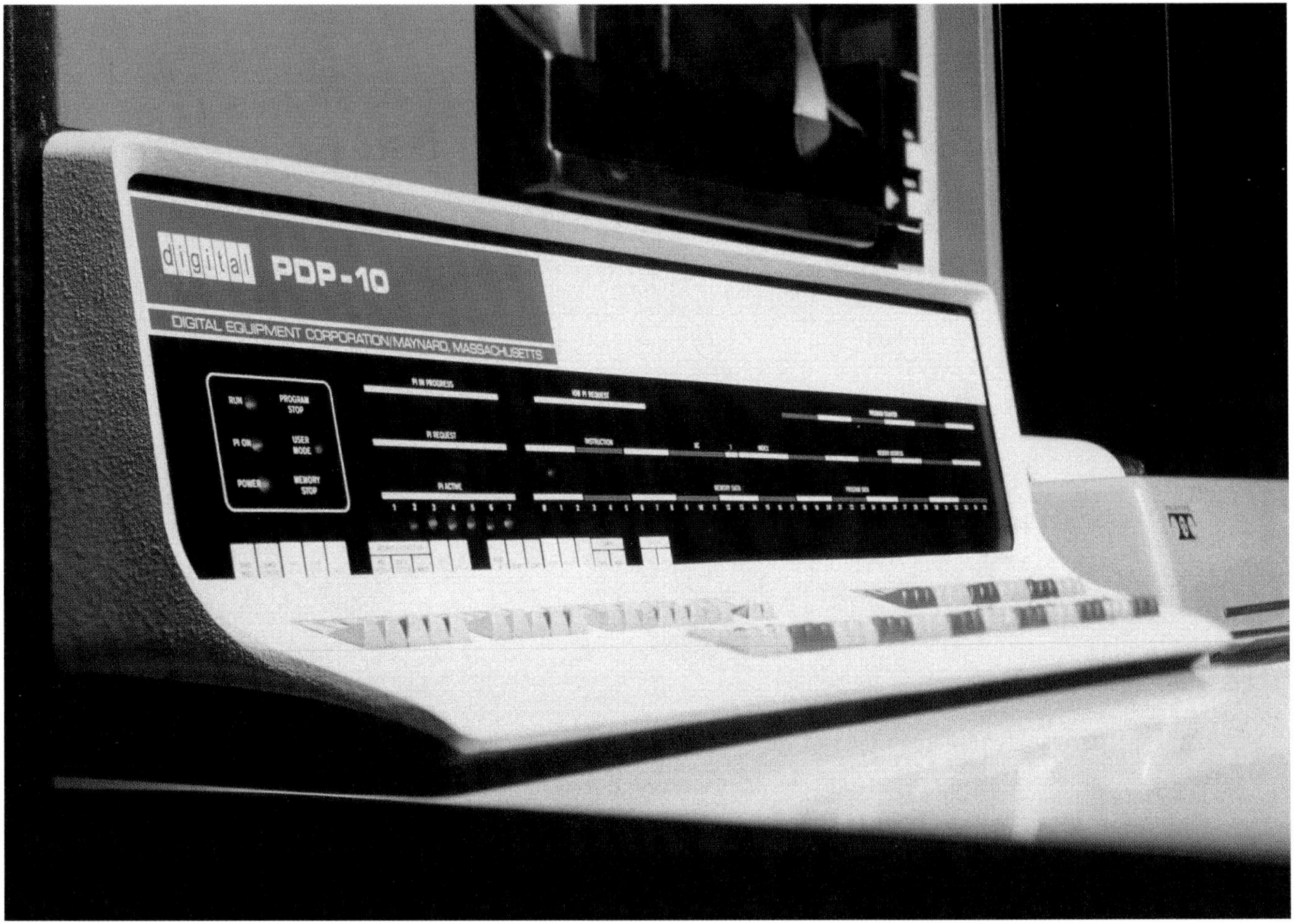

THE OPERATING CONSOLE OF A PDP-10. **DIGITAL EQUIPMENT CORPORATION** USA **1966**

FRONT PANEL OF A PDP-11. **DIGITAL EQUIPMENT CORPORATION** USA **1970**

THE PDP-11 WITH TAPE DRIVES, OPERATING CONSOLE, AND A LINE PRINTER.
DIGITAL EQUIPMENT CORPORATION USA **1970**

digital

PDP-11 INSTALLATIONS WITH VARIOUS MAGNETIC TAPE UNITS AND OPERATING CONSOLES IN THE FOREGROUND. **DIGITAL EQUIPMENT CORPORATION** USA **1970**

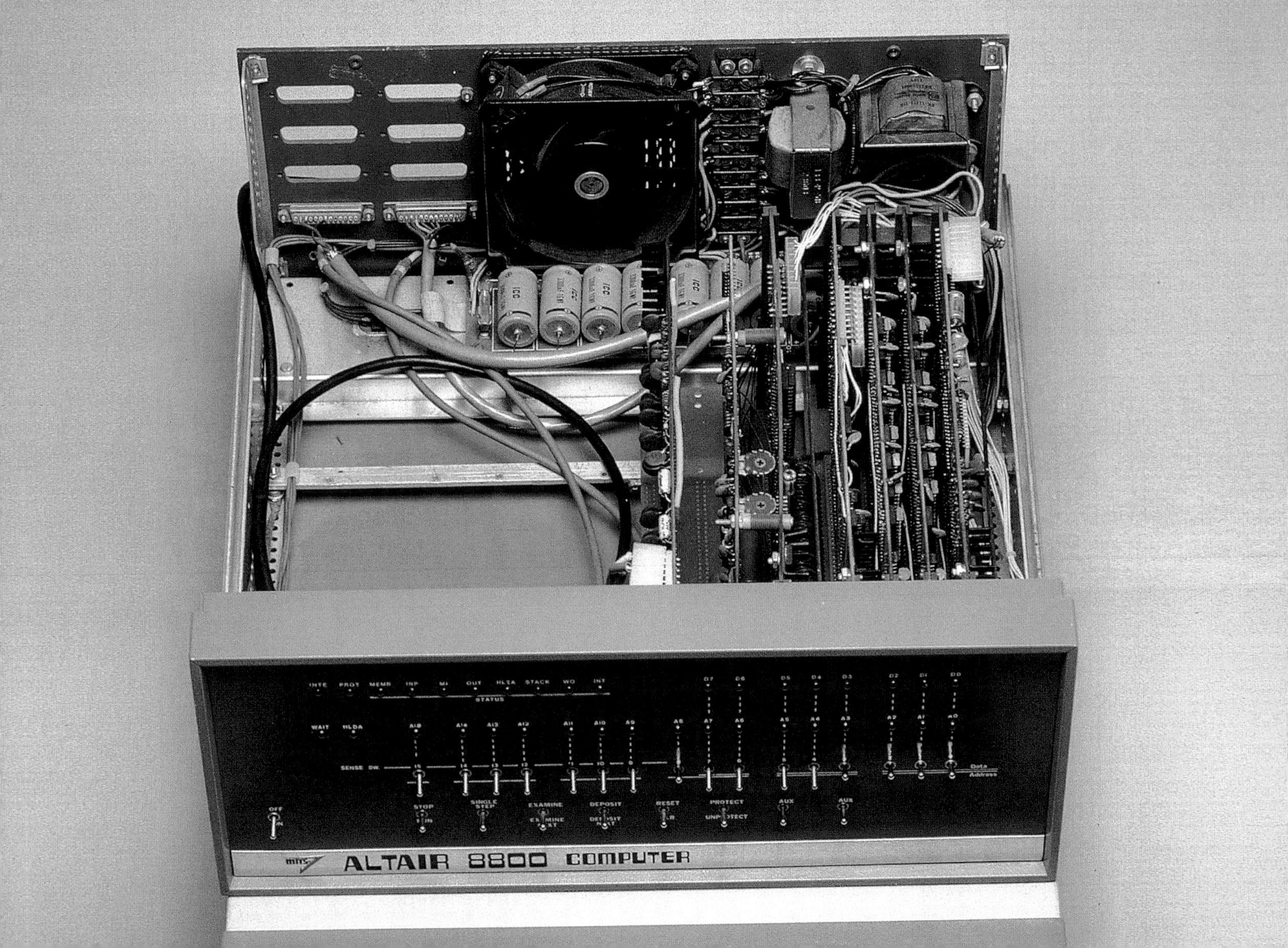
mits
ALTAIR 8800 COMPUTER
INTE PROT MEMR INP MI OUT HLTA STACK WO INT
STATUS
WAIT HLDA
SENSE SW.
STOP
SINGLE STEP
EXAMINE
DEPOSIT
RESET
PROTECT
UNPROTECT
AUX
AUX
OFF
Data
Address

4.0
THE MICROCOMPUTER

"THERE IS NO REASON
ANYONE WOULD WANT A COMPUTER
IN THE HOME."

KENNETH OLSEN, DIGITAL EQUIPMENT CORPORATION, 1977

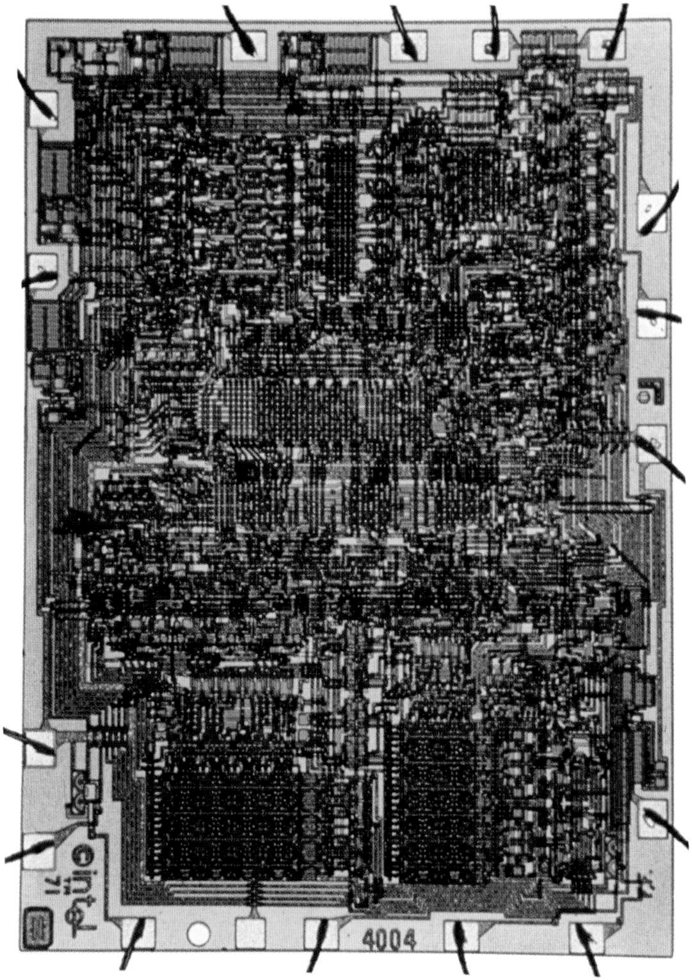

<< THE START OF A NEW EPOCH: THE ALTAIR 8800 COMPUTER KIT. **MITS** USA **1975**

CIRCUITRY OF THE 4004 MICROPROCESSOR. **INTEL** USA **1971**

4.1 THE BIRTH OF THE MICROPROCESSOR

In 1971 the computer industry appeared to be up against the limits of performance, but an invention made that year was to shake it to its very foundations, and also to shape the last two decades of the century in a way that possibly only the steam engine or the dynamo had before. The Intel company succeeded in building the world's first microprocessor, the model 4004. This combined the electronic circuits of the arithmetic unit on a single piece of semiconductor. As an advertisement for the 4004 read: "Announcing a new era of integrated electronics ... a micro-programmable computer on a chip."

Its successor, the 8080, released in 1974, contained 6,000 transistors and was 20 times faster than the 4004. This compact electronic component became the technological basis for the first computers intended for private use, the microcomputers.

What set off the avalanche was a picture of the Altair 8800, a kit costing $400, on the cover of *Popular Electronics* in late December 1974. Although even an experienced do-it-yourselfer needed over a hundred hours to assemble this little computer, and the Altair possessed neither a keyboard nor a monitor, it was a great commercial success in the USA and led to a whole generation of pioneers. After all, it was the first computer that was so small and cheap that an individual could own one – even if nobody really knew at that stage what an individual would want with a computer.

However, things changed rapidly when Paul Allen and Bill Gates – just a few months before they founded their own company – rewrote the freely available programming language BASIC for the Altair. Unlike cryptic machine code, or the relatively complicated FORTRAN and Algol languages, BASIC was simple in structure and easy to learn, so that even an inexperienced Altair owner could write simple programs and run them successfully on his computer. More complex programs were either typed up laboriously from books or magazines, or loaded from a tape cassette.

The surprisingly successful Altair was soon imitated, for example by the Imsai 8080. Some Intel engineers then founded their own company, Zilog, and built the Z80, a chip that was cheaper and more powerful than its competitor made by their former employer – but fully software-com-

JANUARY 1977
$1.50 in NORTH AMERICA
BYTE
the small systems journal

A BETTER WORLD, THANKS TO COMPUTERS: THE ALTAIR 8800 ON THE COVER OF *BYTE*, THE "SMALL SYSTEMS JOURNAL". **BYTE** USA **1977**

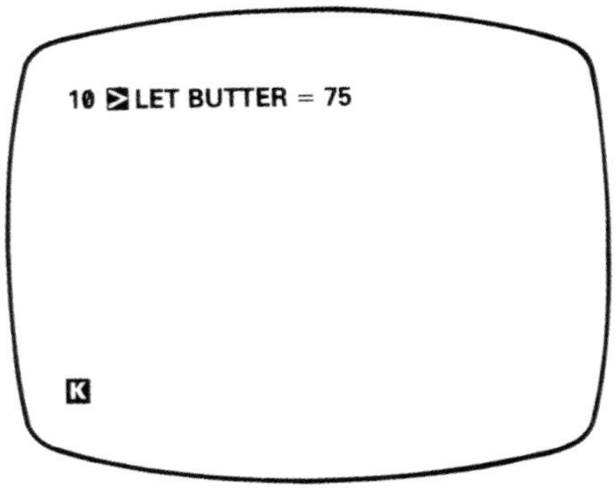

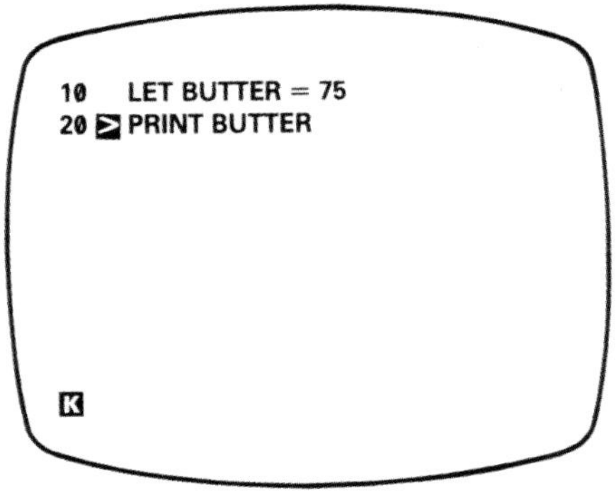

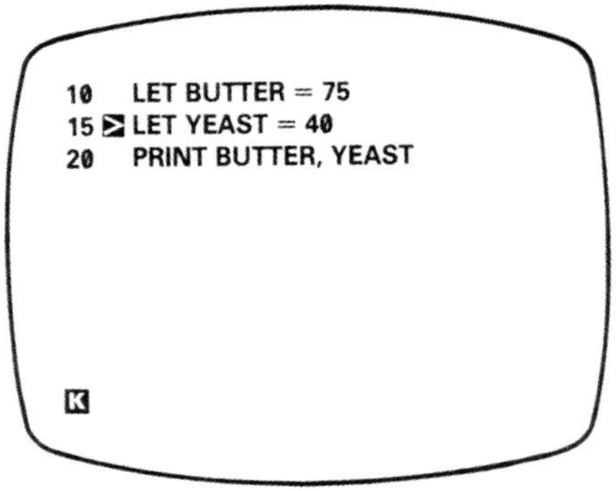

patible with it. The Z80 and its successor the Z81 soon became the processors used by a veritable flood of different microcomputers, such as the ZX81 made by the British company Sinclair. The new microcomputers now entered the home in force.

Shortly before, American amusement arcades, which until then had contained flippers and other mechanical gaming machines, began to install the first commercial computer games – for example Atari's Pong, an electronic variant of table tennis. These highly popular machines were soon adapted into 'video games consoles' for the living room, for example the Magnavox Odyssey or the VCS-2600 made by Atari.

These computer games had impressive user interfaces. Graphics and sound appealed to the senses, while the user interacted with the game by means of new input devices, the joystick and the tracker ball, with which the figures in the game were moved in two dimensions and could be made to jump over an obstacle or fire a weapon, for example. The joystick, in form and function a miniature version of the control stick in an aircraft, was a reminder of the early attempts by the Luftwaffe in the Second World War to control anti-aircraft missiles in flight.

The games were easy to operate, and the simple rules could be learned in a very short time just by watching someone else at play. Computer games held a great fascination for the infant microcomputer industry, so that the first applications were games programs, still very rudimentary but already characterised by the use of colour, sound, and high-speed action.

4.2 THE HOME COMPUTER

Several companies in America, for example the typewriter manufacturer Commodore and the electronics chain Tandy (RadioShack), soon brought out their own microcomputers. Over 10,000 of Tandy's TRS-80 were sold in the first month, far exceeding the expectations of 3,000 a year.

A lively software industry grew up for games and other applications. Joysticks became a standard input device to match up to the demands of the fast games. In contrast to the large-scale computers, which were still horrendously expensive, nearly all the microcomputers used sound and colour graphics, which was partly the reason they were not taken seriously by the major manufacturers – what, for heaven's sake, would a real computer want with all these gimmicks? Nobody except a clairvoyant could have suspected that within a few years a microcomputer would be found on every desk. The uses for the new "home computers", as they

BASIC 1.0 FOR THE ALTAIR. **MICROSOFT** USA **1975**

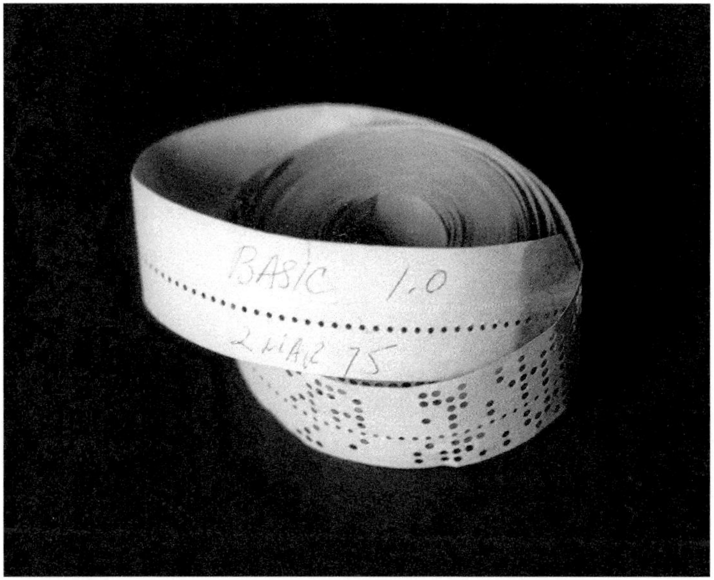

FROM THE BASIC MANUAL FOR THE ZX81 HOME COMPUTER.
SINCLAIR GREAT BRITAIN **1981**

were often known, were summed up by the German computer magazine *Chip* in 1980: chess, family games, music, model-making, hi-fi, drawing and graphics, navigation, learning, handicrafts, programming, and writing.

Soon the large number of different microcomputers became a problem, since every manufacturer used his own 'dialect' of BASIC. The software producers had to tailor their programs for each individual variant – Commodore BASIC, Apple BASIC, or Tandy's TRS-BASIC. The computer scientist Gary Kildall then designed the first operating system for small computers, with the name CP/M (Control Program for Microcomputers), which soon became the standard for over a hundred different types of computer. CP/M was the model for all later operating systems, such as MS-DOS. On the one hand it was a software interface that allowed the user to run standard programs. But it was also a hardware interface that organised the way the computer cooperated with diskette drives, for example. The 'floppy disk', introduced by IBM in 1971, was gradually replacing the cumbersome magnetic-tape and paper-tape storage in mainframes and minicomputers; soon it would become the standard storage medium for microcomputers, displacing the cheap but less convenient cassette drives.

The invention of the microchip, and the resulting availability of cheap computers, set off an avalanche of supply and demand, a boom that was to change the role and the image of the computer forever. The implied slogan of this microcomputer revolution was "computers for everyone", diametrically opposed to the centralised power of the mainframe world.

The wide variety of the microcomputer's applications and abilities was in great contrast to the size and price of this generation of computers: creating music and graphics, simple text editing and accounting, learning foreign words, or even controlling a model railway or the heating system – there were many possible uses.

The affordable price and understandable operation of microcomputers, compared to earlier generations, dramatically increased and thus diversified the circle of users. The low cost and compact dimensions made the microcomputer the first privately owned, and therefore personal, computer. Thanks to the simplicity of BASIC it was also relatively easy to use. All this made it a democratic computer for many people – though by no means for everyone. With the gradual emergence of a software industry for games and other programs, the circle of computer users became further split into programmers and users of games and hobby programs.

In the meantime, computers were no larger than a ream of paper, so could easily fit on a desk or in the corner of the living room. Most of the interaction with the computer now took place by means of the monitor

ONE OF THE FIRST VIDEO GAMES: PONG (FOR TWO PLAYERS). **ATARI** USA **1973**

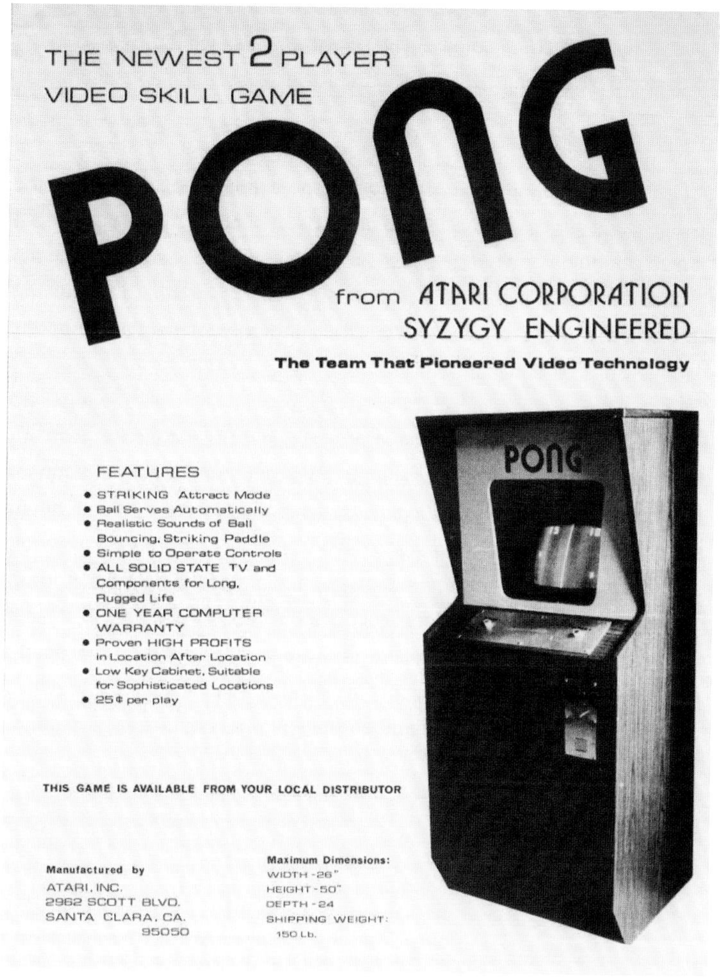
THE NEWEST 2 PLAYER
VIDEO SKILL GAME
PONG
from ATARI CORPORATION
SYZYGY ENGINEERED
The Team That Pioneered Video Technology
FEATURES
• STRIKING Attract Mode
• Ball Serves Automatically
• Realistic Sounds of Ball Bouncing, Striking Paddle
• Simple to Operate Controls
• ALL SOLID STATE TV and Components for Long, Rugged Life
ATARI'S NEW VIDEO GAME
2 or 4 PLAYERS
featuring new giant screen
• ONE YEAR COMPUTER WARRANTY
plus all the features of
the original PONG.
2 players for 25¢
4 players for 50¢
operator adjustable to
4 players for 25¢
specifications:
height — 58"
• Proven HIGH PROFITS in Location After Location
• Low Key Cabinet, Suitable for Sophisticated Locations
• 25¢ per play
PONG
THIS GAME IS AVAILABLE FROM YOUR LOCAL DISTRIBUTOR
Manufactured by
ATARI, INC.
14600 winchester blvd
los gatos, ca 95030
(408) 374-2440
2962 SCOTT BLVD.
SANTA CLARA, CA.
95050
Maximum Dimensions:
WIDTH -26"
HEIGHT-50"
DEPTH -24
SHIPPING WEIGHT:
150 Lb.

PONG DOUBLES (FOR FOUR PLAYERS). **ATARI** USA **1973**

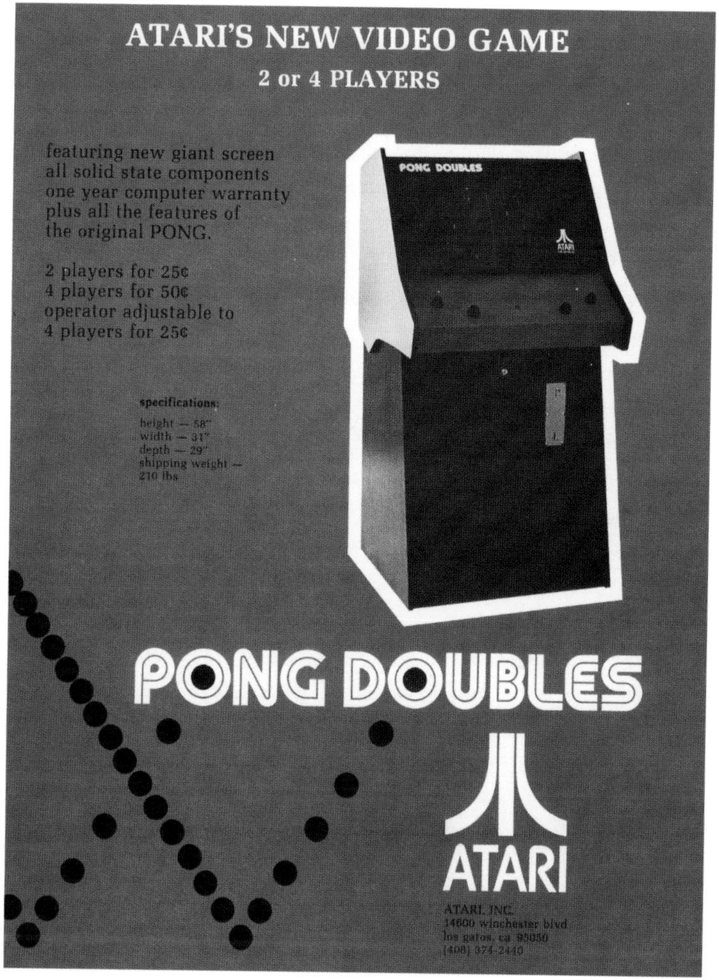

(often a TV set), in the form of short command lines entered on the keyboard (which was usually incorporated in the case of the computer). These were made up of simple BASIC instructions such as LIST, PRINT, LOAD, SAVE, or RUN; the command interface thus allowed one to enter programs and to execute them. At first the interaction and communication with the programs was by means of the command line, but soon the menu technique became popular. By analogy with the bill of fare in a restaurant, the prepared computer menu offers a list of available options; the user selects one by moving a cursor up or down, or by typing a single letter or digit.

The fact that the microcomputer was used mainly for playing games was due mainly to the possibilities opened up by its output interface: it was the first time that computers had possessed sound and colour graphics. A colour TV could be connected as an output device, so the microcomputer offered a considerable number of means of input and output for interaction with the user.

The applications that were opened up, and the resulting rapid growth in the circle of potential users, provided an incredible impetus for the growth of a new computer industry. However, the traditional manufacturers of larger computers did not appreciate the extent of the new threat to their supposedly secure living, or not until it was too late for some of them.

4.3 THE PERSONAL COMPUTER

The transition from early microcomputer to home computer to personal computer was a continuous one, finally manifesting itself in a more 'grown up' or 'professional' structure of the computers and their programs. The manufacturers increasingly rid themselves of the 'hobbies and games' image and appeared in a more serious light in order to tap the lucrative new market of small companies, individual offices, and the self-employed.

In 1976, the two former Atari employees Steven Wozniak and Steve Jobs announced their first computer, the Apple I, which they built themselves. It consisted of a plain wooden case; the keyboard was separate, while a TV served as the monitor. The first consignment went to the Byte Shop in Mountain View, California, probably the first computer shop anywhere, which had ordered 50 computers at a price of $500 ready-assembled.

The unexpected success of the Apple was far exceeded when its successor the Apple II appeared a year later. This could be described as the first genuine personal computer, and that is precisely how the company advertised it. It had an attractive plastic case with a built-in keyboard; this was the first time that injection moulding had been used for a computer to achieve an ergonomic and human-oriented shape. It also possessed sound and colour graphics. A special feature was its 'open architecture' which allowed other companies to develop additional plug-in boards that considerable extended the scope of the computer.

In spite of extreme competition from the CP/M computers, the Apple II soon adopted a vanguard role in the PC revolution. That was not so much a result of technological superiority, but more thanks to a single program that suddenly made the PC more useful than an inflexible and expensive mainframe computer. In 1979 Dan Bricklin wrote the spreadsheet program VisiCalc for the Apple II, the first usable office application for any microcomputer.

VisiCalc was an enormous success, partly on account of its performance, but also thanks to a brilliant user interface, in which numbers were arranged in a table of rows and columns just as on a sheet of paper. Complex calculations could then be carried out simply and in a very clear form. The VisiCalc operating concept was based on the idea of a spreadsheet, borrowing a familiar term from the real world to simplify things for the computer user. For an investment of about $2,500 for the hardware and an additional $100 or so for the software, a small business could therefore buy a computer accounting system that would otherwise have cost twenty times as much. For the first time in the history of computing, the program was at least as important as the computer on which it ran.

GAMES TITLES FOR THE TRS-80. **TANDY RADIOSHACK** USA **1977**

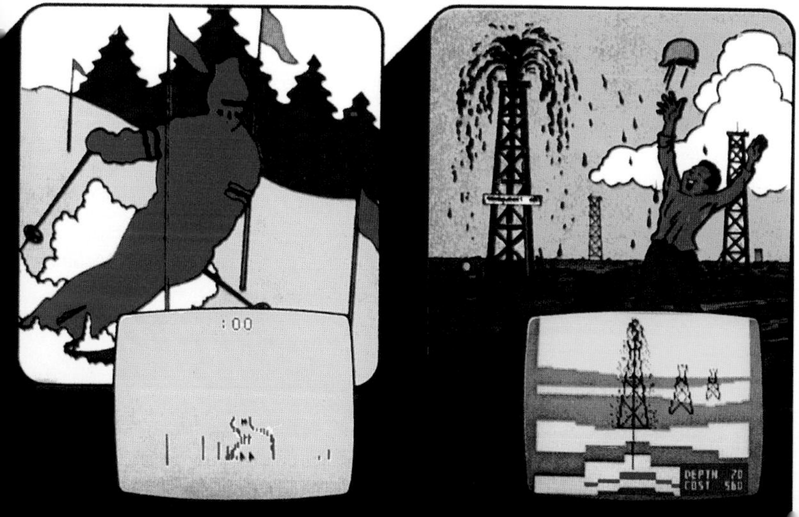

VCS 2600 GAMES CONSOLE. **ATARI** USA **1977**

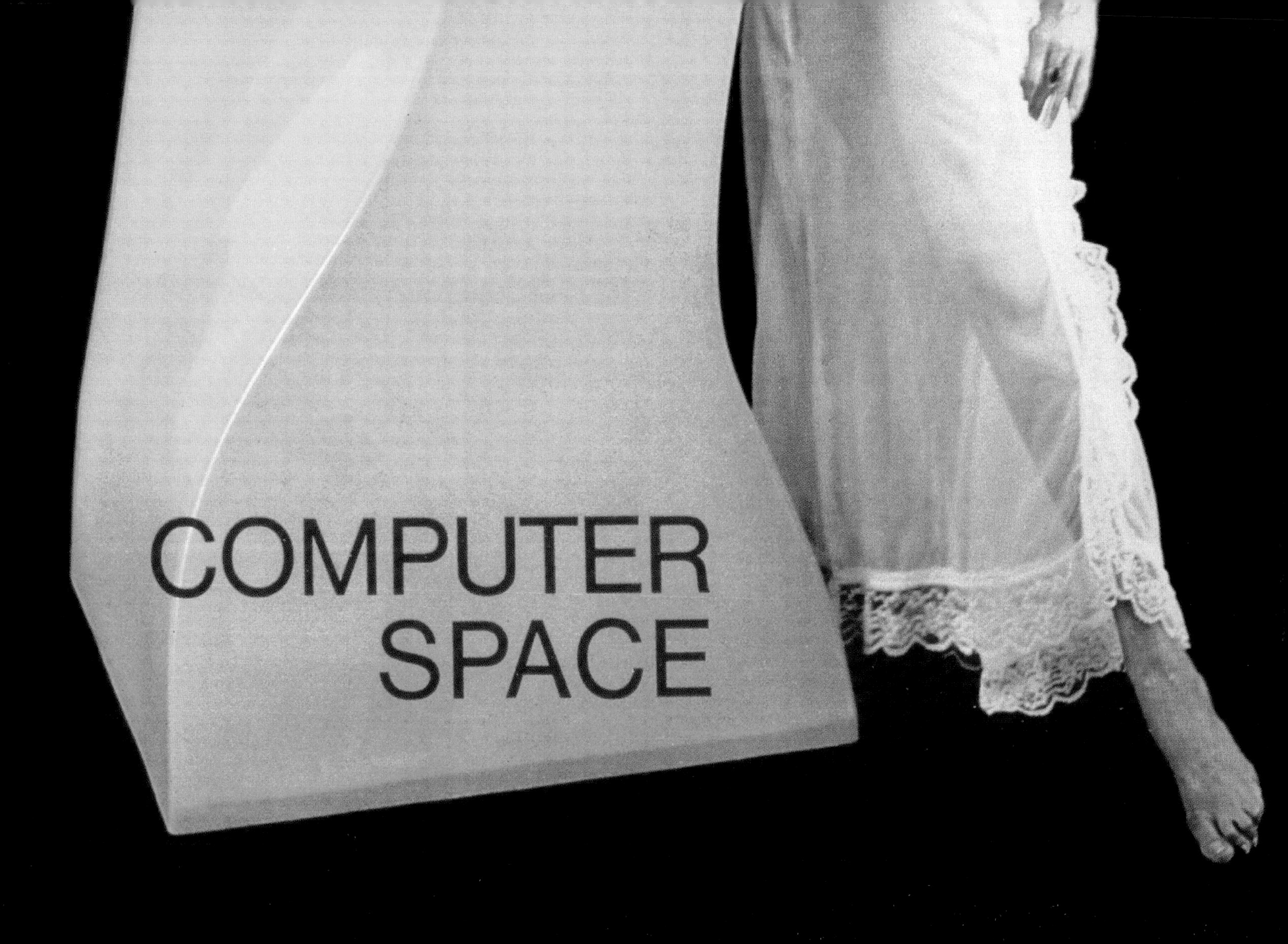
COMPUTER
SPACE

‹‹ COMPUTER SPACE, THE WORLD'S FIRST VIDEO GAME, BY NOLAN BUSHNELL WHO LATER FOUNDED ATARI. **NUTTING ASSOCIATES** USA **1969**

PET 2001. **COMMODORE** USA **1977**
VC 20. **COMMODORE** USA **1981**

CBM. **COMMODORE** USA **1979**
C 64. **COMMODORE** USA **1982**

TI-99/4A. **TEXAS INSTRUMENTS** USA **1981**
ATARI 800 XL. **ATARI** USA **1983**

4.4 "A MASERATI FOR YOUR MIND."

Apple, 1983

In the same year there followed the first 'word processing' programs, for example WordStar by Micropro International. WordStar replaced the line editors that had originally been intended for programming and not for producing whole paragraphs of text. Their line-oriented principle meant that the user could write only a line of text at a time; he then had to save it by pressing a command key before he could see a number of lines. The simple typewriter – using sequential input of text and mechanical deletion of mistakes with the whole page in view – was far superior to the line editors.

WordStar, as the model for all later text-editing programs, set a new standard of user-friendliness. Its clear user interface, using highlighting or colour to distinguish different blocks of text, presented a menu of commands and a paragraph or two of text at a time – not exactly "what you see is what you get", but a good first approximation. The most useful of its numerous options was the ability to move a block of text to any other place in the document, something that has affected our entire way of writing: hardly anything characterises the computer age better than the words 'copy' and 'paste'. WordStar became one of the great software triumphs of the 1980s, even more popular than VisiCalc. In 1980 Seagate developed the first hard disc for personal computers. With a very modest capacity and a price of about $6,000 it was beyond the means of most users, but ten years later it had become part of the standard equipment of any PC.

The structure of the PC market, until then dominated by Apple, began to change when IBM brought out its own PC in 1981 – extraordinarily late. Even more than the Apple II, it was based on an open architecture that was eagerly copied by vast numbers of smaller manufacturers. The very fact that it was made by IBM led to a second wave of cloning, establishing a new de-facto industry standard. Whereas in 1982 Apple still had a market share of 26%, compared to IBM's 17%, the growing competition and resulting price war brought a flood of inexpensive computers on the market, with the result that within a few years the IBM architecture had become the absolute standard for personal computers, with a market share of almost 90% at the turn of the millennium.

A new operating system for the IBM PC also began to dominate the market: Microsoft's MS-DOS. Microsoft was strategically far-sighted and retained the marketing rights for the operating system that was soon running on almost every IBM-compatible computer. The main job of DOS (disk operating system) was to organise read/write operations on the diskette drive, manage files, and generally take care of input and output.

DOS was effectively an extended version of CP/M. It was based on command lines, and the user had to observe a strict syntax consisting of an abbreviated command, generally followed by one or more operands or parameters. Compared to BASIC, which was almost like English, the cryptic DOS was something of a backward step. For example, tricks were required to type a backslash (\) which was a fundamental part of DOS syntax and not at all the same as /. The command syntax was not always easy to remember, and often one had to refer to the manual to carry out a simple operation. There was a built-in help system, at least in later versions, but that was not much use if one had forgotten how to call it up!

THE OLIVETTI M 20 WAS ONE OF THE FEW EARLY PERSONAL COMPUTERS WITH GRAPHICS.

4.5 THE FIRST PORTABLE

The first portable computer, the Osborne I, also came out in 1982. For $1,800 one became the proud owner of a CP/M computer with two diskette drives, 64 kilobytes of store, and an acoustic coupler, the forerunner of the modem. The other unusual feature was that Adam Osborne included an extensive package of software, worth almost as much as the computer itself. The main disadvantage, besides the weight of 12 kg, was the black-and-white screen not much larger than a credit card.

The professional aspirations of the IBM PC, the availability of programs for almost every imaginable purpose, and the wave of clones it set off, were factors that led to it becoming very common in offices and in the home. The PC acquired the reputation of a maid of all work, though its critics dismissed it as nothing more than a sophisticated typewriter. In 1982, *Time* magazine broke with its tradition of nominating a personality of the year from the world of politics, culture, science, or business, and instead declaring the computer “machine of the year”.

The PC era was accompanied by the rise of a software industry developing applications programs for office use, starting with text editors and spreadsheet programs. The business applications began to represent a serious threat to minicomputers and mainframe computers, emphasizing the growing importance of software compared to hardware.

The main change in the user interface, compared to home computers, was the use of an operating system, even if the DOS-type command syntax was generally less convenient than the BASIC programming language. Text remained the basis of interaction with the computer, still with a strict distinction between text and graphics modes, the programs having to switch back and forth between them.

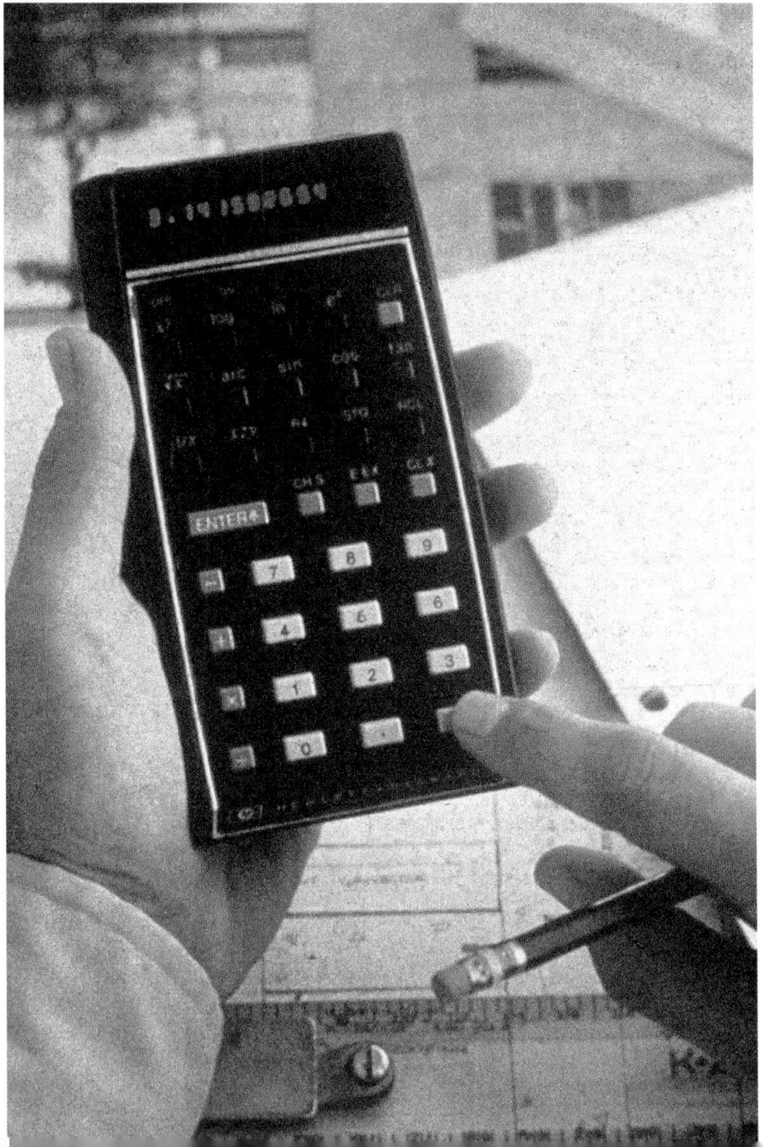

THE HP 35, THE FIRST PROGRAMMABLE POCKET CALCULATOR. **HEWLETT PACKARD** USA **1972**

MAGNETIC STRIP FOR THE TI 59, FOR READING AND WRITING SOFTWARE

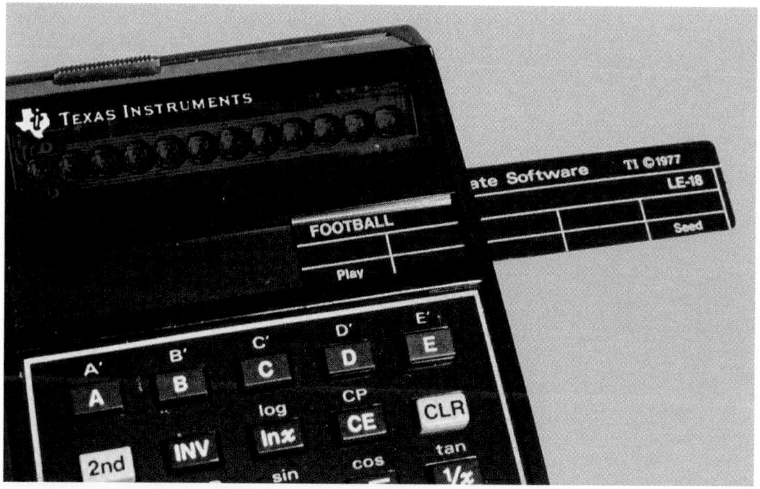

IMSAI 8080
PROGRAMMED OUTPUT
STATUS BYTE
DATA BUS
ADDRESS BUS

"EXPERIENCE THE EXCITEMENT OF OWNING THE WORLD'S FINEST PERSONAL COMPUTER"

ADVERTISEMENT FOR THE IMSAI 8080

THE IMSAI 8080 IS A DIRECT COPY OF THE ALTAIR 8800 BUT WITH NUMEROUS IMPROVEMENTS. IT ORIGINALLY COST $400 IN KIT FORM OR $620 ASSEMBLED, BUT THE GREAT DEMAND SOON PUSHED UP THE PRICE TO $600 AND $930 RESPECTIVELY. **IMSAI** USA **1977**

Sol Terminal Computer
OKIDATA 110

FIRST INTENDED PURELY AS AN INPUT TERMINAL, THE SOL TERMINAL COMPUTER WAS LATER PRODUCED AS A COMPUTER IN ITS OWN RIGHT. ITS DESIGNER, LEE FELSENSTEIN, WAS ALSO CHAIRMAN OF THE HOMEBREW COMPUTER CLUB. THIS ILLUSTRATION SHOWS THE SOL WITH EXTENSIVE ACCESSORIES, EXTENSION STORE, DRIVES, AND OTHER PERIPHERALS. **PROCESSOR TECHNOLOGY** USA **1977**

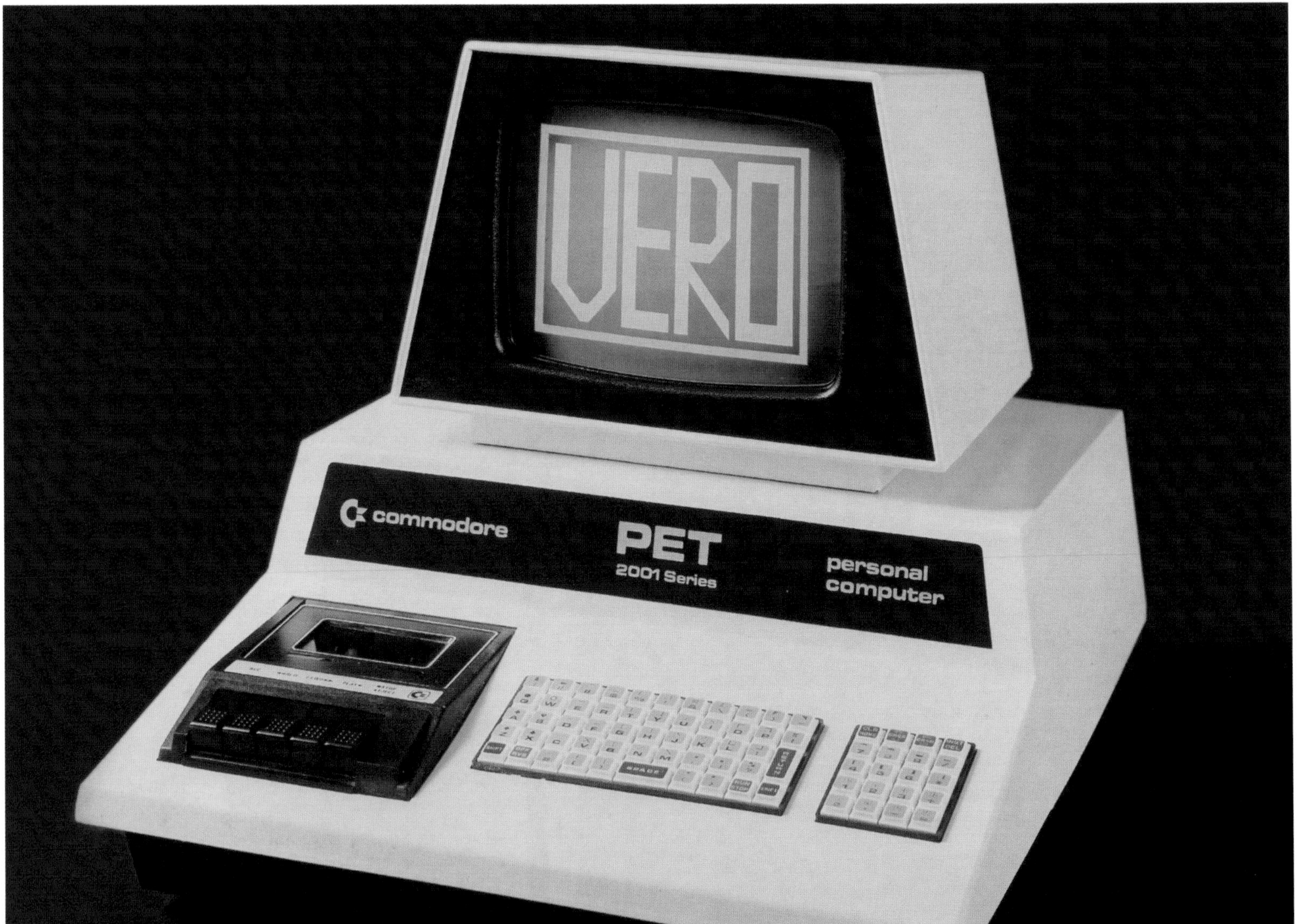
VERO
commodore
PET
2001 Series
personal
computer

PET 2001

RÜDIGER GANSLANDT

THESE DAYS, PERSONAL COMPUTERS NO LONGER REPRESENT A CLEARLY DISTINCT CATEGORY. THE TERM WAS DEVISED TO DIFFERENTIATE THEM FROM THE HOME COMPUTERS, BUT NOW THAT THOSE HAVE MORE OR LESS DIED OUT THE NAME STANDS FOR ANYTHING BUILT TO THE IBM OR MACINTOSH STANDARD AND PRO-VIDING COMPUTING POWER ON A DESK. THE ONLY POSSIBLE CONFUSION COULD BE WITH P.C., NORTH AMERICA´S ATTEMPT "ABOUT ELEVEN YEARS LATE" TO INTRODUCE A KIND OF ORWELLIAN NEWSPEAK UNDER THE LABEL "POLITICAL CORRECTNESS".

REMINISCING ABOUT THE PET 2001 TAKES US BACK TO THE DAYS BEFORE EVEN THE TERM PC WAS INVENTED. "PERSONAL ELECTRONIC TRANSACTOR" WAS THE NAME ON COMMODORE´S COMPUTER, WHICH TOGETHER WITH THE TRS-80 BY RADIO SHACK AND THE APPLE II BLEEPED IN THE AGE OF SINGLE-USER COMPUTERS IN 1977. IN THE LONG RUN THE COMPANY MUST HAVE FOUND THE RATHER ABSTRACT DESIGNA-TION TOO UNWIELDY, FOR A COUPLE OF YEARS LATER IT BORE ONLY THE ABBREVIATION PET, TOGETHER WITH THE TYPE NUMBER 2001, AND NEXT TO IT THE DESCRIPTION "PROFESSIONAL COMPUTER".

THAT WAS NOT TOO GREAT A CLAIM WHEN MEASURED AGAINST THE PERFORMANCE OF THE CONTEMPORARY "SUPERBOARDS": CIRCUIT BOARDS ON RUBBER FEET, WHICH IN THE STANDARD VERSION COULD OFTEN UNDERSTAND AND DISPLAY ONLY HEXADECIMAL GIBBERISH – LUMINOUS RED DIGITS INTERSPERSED WITH THE LETTERS A TO F. YET, COMPARED TO THE OPEN SYSTEM ARCHITECTURE AND GENEROUS STORAGE CAPACITY OF THE APPLE II, THE EPITHET "PROFESSIONAL" WAS SOMEWHAT DARING.

WHAT DID THE PET 2001 OFFER TO SUPPORT ITS CLAIM? FIRST OF ALL, A METAL CASE IN ANGULAR BLACK-AND-BEIGE DESIGN, WEIGHING 20 KILOGRAMS AND CONTAINING THE COMPUTER, KEYBOARD, AND " IN A KIND OF CHOPPED-OFF PYRAMID ON TOP " A SMALL MONITOR. THE BROCHURES USUALLY SHOWED THE SCREEN WITH NOBLE-LOOKING GREEN CHARACTERS AND A CONFIDENCE-INSPIRING TYPEWRITER KEYBOARD.

MY PET, BOUGHT SECOND-HAND, WAS THE MORE SPARTAN ORIGINAL VERSION WITH A BLACK-AND-WHITE SCREEN, A MINI KEYBOARD WITH DIFFERENT COLOURED LETTERS, AND A BUILT-IN CASSETTE RECORDER FOR MASS STORAGE, KNOWN AS THE "DATASETTE".

A GREATER PROBLEM WAS WHAT WAS INSIDE. THE PET 2001 CAME WITH 13 KILOBYTES OF READ-ONLY MEMORY FOR THE OPERATING SYSTEM AND THE READY-INSTALLED BASIC, PLUS 8 KILOBYTES OF USABLE STORE – STATIC RAM CHIPS WITH A HIGH CURRENT CONSUMPTION THAT AFTER A SHORT TIME BECAME TOO HOT TO TOUCH, FREQUENTLY BURNED OUT, AND FOR WHICH REPLACEMENTS WERE NO LONGER AVAILABLE AFTER THE EARLY 1980S. THE SCREEN COULD DISPLAY FORTY CHARACTERS ON A LINE, A CHOICE OF CAPITAL LETTERS OR PREDEFINED GRAPHICS SYMBOLS; LOWER-CASE LETTERS REQUIRED ONE TO GET TO INTIMATE GRIPS WITH THE SOFTWARE INNARDS OF THE MACHINE.

AND THE AVAILABLE SOFTWARE? SERIOUS PROGRAMS FOR ENGINEERS AND BUSINESSMEN WERE REPUTEDLY AVAILABLE ON DISKETTE AT A HIGH PRICE. FOR A NORMAL MORTAL LIKE MYSELF, WITH ONLY A CASSETTE DRIVE, THERE WAS NOT MUCH MORE THAN A COUPLE OF MEAGRE UTILITY PROGRAMS. IN THE DAYS BEFORE MAGAZINES PRINTED PROGRAM LISTINGS THAT ONE COULD TYPE IN, THE ONLY ALTERNATIVE WAS WRITING ONE'S OWN PROGRAMS. WHAT MOTIVATED ME WAS AN ABSTRACT QUESTION: TO WHAT EXTENT COULD EVERYDAY (AND CORRESPONDINGLY NEBULOUSLY FORMULATED) PROBLEMS BE SOLVED WITH THE RIGOROUSLY FORMALISED TOOLBOX OF A PROGRAMMING LANGUAGE – HOW MANY MECHANIZABLE RULES WERE CONCEALED IN EVERYDAY LIFE, AND HOW MUCH INTELLIGENCE IN THE COMPUTER?

WITH AN AVAILABLE STORE OF 8 KILOBYTES IT COULDN'T BE ANY VERY COMPLEX PROGRAMS. ALL THE SAME, I WAS ABLE TO SHOW THAT IT'S ASTONISHINGLY EASY TO TURN THE COMPUTER INTO AN ALMOST UNBEATABLE PLAYER OF NOUGHTS AND CROSSES, OR TO WRITE AN I CHING PROGRAM. EVEN VERSIONS OF PARRY AND ELIZA, THE FIRST TENTATIVE AMERICAN ATTEMPTS AT ARTIFICIAL INTELLIGENCE, COULD BE PROGRAMMED IN COMMODORE BASIC. IN ENGLISH, AT ANY RATE: THE VAGARIES OF GERMAN GRAMMAR SOON SHOWED UP THE LIMITS OF COMPUTER INTELLIGENCE – OR AT LEAST OF MY PROGRAMMING ABILITIES.

FOR A LANGUAGE STUDENT AND A MEMBER OF THE ´68 GENERATION TO OWN A COMPUTER CAUSED ADVERSITIES OF QUITE A DIFFERENT KIND. FOR FELLOW STUDENTS (OF BOTH SEXES) WITH A WELL-DEVELOPED SOCIAL AWARENESS, SUCH A MACHINE WAS A WORK OF THE DEVIL AND POSSESSING ONE MADE ME A LACKEY OF CAPITALISM AND TECHNOLOGY, A CRIME THAT NOT EVEN THE MOST ABJECT SELF-CRITICISM COULD ATONE FOR, SO I WAS INEVITABLY EXCOMMUNICATED FROM THE GROUP. SOME OF MY CRITICS LATER CAME ALONG FULL OF CONTRITION AND BEGGED TO BE ALLOWED TO USE THE TEXT PROCESSOR FOR THEIR MA THESES, OR REPORTED HAVING EXPERIENCED A DIGITAL AWAKENING IN THE COURSE OF RETRAINING SCHEMES FOR UNEMPLOYED TEACHERS. BUT THAT WAS A LATER CHAPTER IN MY LIFE. THE PET, IF YOU DIDN´T LOOK TOO CLOSELY, WAS A PC – P.C. IT WAS CERTAINLY NOT.

THE SINCLAIR ZX81. **SINCLAIR** GREAT BRITAIN **1981**

THERMAL PRINTER AND
'RAM PACK' EXTENSION STORE

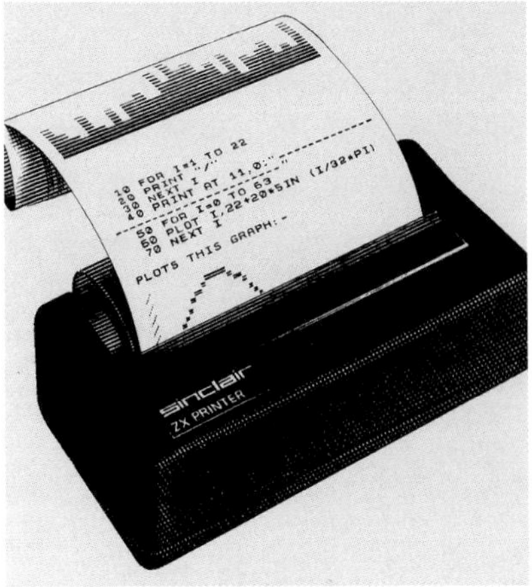

QL HOME COMPUTER. **SINCLAIR** GREAT BRITAIN **1984**

DATA MEDIUM FOR THE MICRODRIVE MAGNETIC TAPE DEVICE

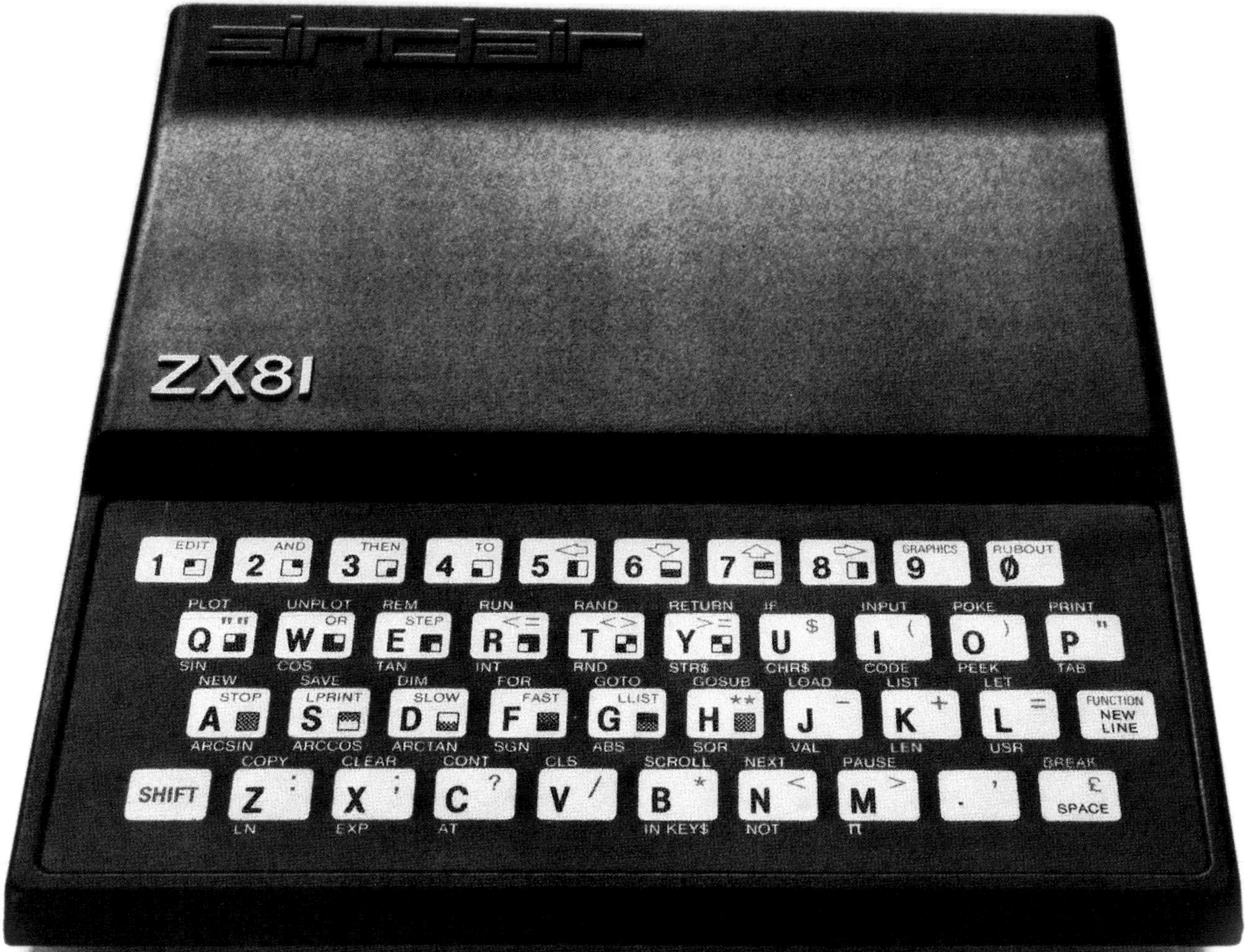
sinclair
ZX81
1 EDIT 2 AND 3 THEN 4 TO 5 6 7 8 9 GRAPHICS 0 RUBOUT
PLOT UNPLOT REM RUN RAND RETURN IF INPUT POKE PRINT
Q W OR E STEP R <= T <> Y >= U $ I (O) P "
SIN COS TAN INT RND STR$ CHR$ CODE PEEK TAB
NEW SAVE DIM FOR GOTO GOSUB LOAD LIST LET
A STOP S LPRINT D SLOW F FAST G LLIST H ** J - K + L = FUNCTION NEW LINE
ARCSIN ARCCOS ARCTAN SGN ABS SQR VAL LEN USR
COPY CLEAR CONT CLS SCROLL NEXT PAUSE BREAK
SHIFT Z : X ; C ? V / B * N < M > . , £ SPACE
LN EXP AT IN KEY$ NOT π

SINCLAIR ZX 81

THOMAS J. SCHULT

WHAT I REALLY WANTED WAS A POCKET CALCULATOR, A PROPER PROGRAMMABLE ONE. THE "ELECTRONIC CALCULATOR" I OWNED AT THE TIME, IN THE EARLY 1980S, CALLED ITSELF PROGRAMMABLE BUT ITS COMMAND LANGUAGE ALLOWED NEITHER LOOPS NOR CONDITIONAL JUMPS: NO REPETITION AND NO IF-THEN, A BIT LIKE A CAR THAT CAN ONLY GO STRAIGHT AHEAD.

BUT THERE WERE OTHERS. I FOUND THAT OUT FROM AN OLDER BOY I MET ON VACATION AT A NORTH SEA RESORT WHO SHOWED ME HOW HE COULD LAND ON THE MOON WITH HIS CALCULATOR. VISUALLY IT WASN'T VERY SOPHISTICATED, BUT THE RHYTHMICALLY GLOWING RED NUMERALS IN THE DISPLAY ANNOUNCED THE ALTITUDE AND THE FUEL RESERVES. YOU COULD ACTUALLY CONTROL SOMETHING.

SO IT HAD TO BE A MOON-LANDING CALCULATOR. JUST THEN THERE APPEARED IN THE NEWS MAGAZINE *SPIEGEL* A FULL-PAGE ADVERTISEMENT SHOWING A SERIOUS-LOOKING BUSINESSMAN HUNCHED OVER A SMALL BLACK THING ON HIS DESK. NEXT TO IT WAS SOME BLURB ABOUT AN INCREDIBLE 400 MARKS FOR A REAL COMPUTER: THE SINCLAIR ZX81. I TORE OUT THE AD AND TOOK IT TO SCHOOL WITH ME. I ASKED GREGOR, WHO I RECKONED HAD MORE TECHNOLOGICAL COMPETENCE THAN ANYONE THERE, WHAT YOU COULD DO WITH A COMPUTER LIKE THAT. HIS ANSWER TOOK ME ABACK: "EVERYTHING!"

SO THAT SETTLED IT. SOON AFTERWARDS I TOOK MY NEW POSSESSION TO SCHOOL, WRAPPED IN A WOOLLY HAT, FOR GREGOR TO ADMIRE.

MY FIRST PROGRAM FOR THE BUILT-IN BASIC INTERPRETER HAD THE EFFECT OF WRITING AN ENDLESS SEQUENCE OF QUESTION MARKS ON THE ZX81 MONITOR. LOOKING BACK, I CAN'T EVEN ATTEMPT TO FATHOM OUT THE SENSE OF THAT. IT WAS THE SHEER FASCINATION OF GETTING A PIECE OF DEAD MATTER TO DO WHAT I TOLD IT, AND IN THEORY, GO ON DOING IT FOR EVER. "MONITOR" IS TOO GRAND, OF COURSE:

IT WAS AN OLD BLACK-AND-WHITE TELEVISION, AND MY EYES WATERED BECAUSE I WAS MUCH TOO CLOSE TO IT.

WAS THE SINCLAIR ACTUALLY ANY USE? YOU COULDN´T EVEN WRITE A LETTER WITH IT. ADMITTEDLY YOU COULD BUY A PRINTER, BUT I WOULDN´T HAVE WANTED TO SEND THE RESULTS TO ANYONE. IT REQUIRED ROLLS OF SPECIAL SILVERY PAPER, ABOUT AS WIDE AS A SUPERMARKET TILL SLIP. ANYWAY, THERE WAS NO TEXT EDITOR. I WOULD HAVE HAD TO CONCEAL MY MESSAGES IN THE OPULENT VOCABULARY OF SINCLAIR´S BASIC DIALECT (SLOW STEP, THEN PAUSE AND RETURN -). GAMES, BORROWED FROM A FRIEND AND WHICH I MANAGED, AFTER SEVERAL ATTEMPTS, TO READ INTO THE SINCLAIR FROM A GRINDING CASSETTE RECORDER, HAD A TRANSITORY APPEAL. AND I NEVER GOT TO THE MOON.

THE PROGRAMS WERE RESTRICTED TO THE TRIVIAL, FOR LACK OF STORAGE SPACE (ONE KILOBYTE IN THE EARLY DAYS). I DIDN´T NOTICE THE SCORN IN GREGOR´S FAINT PRAISE WHEN I TOLD HIM ABOUT MY PROGRAM FOR GENERATING PRIME NUMBERS. INSTEAD OF QUESTION MARKS, IT SHOVELLED ENDLESS NUMBERS ONTO THE SCREEN. I MAY DISCOVER A PATTERN AND BECOME FAMOUS, I THOUGHT.

PERHAPS IT´S ALL TO THE GOOD THAT I DIDN´T. THE KIND OF FAME THAT CLIVE SINCLAIR, THE INVENTOR OF THE ZX81, ATTAINED IN BRITAIN CAN BE SEEN AS A MIXED BLESSING. HE LEFT SCHOOL AT SEVENTEEN, FEELING THAT THE EDUCATIONAL SYSTEM OFFERED TOO LITTLE SCOPE. AFTER THAT HE GAINED A REPUTATION OF FLITTING FROM ONE CRAZY SCHEME TO ANOTHER. HE FOUNDED COMPANIES, WENT BUST, MADE A COME-BACK, INVENTED AND DEVELOPED POCKET CALCULATORS, HOME COMPUTERS, MINI-TELEVISIONS, MOBILE PHONES, ELECTRIC VEHICLES – SENSATIONAL PRODUCTS, A BIT NUTTY, AND ALWAYS CHEAP, SO AS TO GIVE THE MASSES WHAT THEY DESERVED. IN 1983 MAGGIE THATCHER ARRANGED A KNIGHTHOOD FOR HIM, AND TWO YEARS LATER HE WAS BANKRUPT AGAIN.

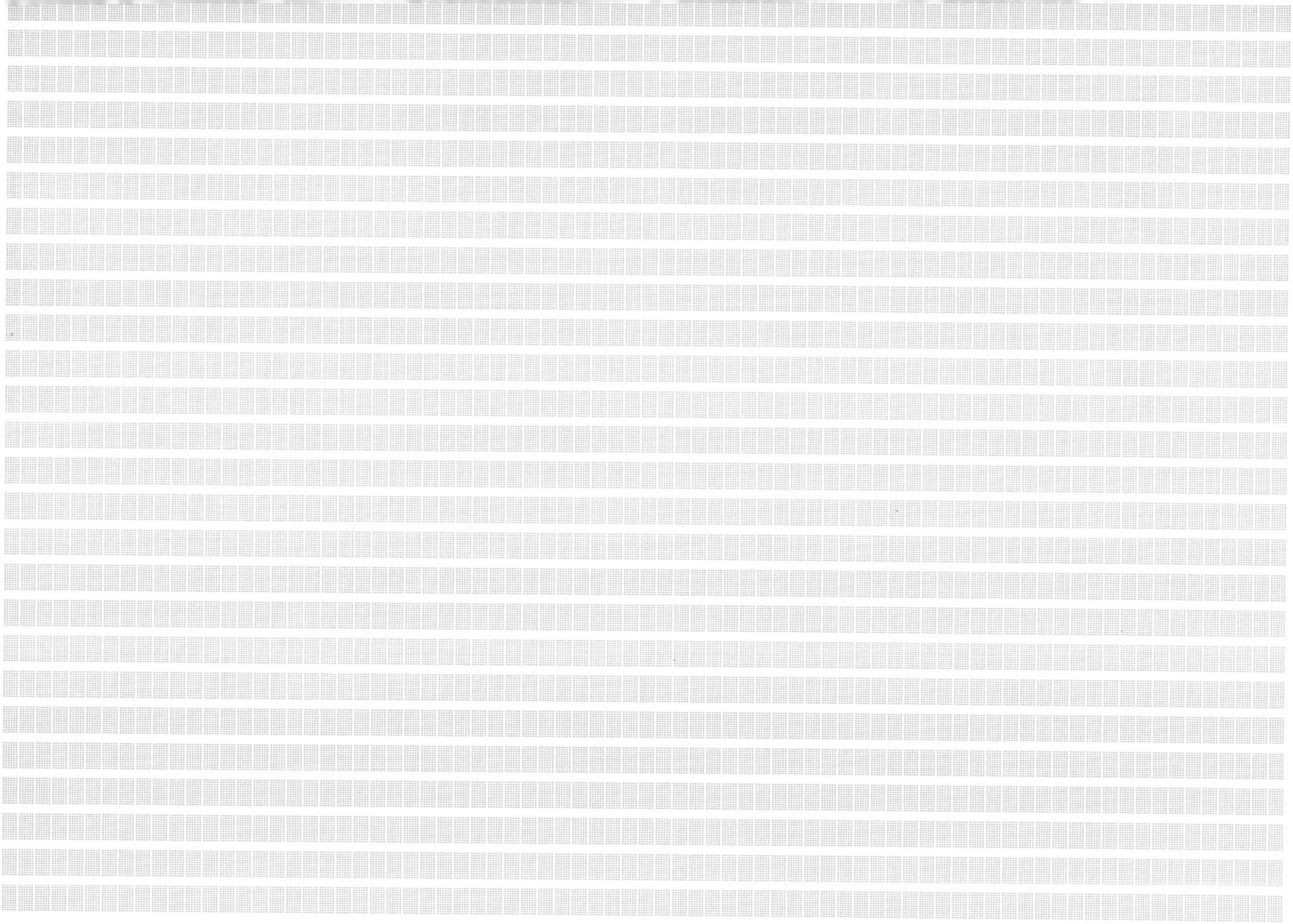

```
\
0 : A9 0 AA 20 EF FF 08 8A 4C 2 0

0000: A9
0.A

0000: A9 00 AA 20 EF FF 08 8A
0008: 4C 02 00


THIS IS WHAT A 6502-COMPATIBLE COMPUTER
DISPLAY LOOKS LIKE. IT IS THE SAME
ONE USED IN THE APPLE-1.
\
THE HEX ABOVE IS A PROGRAM THAT CHECKS
THE DISPLAY AND ATTACHMENTS. FOR MORE IN
FO DOWNLOAD BOINX SOFTWARE'S SIM6502.

\
A LINK TO IT IS PROVIDED IN THE RELATED
LINKS SECTION OF THE APPLE-1 DISPLAY.
```

THE MONOCHROME DISPLAY OF THE APPLE (ABOVE). **APPLE** USA **1979**
APPLE IIE AND APPLE III. **APPLE** USA **1979**

THE APPLE I (ABOVE) **APPLE** USA **1976**
STEVE JOBS AND STEVEN WOZNIAK IN THE LABORATORY (BELOW). **APPLE** USA **1977**

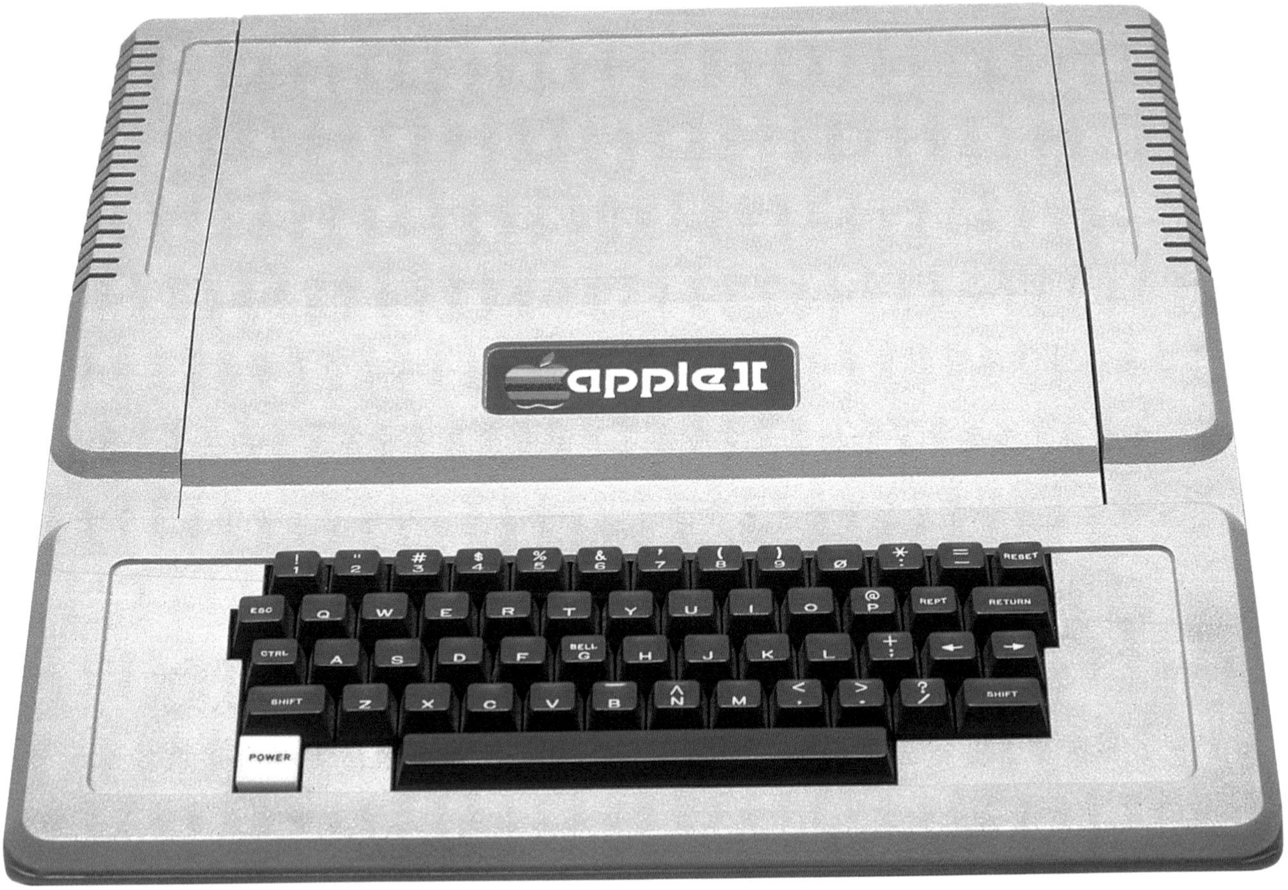
apple][
POWER

APPLE II

WOLFGANG HARZ

THE YEAR WAS 1983, AND MY MIND WAS MADE UP. I BADLY NEEDED A COMPUTER, BUT IT HAD TO BE A "REAL" ONE. AS REAL COMPUTERS ALSO COST VERY REAL AMOUNTS OF MONEY, I JOINED THE RANKS OF LIKE-MINDED PEOPLE WHO WERE GOING TO BUILD THEIR OWN. IN FACT, THE BUILDING WAS LIMITED TO THE POWER SUPPLY AND THE CASE. THE REST WAS JUST SOLDERING COMPONENTS IN THEIR MARKED PLACES ON THE CIRCUIT BOARDS: 1,500 SOLDER JOINTS IN ALL.

IT WAS A COPY OF THE HIGHLY SUCCESSFUL APPLE II, WHICH DOMINATED THE MARKET FOR PERSONAL COMPUTERS BEFORE THE IBM MACHINE CAUGHT ON. EVEN IN THOSE DAYS, MOST NEWCOMERS TO COMPUTERS FOLLOWED THE SAME RULE AS TODAY: YOU BUY THE MODEL THAT OTHER PEOPLE ARE USING. THE REASON WAS OBVIOUS: YOU COULD GET HELP MORE EASILY WHEN YOU NEEDED IT.

THE APPLE II "THE COMPANY WROTE IT APPLE" ATTRACTED SO MANY IMITATIONS BECAUSE IT WAS ASSEMBLED EXCLUSIVELY FROM STANDARD COMPONENTS. NO MICROCHIPS THAT ONLY THE ORIGINAL MANU-FACTURER COULD SUPPLY, NO SID AND VIC AS IN THE COMMODORE C64, BUT JUST PLAIN TTL ICS WHICH COULD BE BOUGHT FROM ANY GOOD ELECTRONICS SHOP. THAT WAS THE STRONG POINT ABOUT THE DESIGN. STEVEN WOZNIAK, CREATOR OF THE MACHINE AND A COFOUNDER OF APPLE COMPUTER INC., CAME FROM THE CALIFORNIA AMATEUR ELECTRONICS SCENE WHOSE AIM WAS TECHNOLOGY FOR ALL. WOZNIAK HIMSELF REALLY ONLY WANTED TO PUT TOGETHER A COMPUTER ON WHICH HE COULD PROGRAM THE PRIMITIVE VIDEO GAME PONG. THAT WAS IN 1976, AND THE RESULT WAS THE APPLE II.

BUT ONCE YOU HAVE A THING LIKE THAT, THEN YOU DISCOVER ALL SORTS OF OTHER THINGS YOU CAN DO WITH IT. TEXT PROCESSING FIRST AND FOREMOST; DATA PROCESSING IN THE TRADITIONAL SENSE WAS SECONDARY – STATISTICS, THAT SORT OF THING. ALL VERY VAGUE. THE FACT THAT IT WAS A BARE MACHINE WITHOUT A STANDARD INTERFACE ONLY MADE IT MORE ATTRACTIVE. SO THE FIRST THING TO

BUY WAS THE LANGUAGE CARD WITH AN EXTRA 16 KILOBYTES OF STORE. THE EXTENSION SLOTS WERE A BLESSING AND A CURSE IN ONE. THERE WERE EIGHT SLOTS CRYING OUT TO BE FILLED. AND FILLED THEY WERE: PARALLEL INTERFACE, SERIAL INTERFACE, 80-CHARACTER BOARD, Z80 BOARD, CLOCK, DISK CONTROLLER, RAM DISK. BY THE TIME I FINISHED, THE COMPUTER WAS FULL TO THE BRIM.

BY THEN, MY APPLE II HAD PRODUCED THREE DIPLOMA THESES AND SEVERAL STUDIES. WHAT FASCINATED ME MOST WAS GRAPHICS PROGRAMMING. THE MACHINE WOULD SPEND NIGHTS ON END CALCULATING FRACTAL IMAGES WHEN CHAOS THEORY BECAME FASHIONABLE IN THE MID-1980S. I LIVED WITH MY APPLE FOR FIVE YEARS, FOR BETTER, FOR WORSE. EVEN TODAY, A COMPUTER WITH ITS FEATURES WOULD BE AN ADVANTAGE. NO FAN, NO WHINING HARD DISK. JUST CALM SILENCE, WHICH STEVE JOBS, THE OTHER APPLE FOUNDER AND AN ADHERENT OF ZEN, INSISTED ON FOR THE FIRST MACINTOSH, THE NEXT-GENERATION APPLE.

THE APPLE II'S SUCCESS, AS WE KNOW FROM HISTORY, CAME WHEN SOME CLEVER PROGRAMMERS INVENTED A SPREADSHEET PROGRAM NAMED VISICALC, AVAILABLE ONLY FOR THE APPLE. IT WAS THE ORIGINAL "KILLER APPLICATION", THE SINGLE SUPER PROGRAM THAT PEOPLE NO LONGER WANTED TO BE WITHOUT AND SO BOUGHT THE COMPUTER IT RAN ON.

BUT THE APPLE WAS POPULAR FOR ITS OWN SAKE. WE COULD SEE THAT IN 1986 WHEN THE GIOTTO SPACE PROBE WAS APPROACHING HALLEY'S COMET. IN THE GERMAN MISSION CONTROL CENTRE IN DARMSTADT STOOD AN APPLE IIE WHICH DISPLAYED THE DATA IN REAL-TIME FROM ONE OF GIOTTO'S ON-BOARD EXPERIMENTS. LOW COST WAS A DECISIVE CRITERION FOR THE IRISH EPONA EXPERIMENT (ENERGETIC PARTICLE ONSET ADMONITOR); OUR BELOVED COMPUTER'S GREAT HOUR HAD COME.

TWO YEARS LATER, WHEN ITS DAY WAS ALMOST OVER, I ACQUIRED A SECOND ONE, AN ORIGINAL APPLE IIE. IT'S STILL WORKING, WITH ITS FAMILIAR RATTLING DISK DRIVES, BUT IS NOW LITTLE MORE THAN A REMINDER OF TIMES PAST. THE SPIRIT OF THE APPLE II LIVES ON IN AN EMULATION PROGRAM RUNNING ON A STANDARD PC – FASTER THAN THE ORIGINAL. EVEN ON A 386DX33 WHICH ITSELF IS

CONSIDERED OLD-FASHIONED NOW. APPLE EVEN BROUGHT OUT AN APPLE II PLUG-IN BOARD FOR THE MACINTOSH LC III, INTENDED MAINLY FOR ALL THE SCHOOLS IN THE USA THAT WERE SO ATTACHED TO THE MASS OF OLD SOFTWARE FOR THE WONDERFULLY SIMPLE APPLE. THE COMPLETE APPLE II, WHICH WHEN IT CAME OUT CONTAINED OVER 150 ICS, HAD SHRUNK TO A SINGLE CHIP ON THAT LITTLE CIRCUIT BOARD. AN APPLE-SPECIFIC CHIP, OF COURSE.

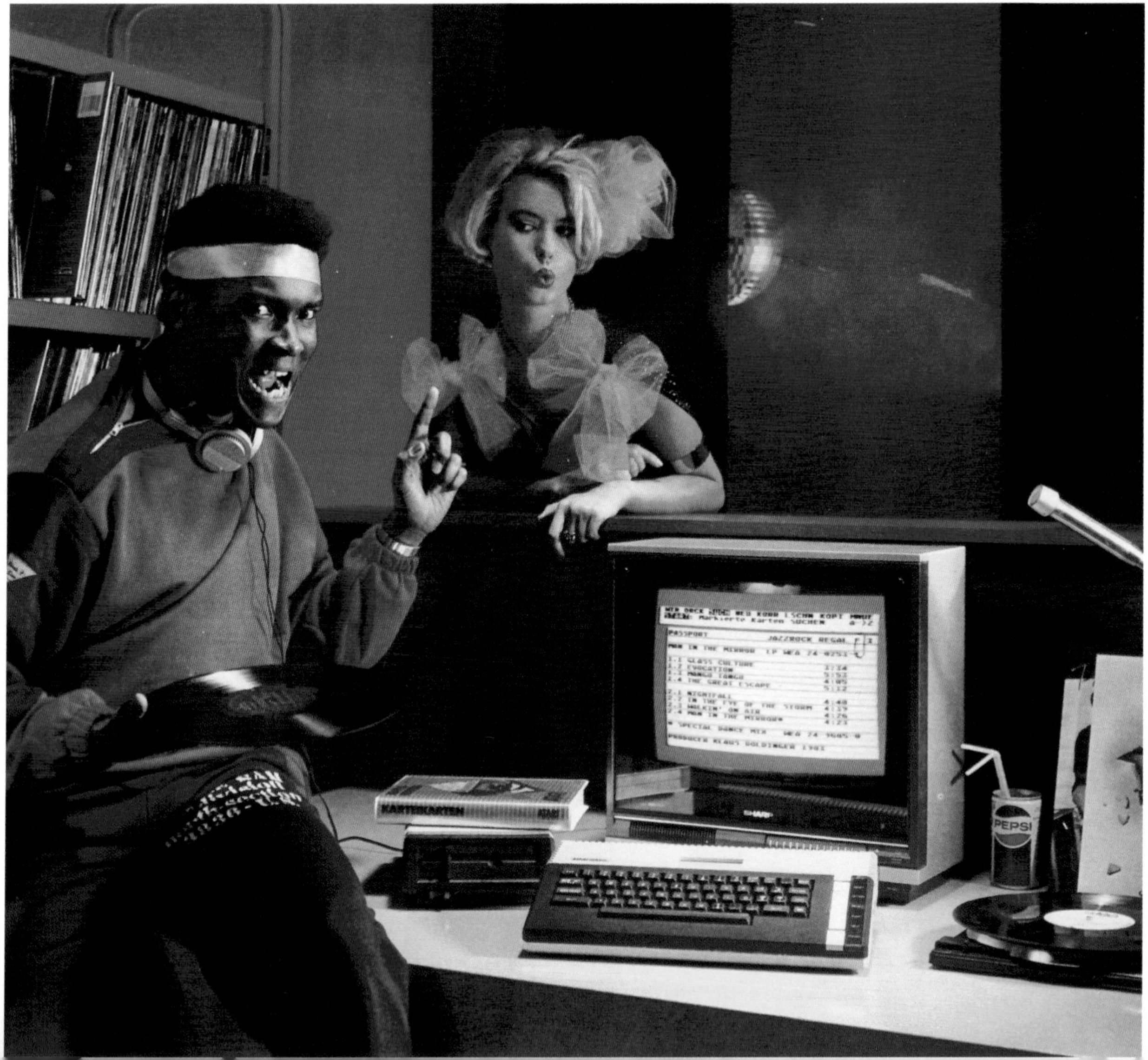
Markierte Karten SUCHEN
PASSPORT
JAZZROCK REGAL
MAN IN THE MIRROR
GLASS CULTURE
EVOCATION
MANGO TANGO
THE GREAT ESCAPE
NIGHTFALL
IN THE EYE OF THE STORM
WALKIN' ON AIR
MAN IN THE MIRROR
SPECIAL DANCE MIX
PRODUCER KLAUS DOLDINGER 1981
KARTEIKARTEN
PEPSI

"WOW! I JUST SAID 'MAN IN THE MIRROR' AND IT REPLIED 'F-3, PASSPORT, PAGE 2, TITLE 4'."

FROM AN ADVERTISEMENT FOR THE ATARI 800 XL

"FASTEN YOUR SEAT BELTS, COMMODORE AND TEXAS INSTRUMENTS FREAKS ...". FROM AN ADVERTISEMENT FOR THE ATARI POLE POSITION GAME. **ATARISOFT** USA **1984**

commodore 64
POWER

COMMODORE C64

GERO VON RANDOW

WE NOW ENTER THE INNER SANCTUM OF THE HARDWARE MUSEUM – PAST A ROW OF PALE-FACED MIDDLE-AGED MEN. THERE WE SEE SOMETHING LOOKING RATHER LIKE A BREAD BIN WITH PUSH BUTTONS, TETHERED TO A TELEVISION SET. IT´S THE C64, THE BEST-SELLING COMPUTER OF ALL TIME, SAID TO HAVE SOLD BETWEEN 17 AND 22 MILLION UNITS FROM 1982 ONWARDS.

THIS „HOME COMPUTER“, AS THEY WERE CALLED IN THOSE DAYS, ENTERED MY LIFE SOON AFTERWARDS, A PRESENT FROM MY PARENTS. I WASN´T PARTICULARLY INTERESTED IN COMPUTERS: I DIDN´T KNOW MUCH ABOUT THEM, AND NEVER ASKED FOR ONE. BUT THERE IT WAS, REPORTING „38911 BASIC BYTES FREE“. THE CHEEK OF IT: THE COMPUTER CONTAINED SOMETHING THAT WAS BEYOND MY KEN! THE CHALLENGE HAD TO BE TAKEN UP, OF COURSE (MY PARENTS WERE NOT SO STUPID, AFTER ALL). AND IF YOU WANTED TO DO ANYTHING WITH THE C64, THERE WERE NO LITTLE ARROWS AND ICONS. YOU HAD TO LEARN A PROPER COMPUTER LANGUAGE – WELL, AT LEAST A FEW EXPRESSIONS IN BASIC.

THEN I FELL DOWN A FLIGHT OF STEPS AND BROKE A LEG, AND SUDDENLY I HAD TIME ON MY HANDS. SO IT WAS THAT THE C64 THAT OPENED THE DOOR TO THE COMPUTER WORLD. RICH LANDSCAPES UNFOLDED BEFORE ME: ADVENTURE GAMES (THE BEST OF THEM WITH TEXT ONLY, BUT STILL A TREASURE CHEST), GAMES OF SKILL (FOR EXAMPLE POGO JOE THE WHOLE NIGHT LONG – QUITE MAD!). DATA TRANSMISSION, TEXT PROCESSING, ROBOTS, COMPOSING MUSIC, PROGRAMMING IN FORTH OR LISP OR ASSEMBLER.

ASSEMBLER? SEMI-COMPREHENSIBLE SYMBOLIC INSTRUCTIONS, NICE FOR THE MACHINE, HARD FOR A HUMAN. IT WAS EVEN HARDER TO PROGRAM THE C64 PURELY IN MACHINE CODE. THE CODES BORE NO OBVIOUS RELATION TO THE SENSE THEY CONTAINED. A SECRET LANGUAGE, ESOTERIC, WONDROUS!

THE OPERATING SYSTEM WAS PERMANENTLY BURNED INTO ROM CHIPS (SAFE FROM VIRUSES!), INDECIPHERABLE BUT PERFECTLY DOCUMENTED. DATA BECKER OF DÜSSELDORF PRODUCED A KIND OF C64 BIBLE, REVEALING WHAT LAY HIDDEN BEHIND EVERY ADDRESS FROM 0000 TO FFFF. THEY COULD BE USED FOR ALL SORTS OF THINGS, EVEN WITH BASIC (BY MEANS OF THE LEGENDARY POKE COMMAND).

THE MACHINE OPENED UP EVER NEW AND EVER DEEPER PLANES TO AN AFICIONADO. ITS CHIPS COULD BE PRECISELY CONTROLLED, AND PARTICULARLY CLEVER WAS THE VIDEO CONTROLLER NAMED VIC. IT HELPED THE CENTRAL PROCESSOR, THE 6510 (A COUSIN OF THE 6502), TO ORGANISE THE SCREEN IMAGE. FOR EXAMPLE, VIC COULD KEEP TRACK OF UP TO EIGHT SPRITES AT A TIME: THEY WERE LITTLE IMAGES THAT THE USER COULD DEFINE AND MOVE ABOUT THE SCREEN, ALSO USING BASIC. THE FIRST C64S HAD A CASSETTE RECORDER AS MASS STORAGE, REJOICING IN THE NAME „DATASETTE". TRYING TO OPTIMISE THE PAINFULLY SLOW WINDING BACK AND FORTH WAS HIGHLY EDUCATIONAL. LATER, A DISKETTE STATION KNOWN AS THE 1541 ALLOWED DIRECT ACCESS TO ANY TRACK. IT GOES WITHOUT SAYING THAT THIS DRIVE WAS ALSO FREELY PROGRAMMABLE – AND INCREDIBLY SLOW.

THE FREAKS BOUGHT THEIR OWN CHIPS, BURNED EPROMS, USED SCREWDRIVERS AND SOLDERING IRONS TO SOUP-UP THEIR C64S. THE OPERATING SYSTEM COULD EASILY BE COPIED TO RAM AND THEN MODIFIED. CHANGING A SOFTWARE POINTER COULD BE LIKE INSTALLING A NEW ENGINE. IN OTHER WORDS, THE C64 WAS A SELF-VARYING MACHINE, THE EPITOME OF THE COMPUTER. (MY BEST PROGRAM WAS AN EMULATION OF A TURING MACHINE, WRITTEN PURELY IN MACHINE CODE. I FINALLY HAD PROOF THAT THE C64 REALLY WAS A COMPUTER.)

FOR YEARS, IT SURFED ON THE PEAK OF A SOFTWARE WAVE. BY THE LATE 1980S IT WAS A TECHNICAL HAS-BEEN, AND HARDLY ANYBODY USED IT FOR THEIR WORK, ERGONOMIC DISASTER AREA AS IT WAS. BUT THE VARIETY OF PROGRAMS KEPT IT ON THE MARKET FOR A WHILE: SPREADSHEETS, TEXT PROCESSING, EVEN A PRIMITIVE KIND OF WINDOWS – THE C64 HAD THEM ALL.

COMMODORE WENT OUT OF BUSINESS IN 1994. UNDAUNTED, A CIRCLE OF FANS KEPT GOING WITH ITS OWN NEWS GROUPS, A MAGAZINE, AND ALWAYS SOME NEW ADAPTATION. IN THE MEANTIME THERE'S AN EMULATION PROGRAM TO TRANSFORM A STANDARD PC INTO A C64 – INCLUDING AN OUTPUT FOR THE 1541 DISKETTE DRIVE. THE C64 CAN NEVER DIE. AT THE END OF TIME, WHEN THE UNIVERSE IMPLODES, COMES TO A STANDSTILL OR THINS OUT TO INFINITY, ONE MESSAGE WILL LIVE ON: "38911 BASIC BYTES FREE".

THE GALAXIAN (TOP) AND FORT APOCALYPSE GAMES FOR THE COMMODORE 64 (BOTTOM). **ATARISOFT** AND **SYNAPSE SOFTWARE** USA **1984** AND **1982** >>

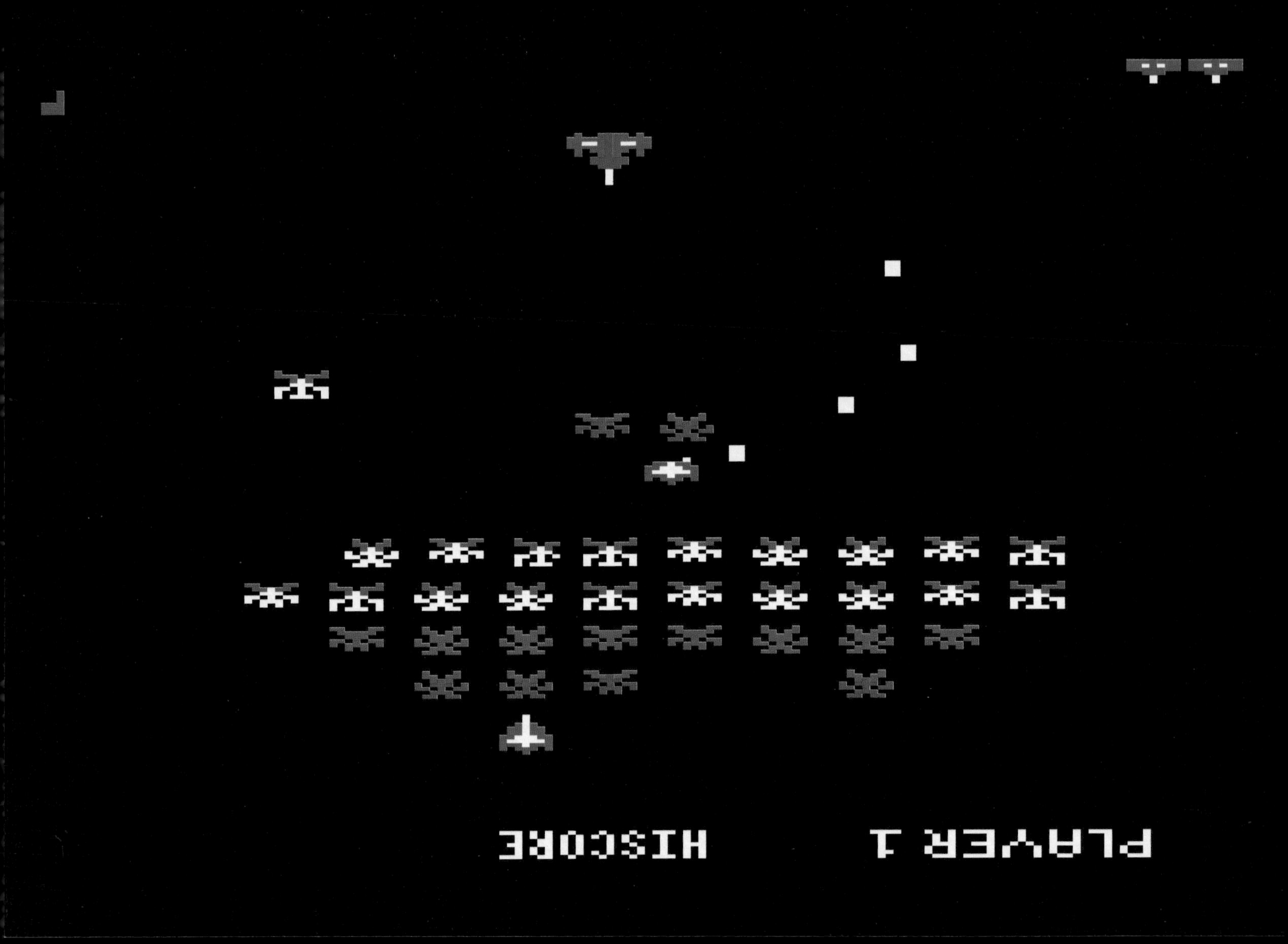
HISCORE
PLAYER 1

SCORE 1580
FUEL
1586
BONUS
9073
NAVATRON

THE ORIGINAL ATARI STANDARD JOYSTICK, THE MODEL FOR ALL LATER JOYSTICK VARIANTS. **ATARI** USA **1977**

THE VCS 2600 VIDEO GAMES CONSOLE IN ITS 6-SWITCH VERSION WITH CORDLESS JOYSTICKS IN THE FOREGROUND. **ATARI** USA **1977**

TOP
OFF
ON
TOP

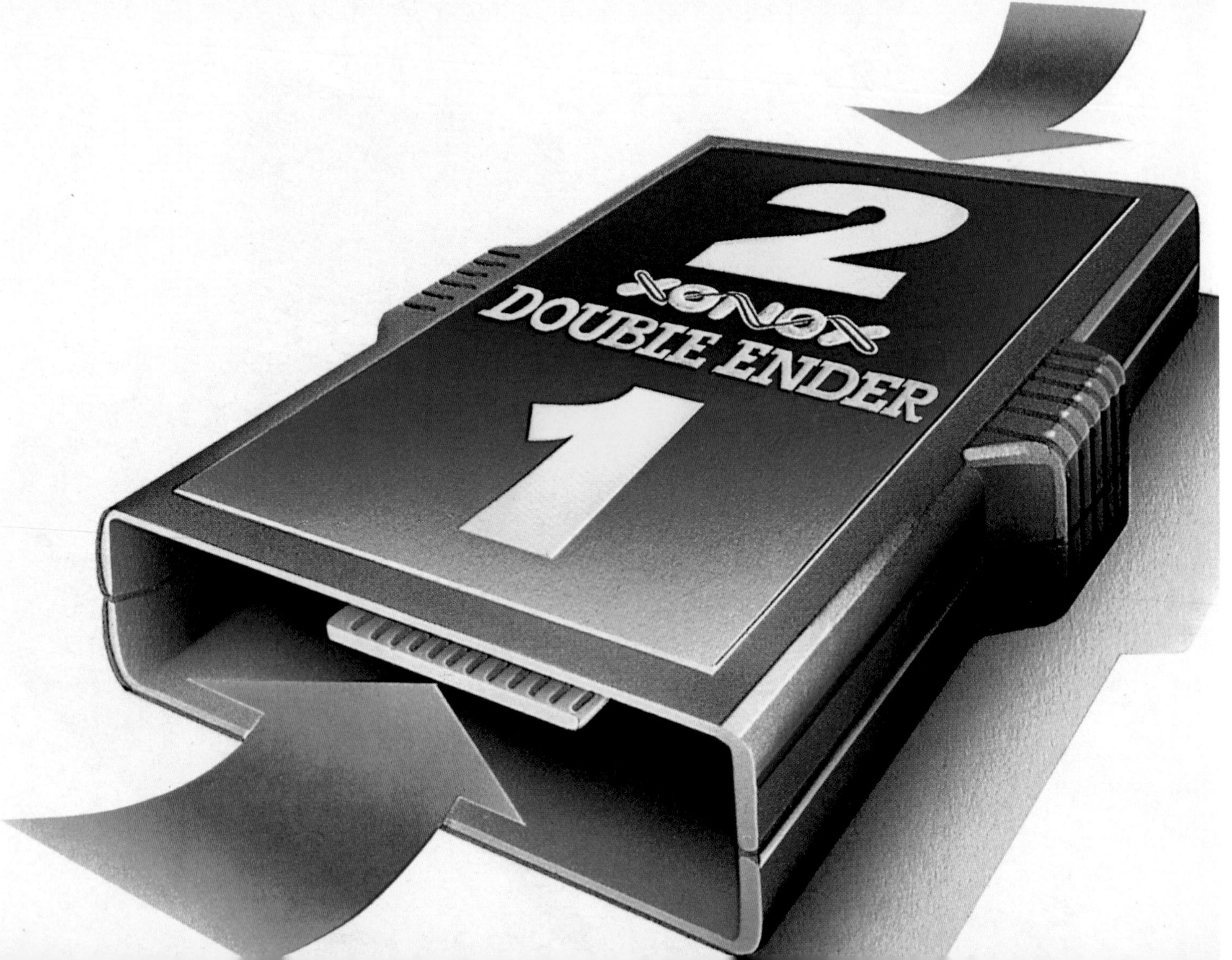
2
XONOX
DOUBLE ENDER
1

THE 'DOUBLE ENDER', AN ATARI CARTRIDGE PLAYABLE IN EITHER DIRECTION FOR THE ATARI (ABOVE). **XONOX** USA **1979**
VARIOUS BADGES FROM ATARI GAMES

"WE ALL LOVE ATARI" PROMOTION WEAR. **ATARI** USA **1982**

ATARI 800. **ATARI** USA **1982**

GALACTIC CHART
ATARI

STILLS FROM THE FILM "TRON", THE FIRST TO USE COMPUTER GRAPHICS AND EFFECTS. **STEVEN LISBERGER** USA **1982**

IMSAI

FUN GAMES TURN INTO SERIOUS REALITY: IN THE HACKER MOVIE “WARGAMES” ENTERING THE SECRET SYSTEM OF THE AMERICAN DEFENCE DEPARTMENT HAS ALMOST FATAL CONSEQUENCES (ABOVE). **JOHN BADHAM** USA **1983**

HACKING IN THE NAME OF THE KGB: STILL FROM THE GERMAN FILM “23 – NOTHING IS LIKE IT APPEARS”, WHICH IS BASED ON A TRUE EVENT (BELOW). **HANS-CHRISTIAN SCHMID** GERMANY **1999**

'BERZERK' TRANSPARENCY. **MILTON BRADLEY** USA **1983**

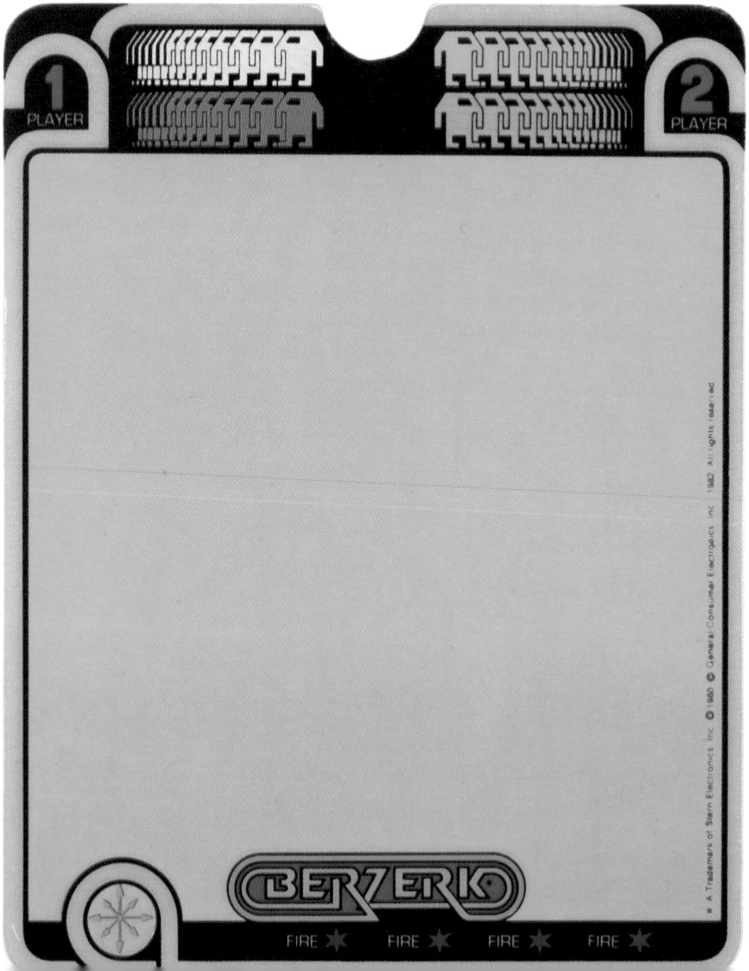

THE VECTREX GAMES CONSOLE. DUE TO ITS LIMITED GRAPHICS, EACH GAME CAME WITH A COLOURFUL TRANSPARENT SHEET. **MILTON BRADLEY** USA **1983**

'SPACE WARS' TRANSPARENCY. **MILTON BRADLEY** USA **1983**

'RIP OFF' TRANSPARENCY. **MILTON BRADLEY** USA **1983**

SYSTEM ONE. **TULIP COMPUTERS** NETHERLANDS **1984** >>

COMPUDATA
TULIP SYSTEM® I

NEU!
64K-Modell
Jetzt mit 10 MBytes
Plattenspeicher
erweiterbar
INTERTEC DATA SYSTEMS
SUPERBRAIN

abc-26
START
STOP
MONITOR
INTENSITY
Ai Electronics
OFF
ON
POWER

<< SUPERBRAIN (TOP), **INTERTEC** USA **1982,** AND ABC 26 (BOTTOM). **ABC ELECTRONICS** USA **1982**

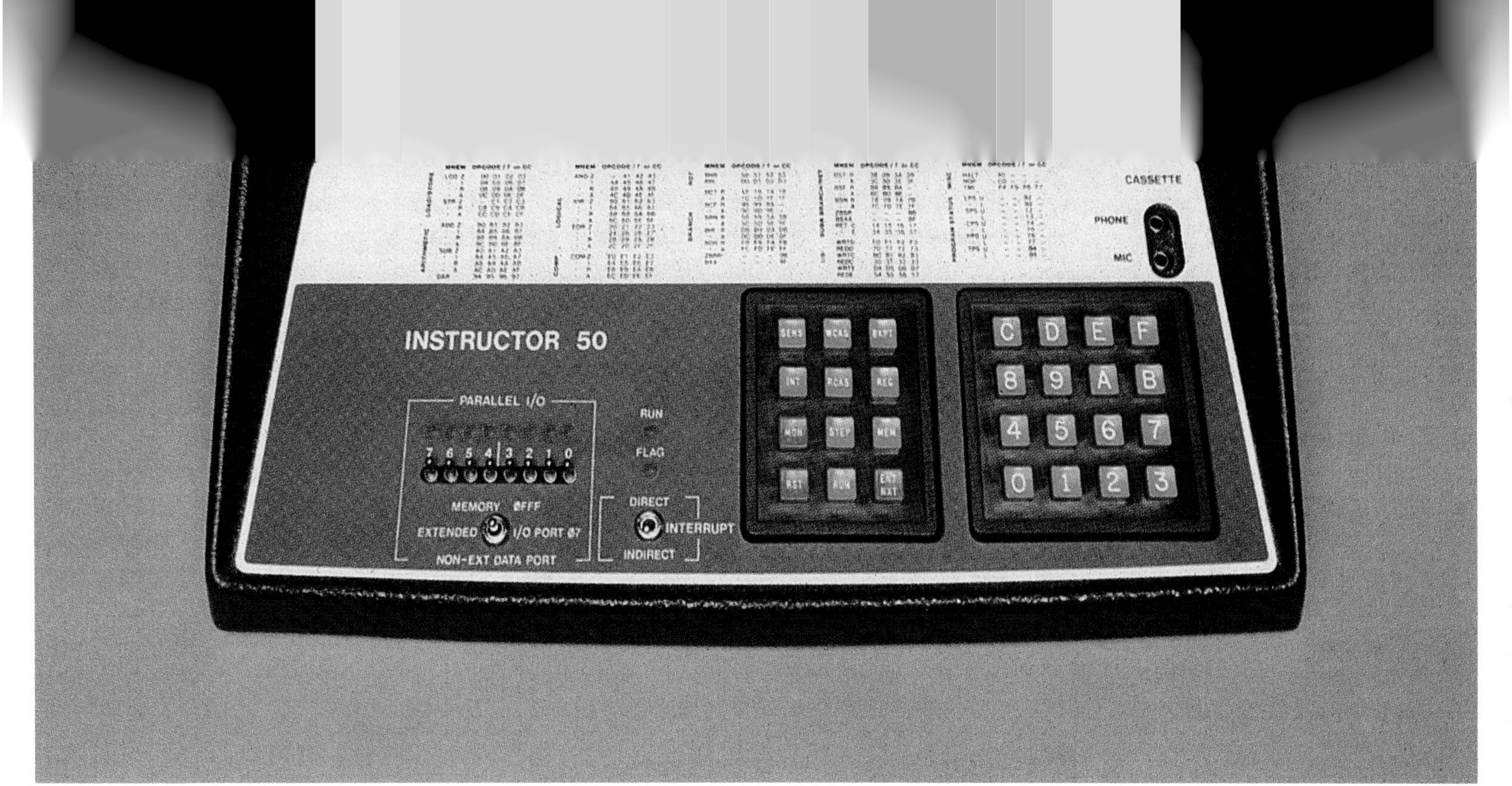

THE INSTRUCTOR 50 COMPUTER HAD TO BE PROGRAMMED ENTIRELY IN MACHINE CODE USING HEXADECIMAL COMMANDS AND ADDRESSES – NOTHING IF NOT INSTRUCTIVE!
SIGNETICS USA **1979**

OSBORNE-1

ADOLF EBELING

BEFORE I TALK ABOUT MY SECOND COMPUTER, AND IN ORDER TO UNDERSTAND WHY I GOT IT, I MUST START BY MENTIONING THE FIRST ONE. THAT WAS A CBM 2001, CHILD OF THE NOW LEGENDARY PET. A MICROCOMPUTER WITH BUILT-IN BASIC, EMPTY APART FROM THAT MEAGRE PROGRAMMING ENVIRONMENT, FILLABLE SOLELY WITH ONE´S OWN CREATIONS, AND CONSEQUENTLY FULL OF IRRESISTIBLE FASCINATION. WHAT JOY TO SEE DECISIONS FLOWING UNHAMPERED BY ANY USEFULNESS, PLAY TRAINS IN THE MOST MODERN AND CAREFREE ELECTRONIC WAY, AND ALL SURROUNDED BY AN AURA OF SERIOUSNESS AND PROGRESS. ART FOR ART´S SAKE, CLEVERLY PACKAGED IN PROGRAM LISTINGS. EVERY INTOXICATION GIVES WAY TO A PERIOD OF SOBERING-UP. IN THIS CASE IT´S CALLED ANALYSING THE UTILITY VALUE, AND THAT WAS PRETTY CLOSE TO ZERO.

COMPUTER NUMBER TWO, WITH THE ´ONE´ IN ITS NAME, WAS TO CHANGE ALL THAT. THIS TIME THE DECISION MUST BE BASED ON COOL REASON RATHER THAN BURNING ARDOUR. IT DID INVOLVE PASSION, AS IT TURNED OUT, THOUGH IN A DIFFERENT SENSE OF THE WORD.

IT REALLY LOOKED VERY DESIRABLE IN ITS GREY-BLUE COAT, A KIND OF RECTANGULAR BUCKET WITH A KEYBOARD AS A LID, THE TWO CONNECTED BY A SPIRAL CABLE. UNDERNEATH THE LID WAS A 5-INCH MONITOR, NOT QUITE AS BIG AS THE PALM OF ONE´S HAND, FLANKED ON EACH SIDE BY A DISKETTE DRIVE, AND A ROW OF CONNECTORS ALONG THE BOTTOM. "OSBORNE I, THE WORLD´S FIRST PORTABLE COMPUTER" IS HOW THE SIGN IN THE SHOP WINDOW DESCRIBED IT.

AND THE MOST UNUSUAL THING ABOUT THIS UNUSUAL MACHINE WAS A SOFTWARE PACKAGE BULGING WITH PROGRAMS: TEXT PROCESSING, SPREADSHEET, DATABASE. AT LAST A COMPUTER ONE COULD REALLY WORK WITH, AT LAST SOMETHING MORE THAN JUST A PROGRAMMABLE TOY. MOBILE, EVEN – SO LONG AS ONE HAD A STRONG ARM AND AN ELECTRIC SOCKET HANDY.

THREE WOMEN AND FOUR MEN WERE THE MIDWIVES AT ITS BIRTH, THE TEAM HEADED BY ADAM OSBORNE, A WELL-KNOWN AUTHOR IN THE FIELD OF ELECTRONICS. ONLY A FEW MONTHS AFTER THE OSBORNE COMPUTER CORPORATION WAS FOUNDED, THE FIRST FIVE PROTOTYPES COULD BE SEEN AT THE WEST COAST COMPUTER FAIR IN THE SPRING OF 1981. THE ORIGINAL SELLING PRICE WAS NEARLY $1,600, THOUGH THE PROGRAMS IT CAME WITH WOULD THEMSELVES HAVE COST $1,500 ON THE OPEN MARKET: WORDSTAR, SUPERCALC, MICROSOFT BASIC, WITH CP/M AS THE OPERATING SYSTEM.

"CP/M WILL SURVIVE, BECAUSE ONLY STANDARDS SURVIVE," WAS OSBORNE'S MAXIM. A FEW MONTHS LATER MS-DOS CAME ALONG AS A WORLD STANDARD AND OUSTED CP/M TO THE GREAT BEYOND, BUT WHO COULD HAVE FORESEEN THAT?

I ORDERED A DAISY-WHEEL PRINTER TO GO WITH IT, THE OLIVETTI PRAXIS 35, READY TO PLUG IN. FOR THE PRICE I PAID, I EXPECTED LOTS OF TYPE TO RATTLE ONTO THE PAPER. IT DID, INTERMITTENTLY. EVEN WITH THE COMPUTER AND THE PRINTER ON THE SAME DESK, THE RIBBON CABLE CONNECTING THEM HAD TO BE A METRE LONG - TOO LONG TO WITHSTAND THE CROSSFIRE OF ELECTROMAGNETIC INTERFERENCE WHEN THE REFRIGERATOR OR FREEZER CAME ON. THE SAD RESULT WAS LETTERS OMITTED OR DUPLICATED, UNLESS I FIRST WENT ROUND THE HOUSE PULLING OUT PLUGS. IF ONLY THAT WERE ALL! BUT THE OSBORNE WAS TOO COMPACT AND OVERHEATED PERMANENTLY AS A RESULT. ADMITTEDLY IT NEVER PASSED OUT COMPLETELY, BUT SOLDIERED BRAVELY ON WITH ITS FUNCTIONS REDUCED TO A MINIMUM. FOR EXAMPLE, IT WOULD SUDDENLY DECIDE IT COULD MANAGE WITHOUT ONE DISKETTE DRIVE. WELL, THE 180 KILOBYTES OF SPACE ON THE OTHER ONE WERE ENOUGH FOR WORDSTAR AND A MEDIUM-SIZED DOCUMENT, BUT I DON'T ENJOY TAKING RISKS, AND THEN THERE'S LAZINESS ON TOP (DO I HAVE TO SPLIT THE FILE YET AGAIN?). AS USUAL IN LIFE, IF SOMETHING CAN GO WRONG IT WILL. GILLS AT THE BACK OF THE CASE DIDN'T ALLOW IT TO BREATHE ANY BETTER - A FAN MIGHT HAVE HELPED, BUT THERE WAS NOWHERE TO PUT IT. EVERY LAST CORNER OF THE CASE WAS STUFFED WITH TWELVE KILOS OF HARDWARE.

ADMITTEDLY, IT WAS THE VERY FIRST PORTABLE COMPUTER, AND INNOVATION ALWAYS DEMANDS ITS TRIBUTE. BUT DIDN´T THEY TEST EVERY SINGLE ONE IN SPECIAL BURN-IN RACKS AT THE OSBORNE HEADQUARTERS IN HAYWARD, CALIFORNIA, THE FUNCTION OF THE DISKETTE DRIVES IN PARTICULAR? AND WEREN´T THE ONES PRODUCED ON A FRIDAY EVEN SUBJECTED TO A 24-HOUR TEST? THAT´S WHAT THEY TOLD US, AT LEAST.

YES, MY VERY OWN OSBORNE WAS SOMETHING SPECIAL. NEITHER A MONDAY MORNING MODEL NOR A FRIDAY AFTERNOON MODEL, BUT A GENUINE SUNDAY´S CHILD THAT GREW UP FREE AND UNINHIBITED IN 1983. ALL THE MORE LOVABLE FOR THAT – AND LOVE, AS WE KNOW, IS BLIND. A LARGE EXTERNAL MONITOR CAME TOO LATE: I ALREADY NEEDED GLASSES BY THEN.

LOCATE 1020 HALF
01010 101 *********** PROGRAMM A U S T GESTARTET ********************
01020 102 EINGABE ANGEBOTSNR (5 STELLEN) :
01030 103 ANGEBOT NR NICHT VORHANDEN, AUFTRAGSNR EINGEBEN :
01040 104 AUFTRAG NR NICHT VORHANDEN, RESTART (Y/N) ?
01050 105 ANGEBOT NR NICHT VORH.(EVTL AUF DISKETTE), RESTART (Y/N) ?
01060 106 QUEUE TABLE VOLL (ENQ IN SYSCOM NICHT MOEGLICH), RESTART (Y/N) ?
01070 107 PROGRAMM AUST IST BEREITS AKTIV, ABBRUCH IST NOTWENDIG
01080 108 ANGEBOT NR BEREITS IN BEARBEITUNG, RESTART (Y/N) ?
01090 109 ANGEBOT NR STATUS IN POSTDAT UNVOLLST., RESTART (Y/N) ?
01100 110 ANGEBOT NR BEREITS IN MASSDAT... LOESCHEN (Y/N) ?
01110 111 DEQ ANGEB. NR IN SYSCOM NICHT MOEGLICH
01120 112 AUFTRAG NR ENTSPRICHT ANGEBOT NR . FORTSETZEN (Y/N) ?
01130 113 ANGEBOT NR IN MASSDAT GELOESCHT
01140 114 ANGEBOT NR IN GLASDAT GELOESCHT
01150 115 VERARBEITUNGSBEGINN VON ANGEBOT NR DURCH PROGRAMM AUST
01160 116 NEU BEGINNEN (Y/N) ?
01170 117 AUFTRAG NR GEHOERT ZU DEM SAMMELAUFTRAG .
01180 118 SOLLEN ALLE AUFTRAEGE MIT KZ VERARBEITET WERDEN (Y/N) ?
01190 119 AUFTRAG NR (ANGEBOT NR)
01200 120 ZUM SAMMELAUFTRAG GEHOEREN FOLGENDE AUFTRAEGE :
01210 121 TECHN. EIGENSCHAFTEN IM INDEX (SUBI) NICHT VOLLSTAENDIG
01220 122 TECHN. DATEN SIND :
1
2
IBM

4878 MONOCHROME DATA MONITOR. **IBM** USA **1982**

THE 3279 AND 5292 COLOUR MONITORS WERE CAPABLE OF DISPLAYING IN RED, YELLOW, GREEN, CYAN, BLUE, MAGENTA, AND WHITE. **IBM** USA **1982** >>

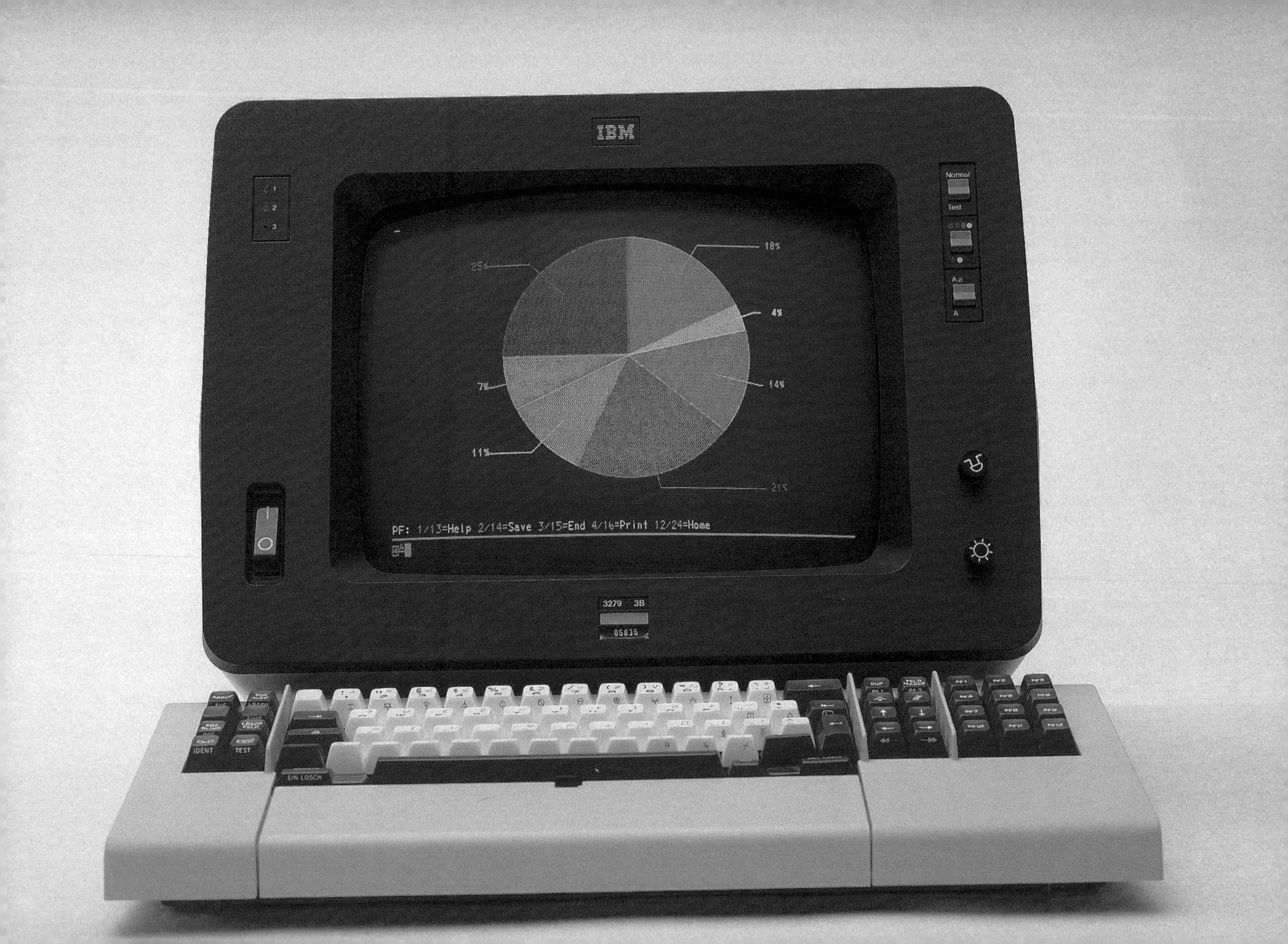
IBM
18%
25%
4%
14%
7%
11%
21%
PF: 1/13=Help 2/14=Save 3/15=End 4/16=Print 12/24=Home
Normal
Test
3279 3B
05835
IDENT
TEST
EIN LOSCH

IBM
K U N D E N S T A M M D A T E N
FORMAT02
Bt-Nr 1 IBM Deutschland GmbH VZ - Frankfurt / Main
Eingabe
KDNR
N a m e
Land PLZ
O r t
11 Barbara Schulze 6500 Mainz
12 Liesel Müller 6500 Mainz
13 Hugo Meier 6000 Frankfurt / Main
14 Walter Schmidt 6000 Frankfurt / Main
15 Inge Bauer 6500 Mainz
16 Erika Fröhlich 6200 Wiesbaden
17
Name Björn Roos
Match-Code Roos
Zusatz Abteilungsleiter
Strasse
Land/PLZ
Ort Wiesbaden
Postfach
Anrede Herr
Vertr-Nr 05
Vertr-Gebiet 07
Titel Dipl. Ing.
Telefon 06121/888888
Telex
Statistik 01
Postleitzahl fehlt

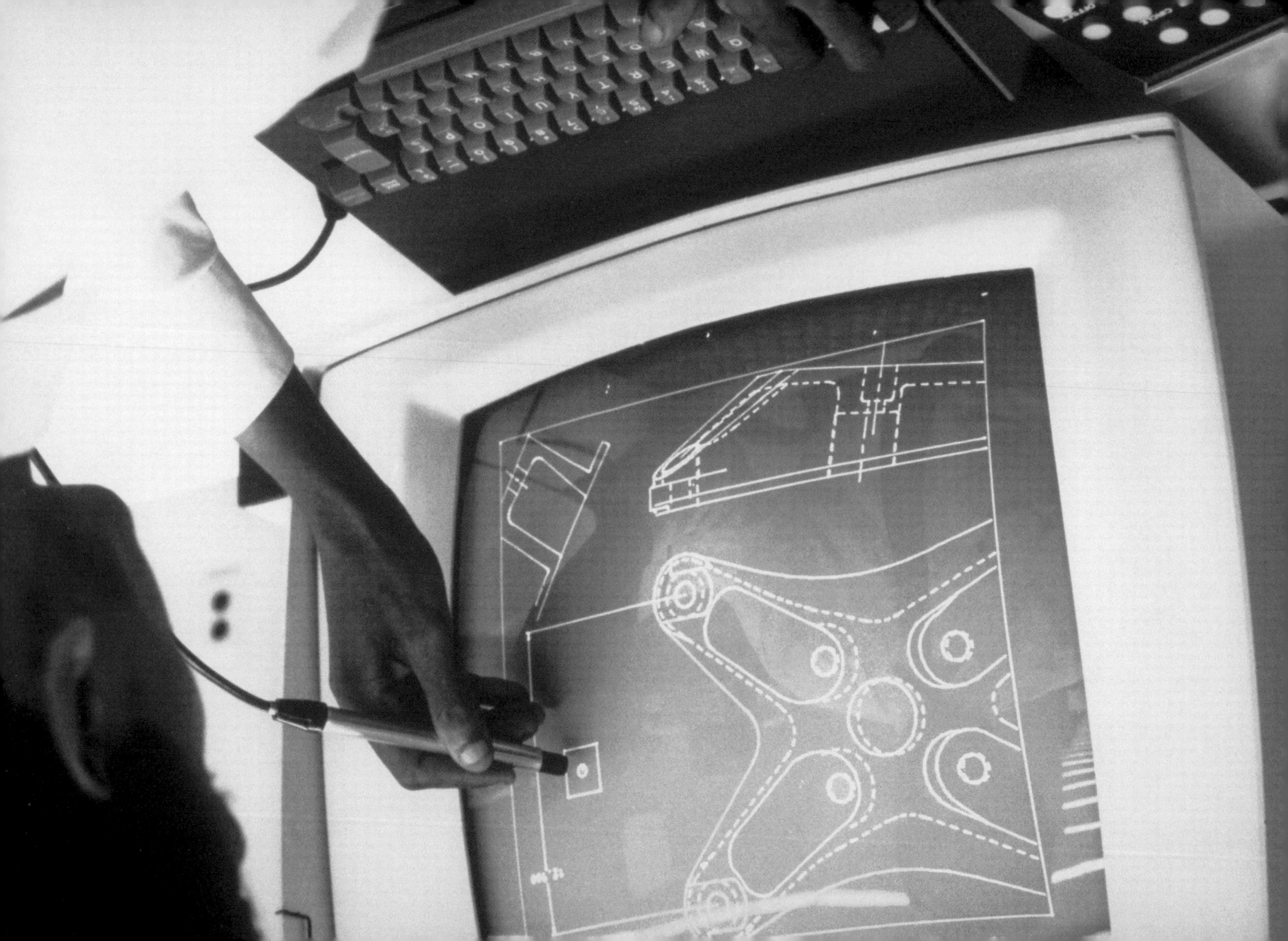

COMPUTER-AIDED DESIGN ON THE SCREEN USING A LIGHT PEN. **LOCKHEED MARTIN** USA **1986**

IT COULD BE OPERATED SIMPLY BY POINTING TO OBJECTS ON THE SCREEN. THE HP 150 WITH TOUCH SCREEN. **HEWLETT-PACKARD** USA **1983**

IBM PC XT (EXTENDED TECHNOLOGY). **IBM** USA **1981**

IBM
SuperScreen
IBM

THE DESKTOP PRO PERSONAL COMPUTER (LEFT) AND PORTABLE PC (RIGHT). **COMPAQ** USA **1984** AND **1982**

TELEVIDEO PORTABLE PC. **TELEVIDEO** USA **1984**

TELEVIDEO TS 804. **TELEVIDEO** USA **1984**

PS/2 MODEL 65 SX/80. **IBM** GERMANY **1986**

THE M21 PORTABLE PC (ABOVE). **OLIVETTI** ITALY **1984,** AND
THE AP PORTABLE PC (RIGHT). **IBM** USA **1987**

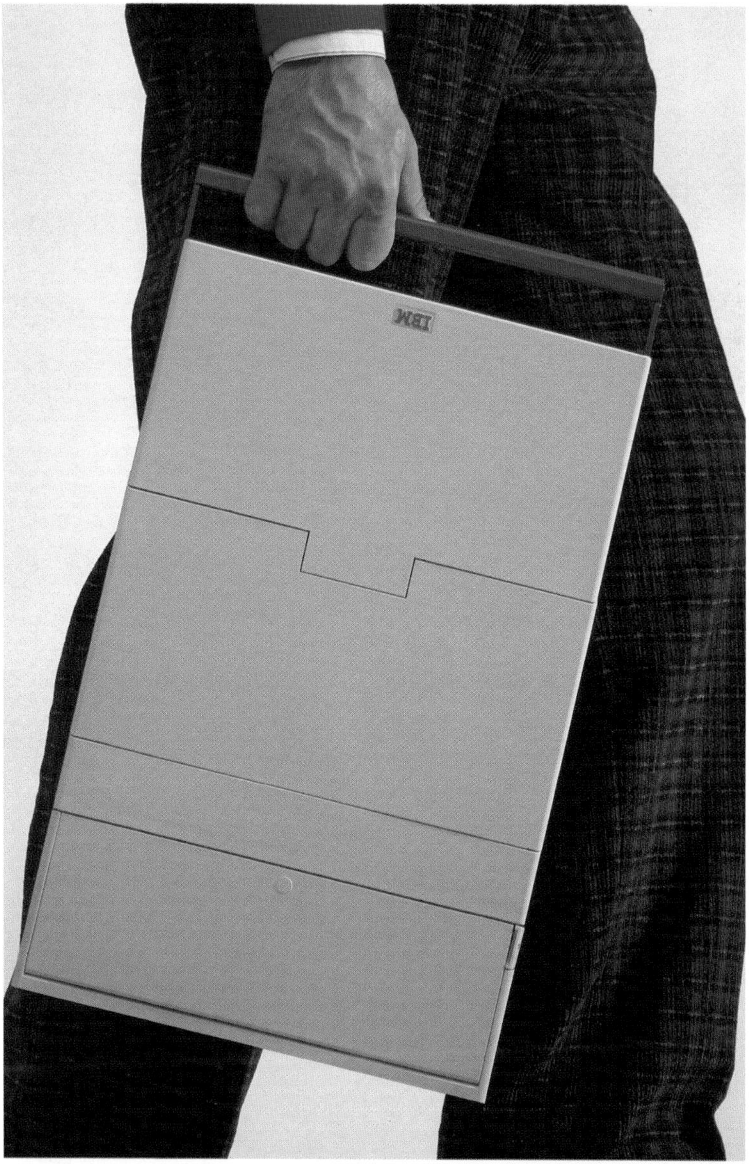

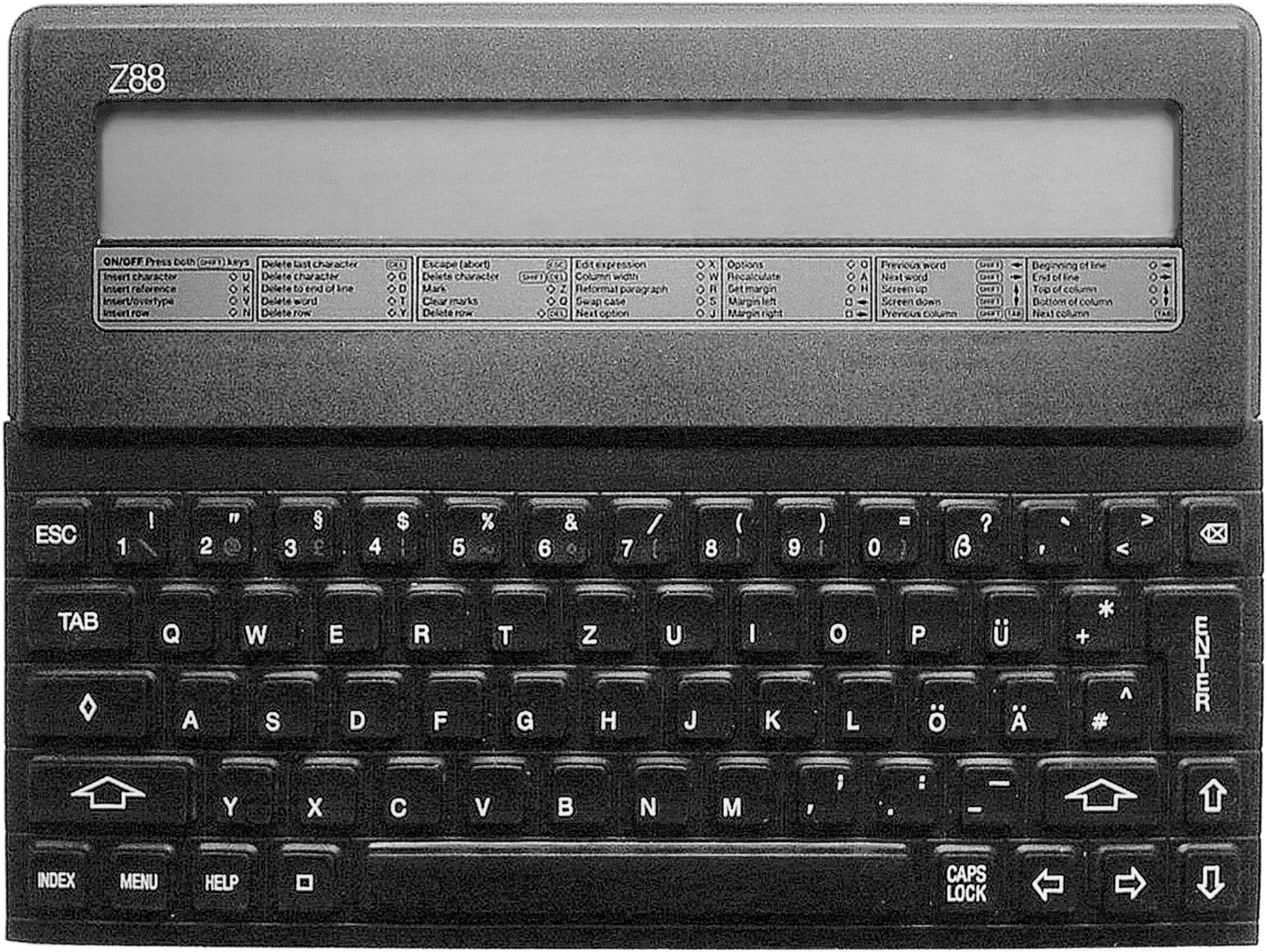
Z88
ON/OFF Press both SHIFT keys
Insert character
Insert reference
Insert/overtype
Insert row
Delete last character
Delete character
Delete to end of line
Delete word
Delete row
Escape (abort)
Delete character
Mark
Clear marks
Delete row
Edit expression
Column width
Reformat paragraph
Swap case
Next option
Options
Recalculate
Set margin
Margin left
Margin right
Previous word
Next word
Screen up
Screen down
Previous column
Beginning of line
End of line
Top of column
Bottom of column
Next column
ESC
TAB
ENTER
INDEX
MENU
HELP
CAPS LOCK

SINCLAIR Z88

KLEMENS POLATSCHEK

THE SINCLAIR Z88 DESCENDED FROM THAT HEAVEN WHERE DWELLS ALL GOOD DESIGN, AND ENTERED INTO A FETISH RELATIONSHIP WITH ME. WE SOUNDED EACH OTHER OUT AT AN OFFICE-EQUIPMENT TRADE FAIR; SOME MONTHS LATER, A DEALER PRODUCED IT FROM THE BOOT OF HIS CAR AT A RENDEZVOUS IN AN UNDERGROUND CAR PARK. THAT´S HOW ONE ACQUIRES THINGS WHICH ARE NOT AVAILABLE THROUGH THE NORMAL CHANNELS.

THE Z88 WAS BLACK AND FLAT, SMALLER THAN A SHEET OF PAPER AND AS THICK AS A FINGER. IT WEIGHED ONLY 900 GRAMS - STILL INCOMPARABLE - AND RAN ON BATTERIES. THE LOWER HALF OF THE TOP SURFACE WAS COVERED WITH A SOFT BLACK RUBBER MAT, WITH BUMPS BEARING LETTERS AND NUMERALS: THIS WAS THE KEYBOARD. A SMALL BOOK WOULD NOT SUFFICE TO DESCRIBE THE BIZARRE FEATURES OF THIS MACHINE. EVEN IN THE DARK IT WAS CLEAR THAT THIS WAS A BRAINCHILD OF A GYRO GEARLOOSE, THE MUDDLE-HEADED GENIUS AND COMPANY FOUNDER CLIVE SINCLAIR OF CAMBRIDGE.

THE LIQUID CRYSTAL DISPLAY, EIGHT LINES OF EIGHTY CHARACTERS, REVEALED A BARE MINIMUM OF INFORMATION - SO LONG AS THERE WAS ENOUGH AMBIENT LIGHT. ON BOARD, IN ROM, WAS EVERYTHING ONE NEEDS FOR WRITING TEXT OR BILLS, OR RECORDING ENGAGEMENTS. THE BASIC VERSION, WITH 32 KILOBYTES OF MAIN STORE, COULD HOLD NO MORE THAN FOUR OR FIVE BRIEF DOCUMENTS. THE BEST THING WAS TO BUY IT WITH ALL THE EXTENSION SLOTS FILLED, ONE OF THEM WITH THE SINCLAIR EPROMS WHICH, ONCE WRITTEN, COULD NEVER BE ERASED EXCEPT UNDER ULTRA-VIOLET LIGHT USING A SPECIAL ADAPTER BOX. THE INVENTOR HAD DECIDED A COMPUTER LIKE THIS HAD NO NEED OF DISKETTES OR SIMILAR CONVENTIONAL CLUTTER FOR STORING DATA.

IT WORKED, AFTER A FASHION. IF YOU WERE CARELESS, THE Z88 WOULD ELEVATE ITSELF INTO A STATE OF ESOTERIC DELIRIUM; AFTER A SOFT RESET IT COULD AGAIN FIND THE FILES IN ITS MEMORY, BUT A

HARD RESET MIGHT CAUSE IT TO FORGET EVERYTHING, INCLUDING THE TIME OF DAY. A TYPICAL CARELESSNESS MIGHT BE TAKING TOO LONG TO CHANGE THE FLAT BATTERIES, OR TRYING TO MAKE THE BUILT-IN UNIVERSAL PROGRAM KNOWN AS PIPEDREAM COPE WITH TEXTS LONGER THAN 300 LINES. AND SO OUR RELATIONSHIP SWUNG BACK AND FORTH. SOMETIMES I STUDIED BRITISH COMPUTER MAGAZINES TO SEE HOW ONE COULD EXPLOIT THE SCIENCE OF APPLIED HIEROGLYPHICS TO RESCUE THE Z88 FROM ITS MENTAL DELUSIONS; AT OTHER TIMES IT REMAINED IN THE DRAWER FOR MONTHS ON END - LATER TO BECOME A CONSTANT COMPANION IN THE OFFICE OR IN BED. FINALLY IT LEFT ME: IT HAD INSISTED ON SPENDING THE NIGHT IN THE TRAVELLING BAG THAT GOT STOLEN.

BUT THE Z88 WAS NOT THE SORT ONE CAN ACCUSE OF INFIDELITY, SO I DECIDED I WANTED ANOTHER. THE IDEA BECAME A QUEST WHEN ONCE IN ENGLAND I STUMBLED ON A DISCOUNT SALE WHERE A CYNICAL BEAU WAS PALMING PEOPLE OFF WITH BRASS-ORNAMENTED SAUCEPANS, UNUSABLE CAMERAS, OR PINCHBECK WATCHES AT INFLATED PRICES. BUT WHAT WAS THAT IN THE CORNER? A PILE OF Z88S IN THEIR ORIGINAL BOXES, EVIDENTLY A JOB LOT ACQUIRED WHEN SINCLAIR´S COMPANY WAS ON ITS LAST LEGS. PEOPLE PEERED INTO THE BOXES WITHOUT SUSPECTING THE TRUTH.

THERE WAS UNFORTUNATELY NO RESCUING THEM FROM THE HANDS OF THIS SWINDLER. BUT THEN I DISCOVERED A HANDWRITTEN SMALL AD IN A BRITISH USED-COMPUTER NEWSLETTER: "Z88" EVERYTHING IN STOCK - RING VIC ON". VIC HAD BEEN A Z88 DEALER FROM THE BEGINNING, AND, SURE ENOUGH, HE STILL HAD SOME. USED AT GBP 40, BRAND NEW AT GBP 80 - NINE YEARS ON. THREE GENERATIONS OF MICROCOMPUTERS HAD COME AND GONE IN THE MEANTIME. "HOW ON EARTH DID YOU GET HOLD OF THEM? WANGLED THEM OUT OF SINCLAIR AT THE LAST MINUTE?" "SOMETHING LIKE THAT", SAID VIC; "I GOT ´EM WHEN THEY HAD ALL THEY WANTED - AND I´D HAD ENOUGH OF THEM." ONE COULD SEE THE CRASH COMING A MILE OFF, I SAID. "YES," REPLIED VIC. THE LAST TIME HE´D PHONED THEM THEY WERE INTERESTED ONLY IN THE SATELLITE DISHES THEY´D CHANGED OVER PRODUCTION TO. "I THINK THEY´VE GIVEN UP THE DISHES NOW, AND ARE MAKING ONLY THE SIGNAL CONVERTERS FOR THEM. I RECKON NEXT YEAR THEY´LL BE MAKING JUST THE SCREWS FOR THE SIGNAL CONVERTERS."

"WASN'T THERE A Z88 CLUB?" "YES, I THINK SO, BUT I MUST BE THE LAST IDIOT WHO'S STILL INTERESTED IN THE Z88." A TRAGEDY THAT SIR CLIVE'S DREAMS HAD TO END LIKE THAT, I SAID. "OH, HE'S ALWAYS FINDING SOMETHING ELSE TO DO", ANSWERED VIC; "NOW HE'S DEAD SET ON ELECTRIC MOTORS FOR BICYCLES. YOU SCREW THE THING ON YOUR BIKE, PRESS A BUTTON, AND IT CATAPULTS YOU THROUGH THE NEAREST SHOP WINDOW."

SO MUCH FOR THE GREAT TECHNOLOGICAL COUP.

5.0
THE DESKTOP COMPUTER

"640 KILOBYTE OUGHT TO BE ENOUGH FOR ANYBODY."

BILL GATES, 1981

<< APPLE USB MOUSE. **APPLE** USA **1999**

MULTICOLOURED COMPUTER GRAPHICS, DRAWN ON A PLOTTER. **1979**

5.1 THE BIRTH OF COMPUTER GRAPHICS

In the computer sciences, graphics always occupied an 'outsider' status; many engineers and scientists dismissed them as an unnecessary gimmick and a waste of resources. Most specialists knew graphics only in the form of computer games, something that raised only a faint smile. Why would one need graphics for serious tasks such as scientific and commercial applications, when there were machine code and assembler, FORTRAN and Algol, and the command-line interface by means of which an expert could breathe life into a computer? For such people, graphics were simply a frivolity.

Once again it was the American armed forces which – more by accident than design – became the midwife for a computer innovation, by providing enormous sums for research at Cambridge (Massachusetts) and Stanford in the 1950s and 1960s. The common goal of the various research projects was to find out more about human interaction with computer-controlled defence systems.

The Lincoln Laboratory, home of the Whirlwind Computer, was one of the establishments that benefited greatly from the extensive funding. There, as part of his doctoral thesis on a graphical man/machine communications system in 1962, Ivan Sutherland developed the Sketchpad program, with which the user could draw pictures on a computer screen in real-time using a light pen. The young researcher was thus an important pioneer of computer graphics.

Intended for very precise technical drawings, Sketchpad could produce drawings at a scale of up to 1:2000. It was possible to zoom in on details and out again, to duplicate elements, to work on them, and finally to store the image. The resulting image, like a drawing made by hand, consisted exclusively of straight lines, because the cathode-ray tubes were programmed for vector graphics. Present-day shapes and patterns, of course, are nothing more than a collection of short line segments, the screen image being built up of numerous horizontal scan lines.

Sketchpad was a milestone in the history of computing, for several reasons. On the one hand it marked the birth of computer graphics; on the other hand the program was very forward-looking and became the model for a whole class of later programs to extend the use of the computer, under the name CAD (computer-aided design). Above all, Sketchpad's graphic interface demonstrated a new form of communication with the computer: by pointing to an object on the screen, the user altered the content of the computer store, with a corresponding change in the screen image, so that he had the feeling he was changing the image directly. For the first time, a computer was operated both interactively and in real-time.

5.2 THE INVENTION OF THE MOUSE

Besides Sutherland's contribution to computer graphics, the work of Douglas Engelbart is to a large extent responsible for the way a modern computer is operated. Even before he joined the US Army as a radar technician, he had come across the article by Vannevar Bush mentioned in chapter 1: Bush's Memex described a man/machine system where the machine was more than just a simple-minded slave. Instead, Memex was to help the human learn, research and process information in general, in order to relieve the human brain, support and 'enlarge' it. The article made a deep impression on Engelbart and was to influence him in much of his later work.

Starting in 1959, the Department of Defense financed his work at Stanford Research Institute (SRI) into "increasing the human intellect": the possibilities of human interaction with a computer. Like Vannevar Bush, he called for computers whose abilities were not restricted to solving mathematical problems but which are able to assist humans in all their activities: "In such a future working relationship between human problem-solver and computer 'clerk', the capability of the computer for executing mathematical processes would be used whenever it was needed. However, the computer has many other capabilities for manipulating and

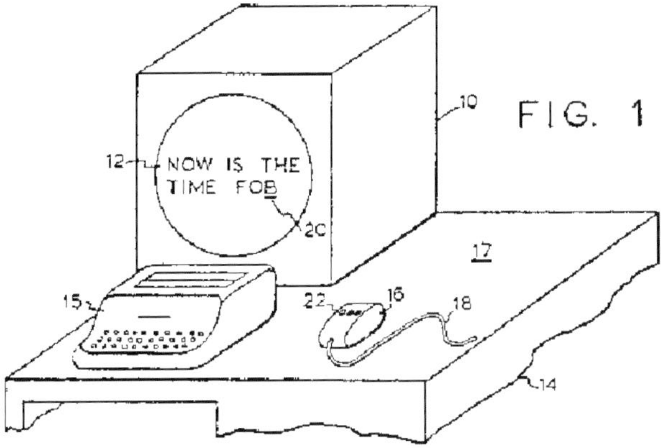

FIG. 1

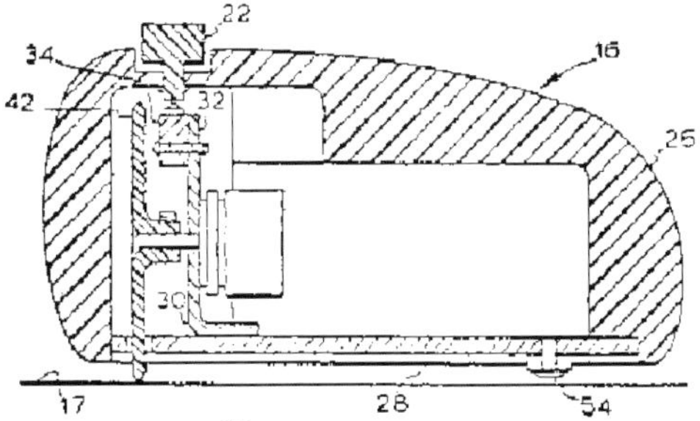

FIG. 2

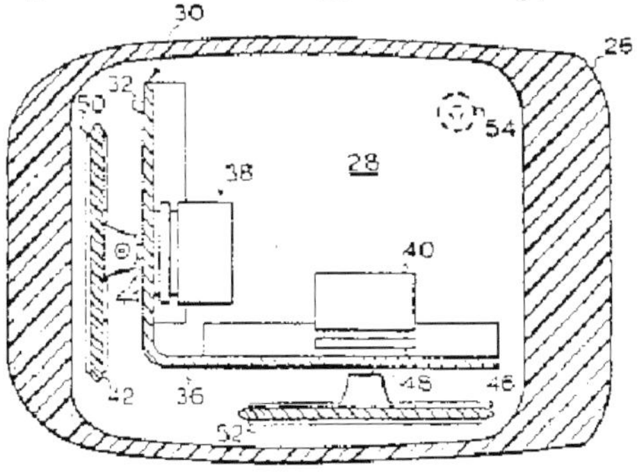

FIG. 3

PATENT SPECIFICATION FOR THE MOUSE. **DOUGLAS ENGELBART** USA **1968** displaying information that can be of significant benefit to the human in nonmathematical processes of planning, organizing, studying, etc. Every person who does his thinking with symbolised concepts (whether in the form of the English language, pictographs, formal logic, or mathematics) should be able to benefit significantly."

In the years that followed, Engelbart designed, built, and tested a number of different input devices intended to make it easier for humans to work with information. It was one of his visions to fly through data space in a computer. Besides various light pens, joysticks, and a strange device operated with the knees, he finally designed an "X-Y position indicator for a monitor system", soon to be nicknamed the mouse. In 1968 Engelbart applied for a patent on a prototype of the position indicator, which in those days had just one button. Later versions all had at least two buttons on them.

At the computer conference in San Francisco in the same year he astonished the specialist world with a 90-minute demonstration of his 'online

THE FIRST MOUSE. **DOUGLAS ENGELBART** USA **1968**

system'. This demonstration has been called the "mother of all presentations" on account of its multi-media nature. For the first time, a computer was controlled, not by punched tape or a telex machine, but by means of his revolutionary device. For good measure, the computer itself was 25 miles away! The demonstration centred on a computer monitor, the screen being divided into several 'windows' with a representation of a teleconference between two people. What caused a stir was not so much the new hardware, but above all the basic concept of manipulating objects on a screen: a way of operating a computer without entering any text commands.

5.3 THE INVENTION OF THE GRAPHICS USER INTERFACE

The Alto computer, introduced in 1974, was the starting point for a further evolution in the man/machine interface: the invention of the graphics interface at the Palo Alto Research Center, or PARC for short. At this research laboratory belonging to the Xerox corporation, some of the most brilliant brains in computer science had been given the brief to develop new computer concepts and technologies, and then to implement them in the form of products.

Many of the PARC scientists had come from Engelbart's Augmentation Research Center at the SRI, or from the government authority ARPA, which at that time was supporting or financing all the important computer research projects at the major universities and institutes.

Thanks to a further PARC development, the line-scan graphics screen, the Alto was the first computer with graphics as a general means of communication with the user. Unlike the vector graphics monitor used by Sutherland and others, a line-scan monitor allows one to address individual points on the screen and set them to various colours or levels of grey. The number of discrete points of light or 'pixels' – a portmanteau word meaning picture elements – depends on the storage space available in the computer and the resolution of the screen. When these were high enough, it became possible for the first time to display photo-like images on the screen.

THE FIRST COMPUTER WITH A GRAPHICS USER INTERFACE: THE ALTO. **XEROX PARC** USA **1974**

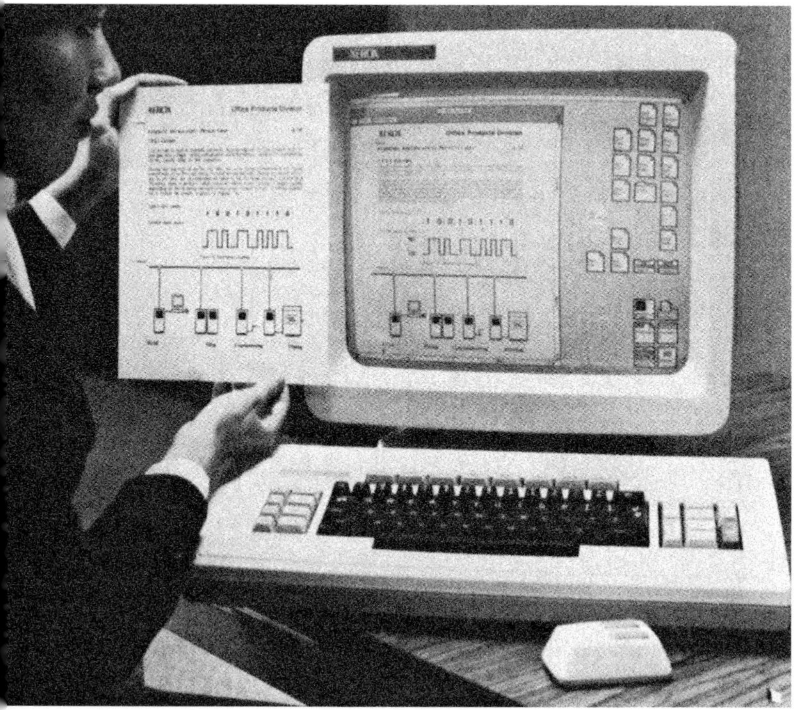

“WHAT YOU SEE IS WHAT YOU GET”: THE 8010 STAR COMPUTER. **XEROX PARC** USA **1981**

Besides the computer itself, the Alto system consisted of a graphics screen in ‘portrait’ format to represent a sheet of paper, and Engelbart’s mouse. The screen display was to change man’s relation to work rather as the invention of the motorcar had changed his relation to travel. It was a simplified two-dimensional representation of an office environment, in the form of a desk on which lay various documents and folders, a pocket calculator, and in the corner a waste-paper basket. Suddenly the main means of interaction with computers, text, was largely banned from this stylised graphical universe.

The small set of activities that could be carried out with a mouse – clicking, dragging and dropping symbols – replaced the strictly linear and complicated syntax of the command-line interface; like the joystick of the early computer games, it was something that even people with no computer experience could quickly understand and learn. Each mouse activity initiated a computer action. The graphics interface increased the user-friendliness and made it easier to operate a computer, which was now done mainly by clicking, moving, and releasing a button. The Alto was so radically new and different that representatives of the computer industry who were regularly given tours of the SRI laboratories were to appreciate its fundamental ideas only years later.

The PARC scientist Alan Kay – largely responsible for designing and implementing the graphics user interface and who can thus be consid-

IT WAS THE FIRST COMMERCIAL COMPUTER WITH A MORE ADVANCED VERSION OF THE ALTO'S DESKTOP INTERFACE: THE APPLE LISA. **APPLE** USA **1983**

ered its real inventor – was inspired in his idea of intuitive operation of a computer by an equally clever idea of Seymour Papert's for programming a computer. Kay and other researchers had been fascinated in the late 1960s to watch how school children were able to use Papert's graphical programming language Logo to write and run their own small graphics programs. In Logo, all the commands were expressed as objects and movements ('turtle graphics'); in the same way, Kay's object-oriented language for the Alto, Smalltalk, translated all the needs of a person using a computer and its programs into simple actions and pictogram-like objects he called icons.

Being small, the icons could not contain a lot of detail; without their legends, in the form of file names, they were also too general to be of much use. Even so, after a short learning phase they allowed an intuitive and almost subconscious operation of the computer, without any need to understand what was really going on inside the machine. The name icon was therefore appropriate, since it fulfilled the traditional task of an icon in conveying a pictorial message to people who did not understand computer instruction codes.

5.4 WYSIWYG

The scientists at PARC also formulated for the Alto the ideal that came to be known as WYSIWYG (what you see is what you get). In the long term, the pioneering idea of seeing the results on the screen before the operation was complete, was to become the general pattern for software operation, leading to a new quality of life in working with computers.

In 1979 Steve Jobs of Apple Computer and several of his staff visited PARC and were given an extensive demonstration of the Alto system. He later recalled: "They showed me really three things. But I was so blinded by the first one I didn't really see the other two. They showed me object-oriented programming, but I didn't see that. They showed me a networked computer system – they had over a hundred Alto computers all networked using e-mail etc., etc. I didn't even see that. I was so blinded by the first thing, which was the graphical user interface. I thought it was the best thing I'd ever seen in my life, and within ten minutes it was obvious to me that all computers would work like this some day."

Jobs immediately took up the revolutionary idea for the successor to the Apple II, which was still under development. In the spring of 1983 his company announced the Apple LISA (Local Integrated Software Architecture), the first commercial computer with a graphics user interface. It is one of the more persistent legends in the history of computing that Apple simply stole the idea from PARC. The truth is that the licensing agreement gave PARC some Apple shares that soon afterwards were worth about 18 million dollars.

The LISA user interface was more than just a successful integration of the SRI and PARC operating concepts, without watering down their strong points; it was also a successful further development. Fundamental elements of present-day desktop interfaces stem from the LISA, for example the fixed menu bar at the top of the screen and the menus that can be 'pulled down' from it. For all its technical brilliance, the LISA was a failure, mainly because of its high price of about $10,000.

In the same year, Microsoft, as ruler of the DOS kingdom, announced its Interface Manager, a graphics user interface for IBM machines. Over two years were to elapse before it was finally available as Windows 1.0.

The breakthrough for graphics interfaces came when Apple presented the Macintosh, which had been developed in parallel to the LISA, to the American television public. The publicity spot, first broadcast during the half-time break in the 1984 Superbowl finals, was set against the background of Ridley Scott's *Bladerunner* and promised a way out of the Orwellian dilemma – a veiled reference to IBM's central power – by means of the new Apple Macintosh computer.

5.5 THE MACINTOSH

The Macintosh's operating system, Mac OS, was a heavily reworked version of the Alto interface, like that of its less fortunate sister model. Apple saw it as the Volkswagen of the computer world, advertising it with the slogan "Introducing Macintosh: for the rest of us". The blurb continued: "In the olden days, before 1984, not very many people used computers. For a very good reason. Not very many people knew how. And not very many people wanted to learn. After all, in those days it meant listening to your stomach growl through computer seminars. Falling asleep over computer manuals. And staying awake nights to memorise commands so complicated you'd have to be a computer to understand them. Then, on a particularly bright day in Cupertino, California, some particularly bright engineers had a particularly bright idea: since computers are so smart, wouldn't it make more sense to teach computers about people, instead of teaching people about computers?"

The Macintosh was a great success, largely thanks to its new graphics interface and mouse control, which met with an enthusiastic reception.

It was so simple to work with that even new computer users got the hang of it straight away. All the technical attributes, with which previous computers had been visibly burdened, were now pushed into the background by the object-oriented interface. And the Macintosh was not only extremely functional; it also aroused people's emotions. It was very good-looking and became the first computer to be included in the Design collection at the Museum of Modern Art in New York.

In 1987 Bill Atkinson wrote HyperCard for the Macintosh: a program for developing future Apple applications that was itself operated entirely via the graphics interface. It was fundamentally different from all previous development programs, because the applications could now be programmed in an object-oriented way via the graphics interface rather than via a command-line interface. Rather like Papert's Logo, it blurred the boundaries between programming and application, making it possible, for the first time, for non-programmers to create simple programs. It thus proved that the task of programming can be resolved into a sequence of interactive dialogues. HyperCard was a great in-house success, and soon afterwards was made publicly available.

The continual technical progress in the years that followed led to ever-faster computers with increasing storage capacity, which made it possible to work at a comfortable pace without having to wait for the system to react. The growing resolution of screens, printers, and scanners resulted in much more sophisticated images, while simulation and modelling could also be carried out on a normal computer.

For example, the PageMaker layout program for producing magazines, catalogues, and even books on a Macintosh marked the advent of desktop publishing in 1985, and also the start of the computer as a publicity and communications medium *per se*. PageMaker, Ventura Publisher, and the present de-facto standard QuarkXPress were to revolutionise the entire graphic art business in the coming years, providing Apple Computer with a secure position in this small but important market. But Microsoft also made use of the new possibilities, so that graphics display and intuitive operation became an integral part of its Windows operating systems and applications such as Word for Windows and Excel.

With this handful of products, Microsoft succeeded in making its mark on the era of the desktop computer and also dominating the entire computer industry, since nobody could now sway the countless clone manufacturers from the IBM standard. The confident claim in an Apple advertisement, “Soon there'll be just two kinds of people: those who use computers and those who use Apples”, began to come true; from this point on the personal computer world was divided into two camps. In some circles the choice of the ‘right’ operating system became akin to a religious creed, as the Italian writer and professor of semiotics Umberto Eco once so appositely remarked.

»THE COMPUTER FOR THE REST OF US« – FOR THE FIRST TIME, IN EFFECT, A COMPUTER COULD BE OPERATED WITHOUT ANY PREVIOUS EXPERIENCE:

The new CD-ROM drives – a development of the audio CD players developed by Phillips and Sony in 1983 – now offered the possibility of retrieving large amounts of data in the form of encyclopaedias, video games, films and the like. And so the existence of this computer, capable of music and graphics, became known as a "multi-media" computer and people first got the idea that a computer can also be a media machine.

The era of the desktop computer followed the model of a computer whose operation was intuitive and child's play. The interface thus became its most important component. The technical aspects retreated into the background; for the first time computers appeared to be the servants of man rather than the other way around. The human senses were now met on more equal terms by a more versatile interface that extended the means of expression of the previous text-oriented interface in a multi-media way.

The computer's outstanding graphics ability, coupled with its rapidly growing speed and storage capacity, allowed completely new tasks such as desktop publishing, or two-dimensional and three-dimensional graphics applications which increasingly also influenced media productions. For the first time, computers shaped people's jobs, not from the programming side, but from the applications side.

"SOON THERE'LL BE JUST TWO KINDS OF PEOPLE: THOSE WHO USE COMPUTERS AND THOSE WHO USE APPLES"

FROM AN APPLE ADVERTISEMENT

APPLE'S FIRST MOUSE: THE DESKTOP MOUSE 1 (LEFT), **APPLE** USA **1983,** AND THE HAWLEY X063X-MOUSE IN VARIOUS COLOURS (BELOW). **MOUSE HOUSE** USA **1981**

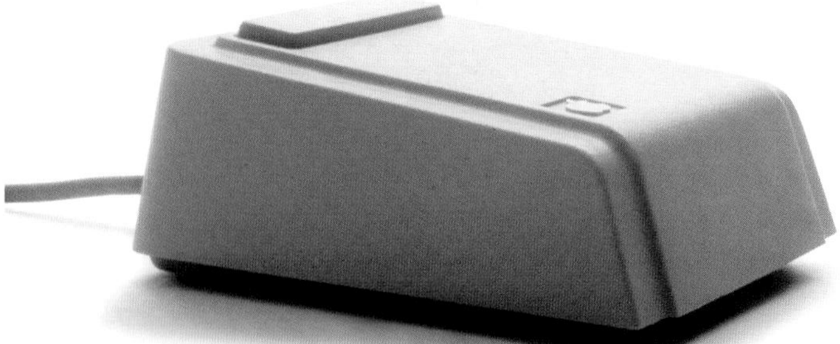

EXPLOSION SKETCH FOR THE FIRST APPLE MOUSE FROM THE DESIGN OFFICE HOWARD KELLEY. **APPLE** USA **1980-82**

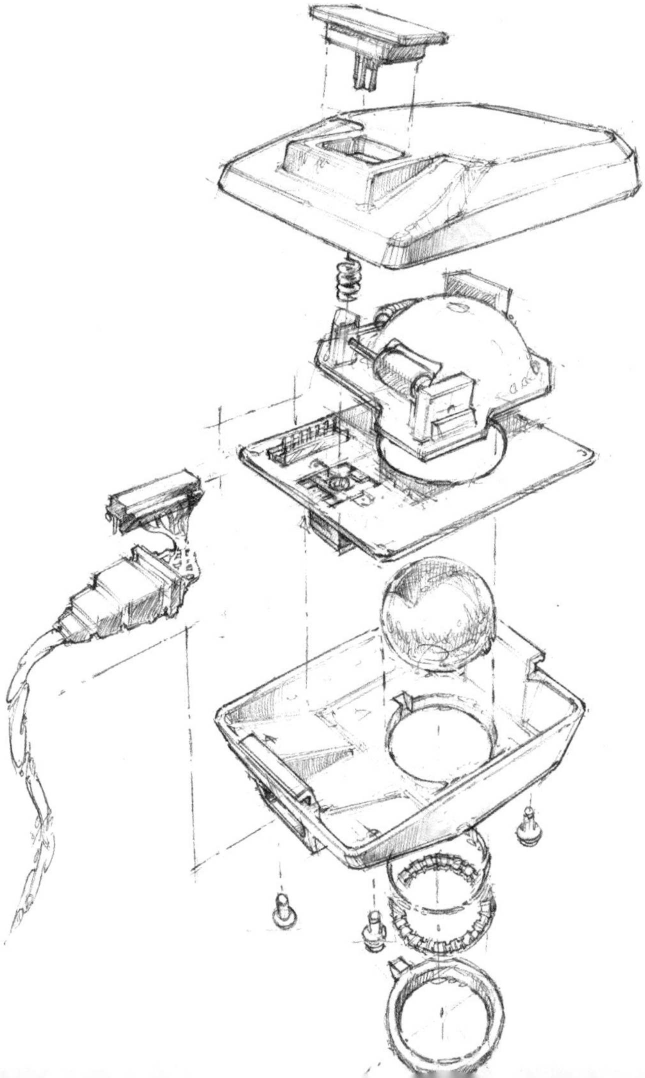

PROGRAM TO CREATE ICONS FOR THE APPLE DESIGNER SUSAN KARE. **APPLE** USA **1985**

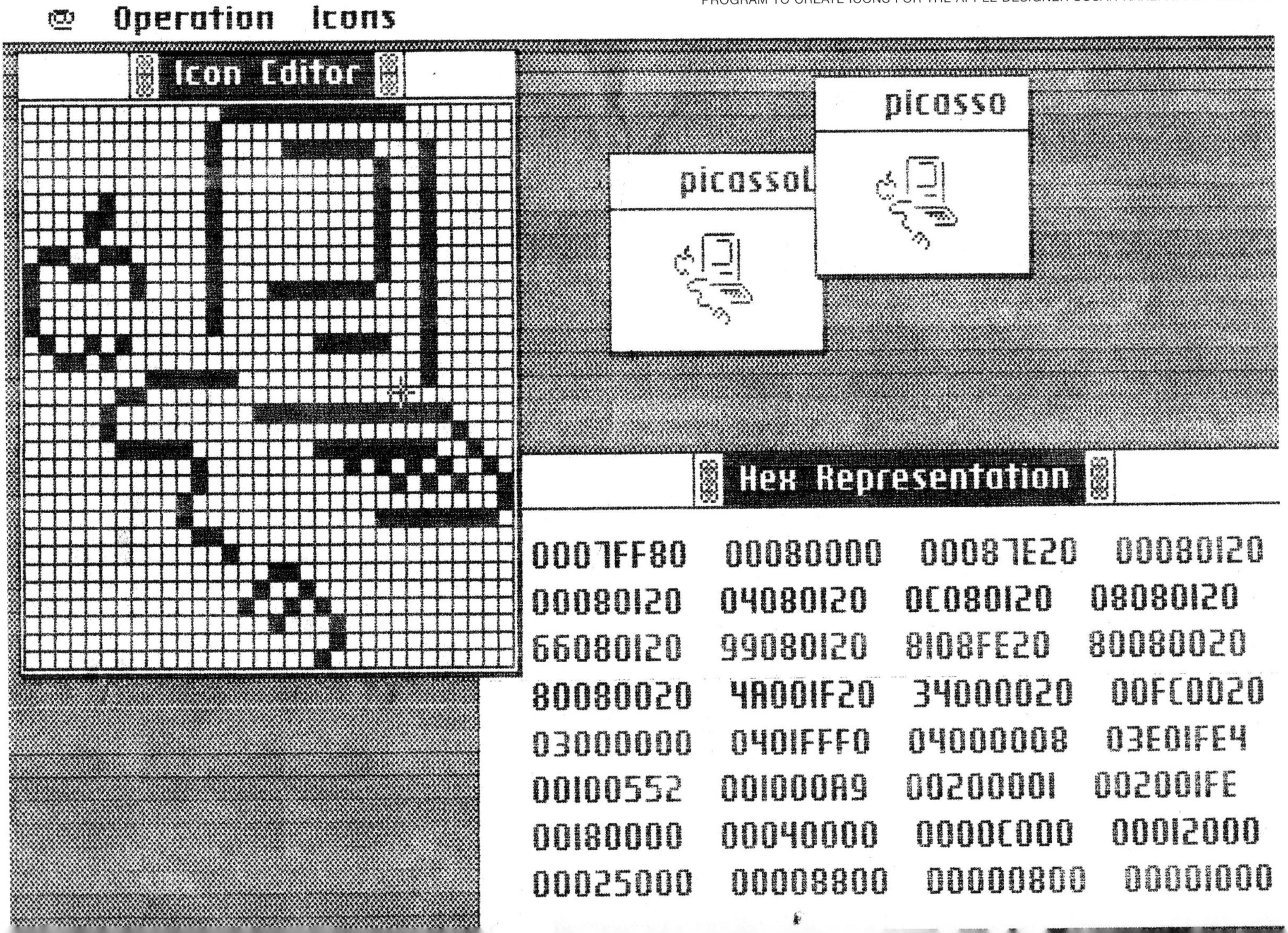

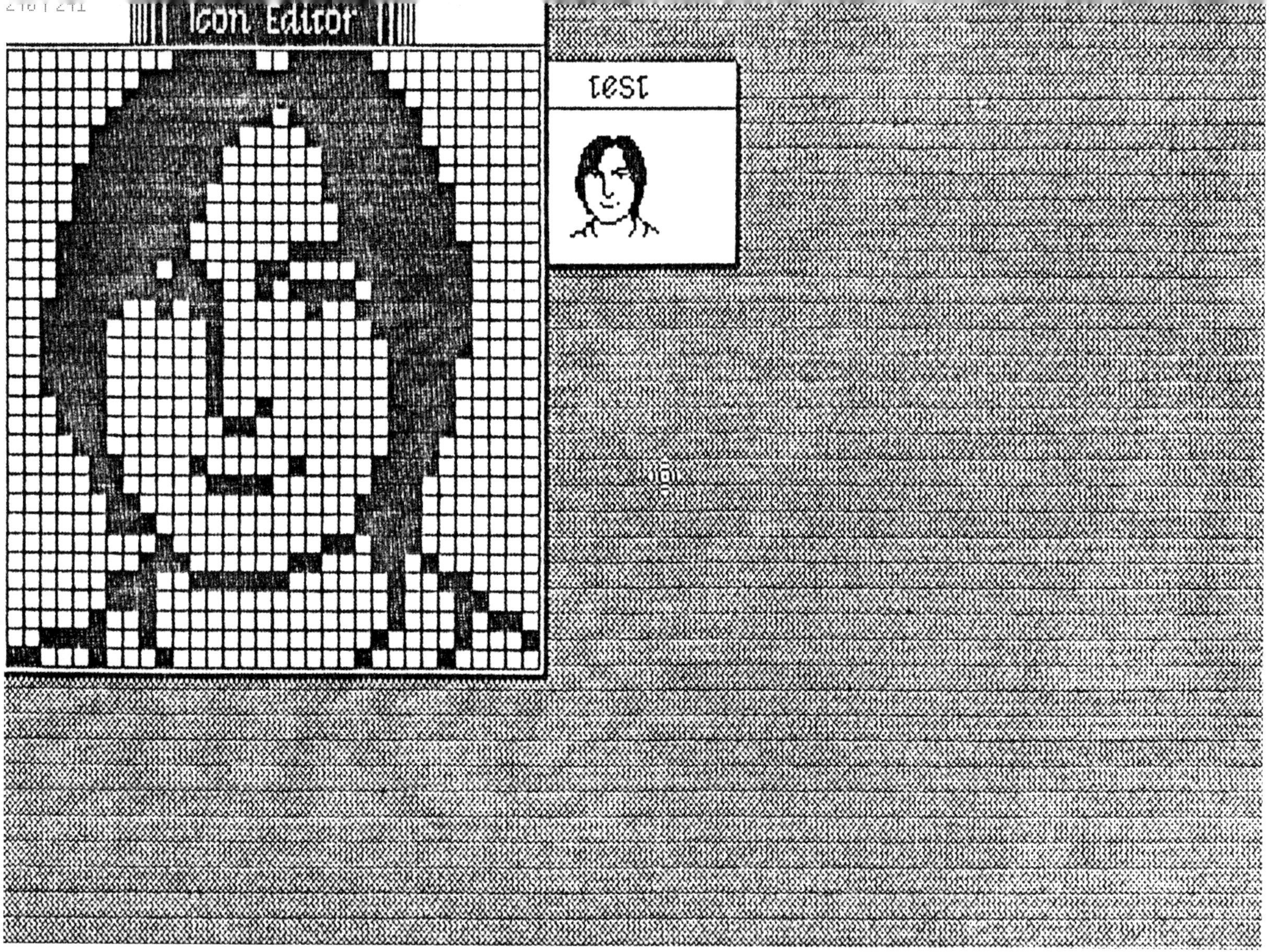
Icon Editor
test

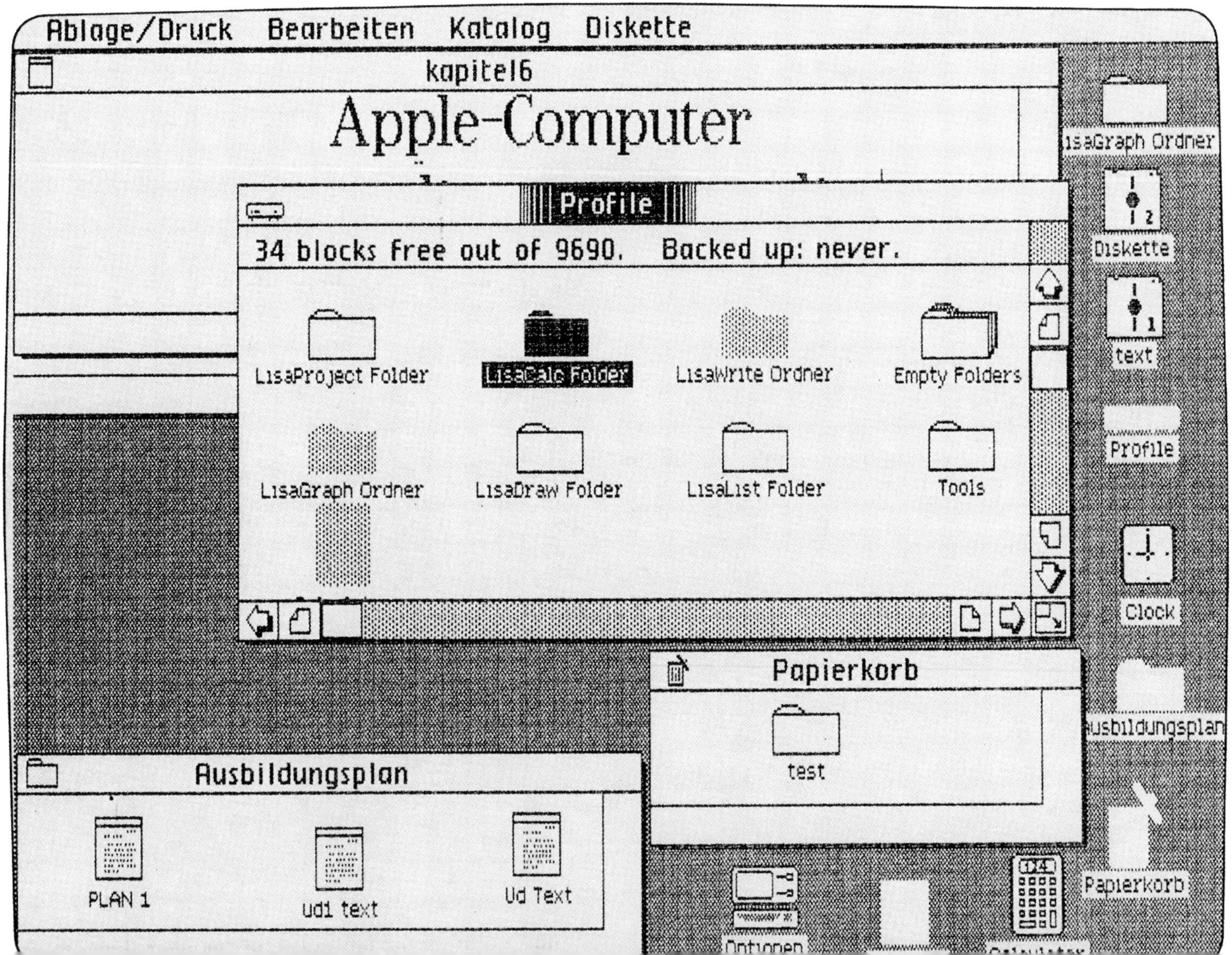
Ablage/Druck
Bearbeiten
Katalog
Diskette
kapitel6
Apple-Computer
Profile
34 blocks free out of 9690. Backed up: never.
LisaProject Folder
LisaCalc Folder
LisaWrite Ordner
Empty Folders
LisaGraph Ordner
LisaDraw Folder
LisaList Folder
Tools
Papierkorb
test
Ausbildungsplan
PLAN 1
ud1 text
Ud Text
Diskette
text
Profile
Clock
Papierkorb
Optionen

MACINTOSH OS 1.0

BORIS GRÖNDAHL

MY FIRST APPLE MACINTOSH STILL SITS ON MY DESK: MODEL SE FROM 1990, ONE OF THE LAST WITH THE CLASSIC CUBICAL SHAPE IN WHICH THE MAC ORIGINALLY CAME ON THE MARKET IN 1984.

I TURN THE SWITCH FROM 0 TO 1, AND IMMEDIATELY THE COMPUTER RESPONDS WITH ITS FAMILIAR START-UP SOUND. AFTER A FEW SECONDS, A SMALL PICTOGRAM OF "THE COMPUTER THAT CHANGED EVERYTHING" (ACCORDING TO STEVEN LEVY) APPEARS ON THE SCREEN, GIVES ME A WELCOMING SMILE. EVERYTHING IS WHERE IT SHOULD BE: THE FAMILIAR MENU BAR AT THE TOP OF THE SCREEN, THE WINDOWS AND ICONS, THE APPLE SYMBOL AT TOP LEFT AND THE WASTE-PAPER BASKET AT BOTTOM RIGHT, LOOKING FOR ALL THE WORLD LIKE AN AMERICAN "TRASH CAN". THE FAMOUS LOOK AND FEEL OF THE MAC WITH THE BRILLIANT PICTOGRAMS BY THE DESIGNER SUSAN KARE.

UP TO NOW, THERE IS NOTHING TO REVEAL THAT THE LITTLE MAC IS RUNNING NOT THE LATEST VERSION OF THE OPERATING SYSTEM BUT THE VERY FIRST VERSION FROM 1984. IT´S NOT HARD TO IMAGINE WHAT A FURORE IT MUST HAVE CAUSED IN THOSE DAYS, TO COPY A FILE BY PICKING IT UP AND DRAGGING IT WITH THE MOUSE, INSTEAD OF TYPING IN A DOS COMMAND SUCH AS C:\COPY TIME.TXT A: IN SPITE OF THE GOOD PRESS IT RECEIVED, THE SALES FIGURES FOR 1984/85 WERE DISAPPOINTING – THEY ROSE ONLY WHEN ALDOUS BROUGHT OUT ITS PAGEMAKER PROGRAM AND OPENED UP THE DECISIVE NICHE MARKET FOR THE MAC: DESKTOP PUBLISHING, DOCUMENT LAYOUT BY COMPUTER, WHICH IN THE SPACE OF TEN YEARS CAUSED SUCH AN UPHEAVAL IN THE FIELD WHERE THE MAC IS STILL THE UNCHALLENGED LEADER.

NOWADAYS ANY PROFESSIONAL USER WOULD LAUGH AT THE ORIGINAL MAC. THINGS WE NOW TAKE FOR GRANTED, SUCH AS THE POSSIBILITY OF HAVING SEVERAL PROGRAMS LOADED AT THE SAME TIME, WERE STILL PIE-IN-THE-SKY IN THOSE DAYS. WITH THE 128 KILOBYTES OF STORE THAT THEY COULD SPARE FOR THIS MACHINE, EVEN A GREY-SCALE MONITOR WAS OUT OF THE QUESTION, LET ALONE A COLOUR ONE.

YET OCCASIONALLY ONE LONGS FOR THE SIMPLICITY OF THOSE DAYS. ONE THING THE EARLY VERSION CERTAINLY WAS NOT: SLOWER. THE CONTINUAL RAPID INCREASE IN THE SPEED OF PROCESSORS, THE STORAGE CHIPS THAT GET CHEAPER ALL THE TIME; WITH THE MAC, TOO, THE IMPROVEMENTS GET EATEN UP BY BLOATED SOFTWARE FULL OF NEW FEATURES OF DOUBTFUL BENEFIT.

FOR EXAMPLE, THE FIRST MAC HAD A "CONTROL PANEL" WHERE ONE COULD SET ALL THE IMPORTANT FUNCTIONS, SUCH AS LOUDSPEAKER VOLUME, SPEED OF THE MOUSE, CURSOR BLINK RATE, AND SO ON. NOW THAT HAS GIVEN WAY TO A WHOLE FOLDER FULL OF CONTROL PANELS FOR EVERY IMAGINABLE PHASE OF THE USER'S LIFE. TOGETHER WITH AN EQUALLY CONFUSING NUMBER OF "SYSTEM EXTENSIONS", WHICH HAVE A HABIT OF SLIPPING UNNOTICED INTO THE SYSTEM FOLDER ON INSTALLATION, THEY REPRESENT A VIPER'S NEST OF INCOMPATIBILITIES WHICH POUR SCORN ON THE ORIGINAL CLAIM OF OPERATION AS SIMPLE AS CHILD'S PLAY. NOT SURPRISINGLY, THE BEST-SELLING PROGRAMS FOR THE MAC ARE PACKAGES THAT SNIFF OUT POTENTIALLY FATAL CONFLICTS IN THE SYSTEMS SOFTWARE.

HOWEVER, NEITHER THE APPLE FOUNDERS STEVE JOBS AND STEPHEN WOZNIAK, NOR ANY OTHER MEMBER OF THE MAC DEVELOPMENT TEAM, COULD CLAIM TO HAVE ORIGINATED THE REVOLUTIONARY METHOD OF OPERATION. THE GRAPHICS INTERFACE, THE 'DESKTOP' METAPHOR, THE WINDOWS AND THE ICONS, BIT-MAPPING (IN WHICH EACH INDIVIDUAL PIXEL ON THE SCREEN IS ADDRESSED DIRECTLY BY THE COMPUTER), THE LOGICAL USE OF THE MOUSE - ALL THAT WAS CRIBBED BY THE APPLE PEOPLE ON A VISIT TO THE XEROX CORPORATION'S PARC LAB.

THE FIRST MAC OPERATING SYSTEM WAS A REVOLUTION IN 1984. BUT IT'S SUSPICIOUS THAT IT STILL LOOKS MUCH THE SAME AS IT DID THEN. THE MAC'S "WOW" FACTOR IS LONG SINCE EXHAUSTED. THE MAC REVOLUTIONISED THE PERSONAL COMPUTER, BUT THE REVOLUTION IS NOW TURNING TO DEVOUR ITS ERSTWHILE LEADER.

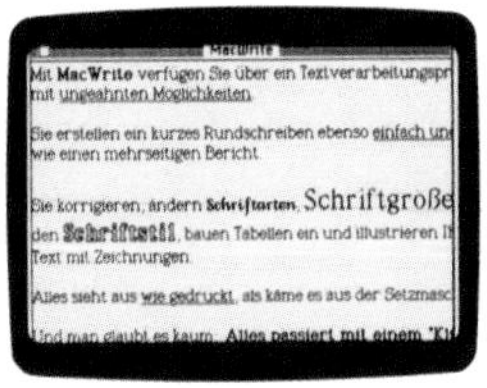
MacWrite
Mit MacWrite verfügen Sie über ein Textverarbeitungspr
mit ungeahnten Möglichkeiten.
Sie erstellen ein kurzes Rundschreiben ebenso einfach un
wie einen mehrseitigen Bericht.
Sie korrigieren, ändern Schriftarten, Schriftgröße
den Schriftstil, bauen Tabellen ein und illustrieren I
Text mit Zeichnungen.
Alles sieht aus wie gedruckt, als käme es aus der Setzmasc

MacPaint

MULTIPLAN
Ein - Ausgabenrechnung

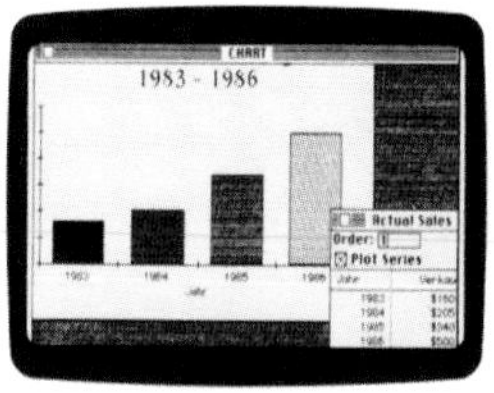
CHART
1983 - 1986
Actual Sales
Plot Series

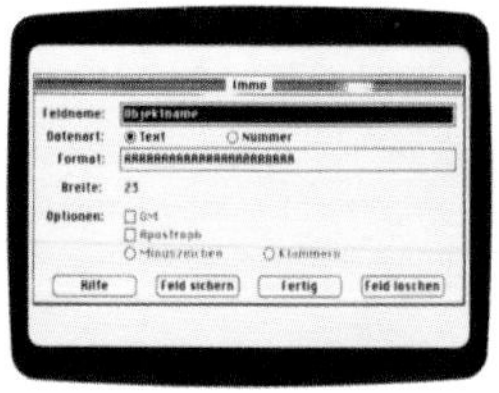
Immo
Hilfe
Feld sichern
Fertig
Feld löschen

MacTerminal
Bearbeiten Befehle Einstellungen Telefon Funktionen
Elektronische Post

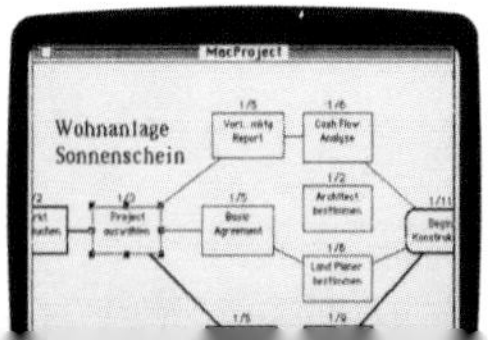
MacProject
Wohnanlage
Sonnenschein

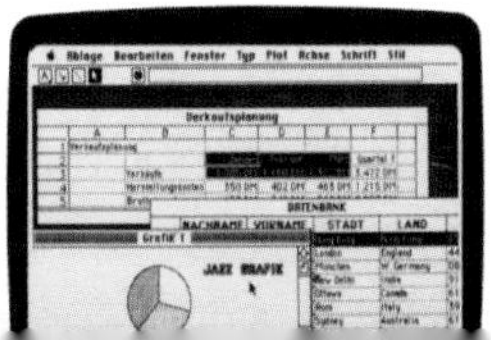
Ablage Bearbeiten Fenster Typ Plot Achse Schrift Stil
Verkaufsplanung
DATENBANK
JAZZ GRAFIK

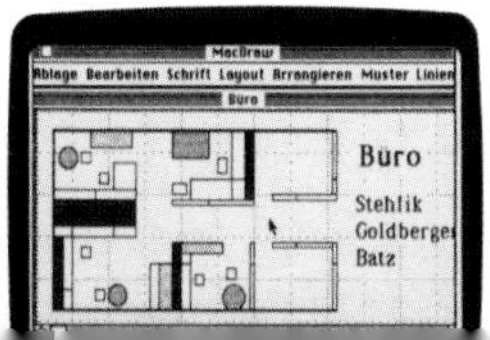
MacDraw
Ablage Bearbeiten Schrift Layout Arrangieren Muster Linien
Büro
Stehlik
Goldberger
Batz

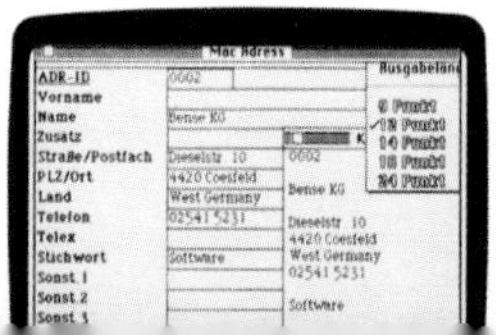
Mac Adress
ADR-ID
Vorname
Name
Zusatz
Straße/Postfach
PLZ/Ort
Land
Telefon
Telex
Stichwort
Sonst.1
Sonst.2
Sonst.3

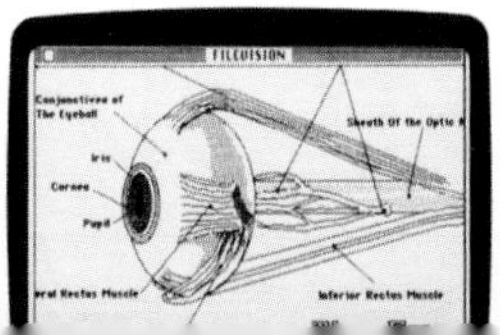
FILEVISION

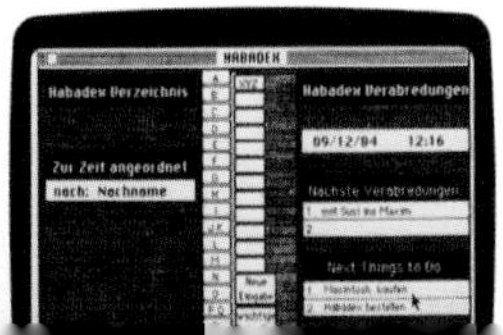
HABADEX
Habadex Verzeichnis
Habadex Verabredungen
Zur Zeit angeordnet
nach: Nachname
Nächste Verabredungen
Next Things to Do

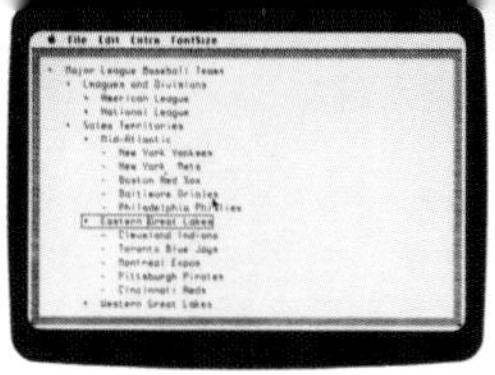

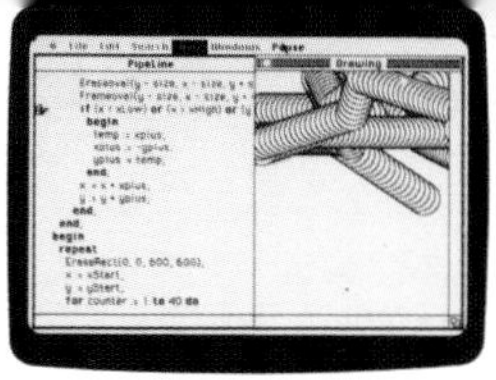
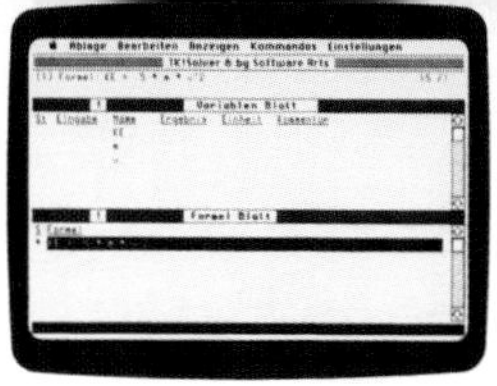
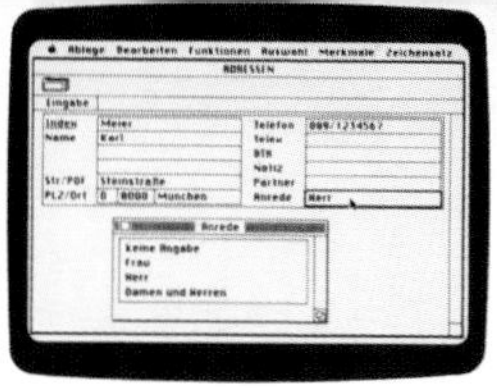

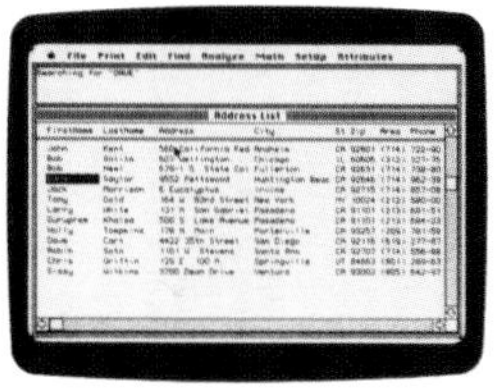
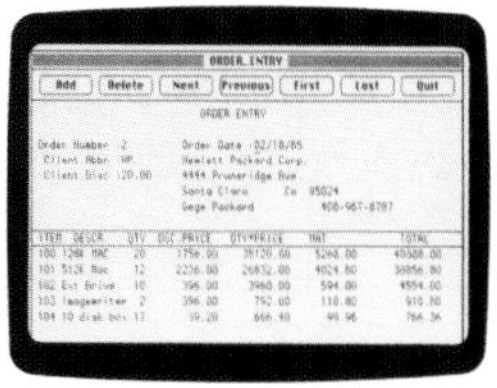
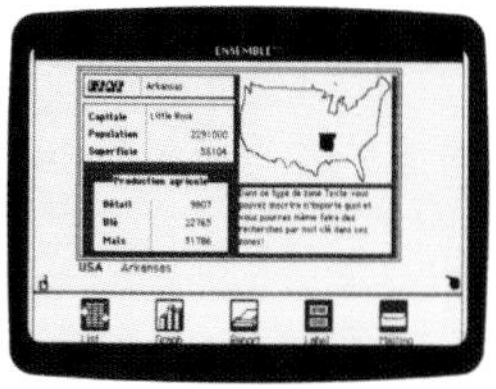

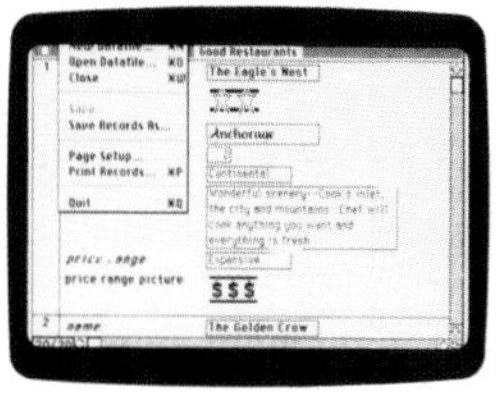
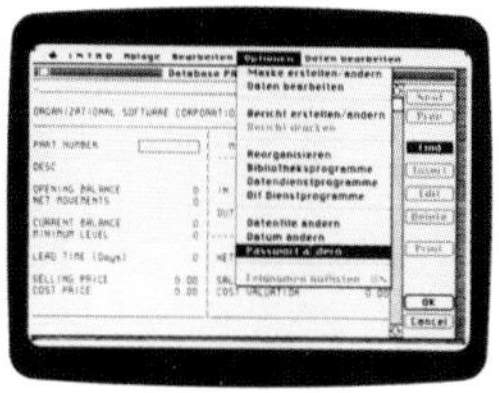

THE MACPAINT GRAPHICS PROGRAM ON A LISA (TOP) **APPLE** USA **1986**, AND THE PHOTOSHOP PROGRAM ON A MACINTOSH (BOTTOM). **ADOBE** USA **1986** >>

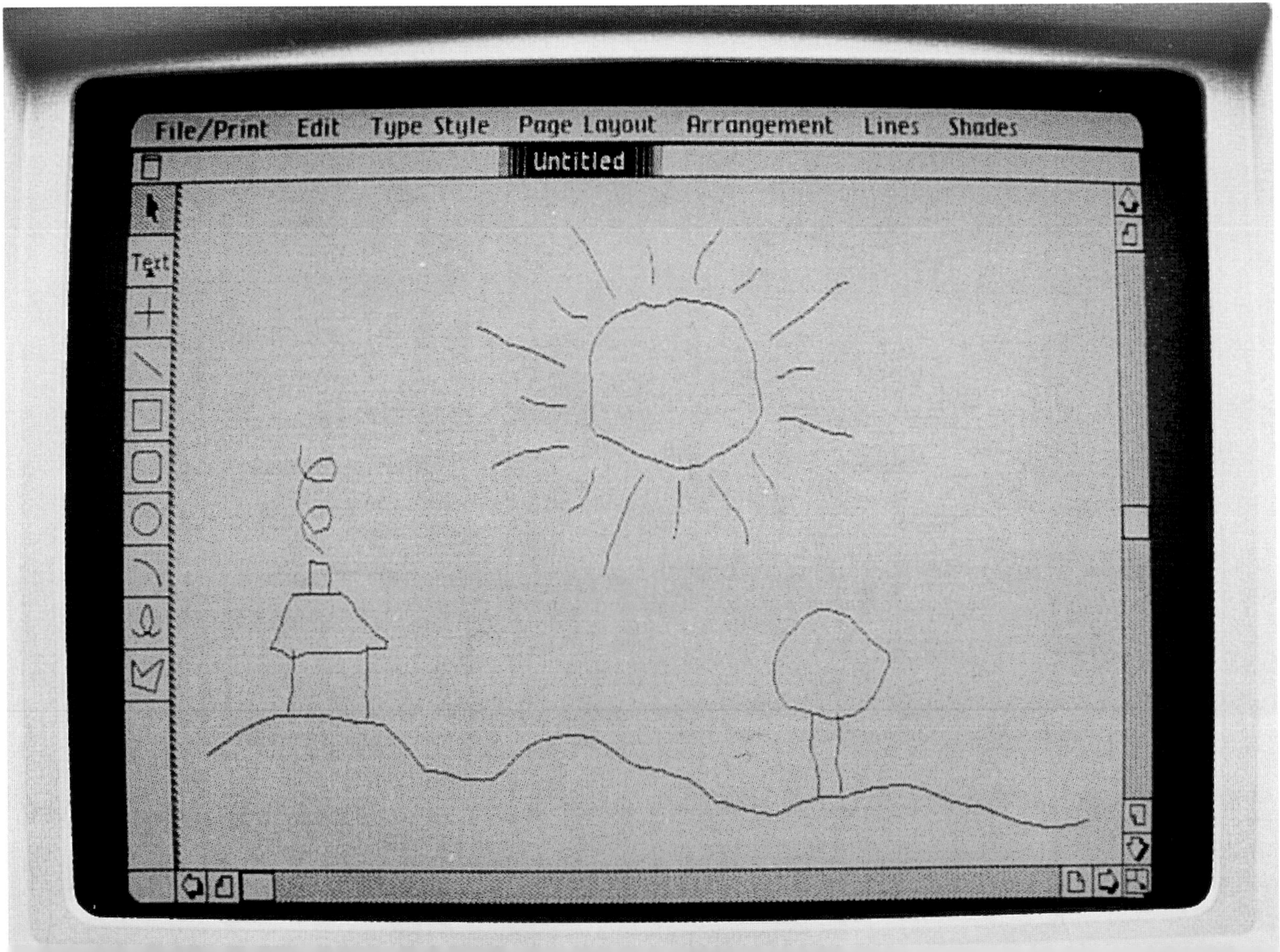
File/Print
Edit
Type Style
Page Layout
Arrangement
Lines
Shades
Untitled
Text

Datei
Bearbeiten
Hilfsmittel
Zeichensatz
Größe
Stil
Widerrufen ⌘Z
Ausschneiden ⌘X
Kopieren ⌘C
Einsetzen ⌘V
Löschen
Invertieren
Konturen ⌘E
Um Horizontale drehen
Um Vertikale drehen
Rotieren
Tennisschuh
Z
Stollen

Bildschirmtext

THE PORTABLE VARIANT OF THE APPLE II: THE APPLE IIC (ABOVE). **APPLE** USA **1984**
AND THE IBM THINKPAD 701 NOTEBOOK COMPUTER WITH FOLD-AWAY KEYBOARD (BELOW). **IBM** USA **1995**

DESKTOP PUBLISHING ON AN IBM PS/2 COMPUTER USING THE ALDUS LAYOUT PROGRAM PAGEMAKER. **ALDUS** USA **1987**

THE MATT BLACK NEXT CUBE WAS STEVE JOBS' NEXT COMPUTER AFTER HE LEFT APPLE. **NEXT** USA **1989**

RELAX
FLOATING

COMPUTER-GENERATED SCENES FROM THE FIRST VIRTUAL REALITY FILM "THE LAWNMOWER MAN". **BRETT LEONARD** USA **1992**

5.6 THE NETWORKED COMPUTER

The Advanced Research Project Agency (ARPA) was set up by the US Department of Defense in 1958 following the Sputnik shock – a few months earlier, the Soviet Union had succeeded in launching the first artificial satellite. The new government agency was intended to carry out research and development in advanced technologies such as space exploration and computers, and also to fulfil military demands for an independent and decentralised communications network in the event of an attack. ARPA's initial annual budget was to be 2 billion dollars, but nearly all of its planned research activities were hived off soon afterwards to the newly founded National Aeronautics and Space Administration (NASA).

The first director of the department that was to design and implement the new network was James Licklider, a visionary who foresaw a global computer network. In a 1960 paper he wrote: "It seems reasonable to envision, for a time ten or fifteen years hence, a 'thinking center' that will incorporate the functions of present-day libraries together with anticipated advances in information storage and retrieval and the symbiotic functions suggested earlier in this paper. The picture readily enlarges itself into a network of such centers, connected to one another by leased-wire services. In such a system, the speed of computers would be balanced, and the cost of the gigantic memories would be divided, by the number of users."

ARPA provided support for several research projects at various universities, all equipped with extremely expensive mainframe computers. ARPA therefore drew up a plan for a network for sending packets of data to and fro, in order to make better use of the computing resources. Once the main technical difficulties had been overcome, above all the difficulties of data transfer, ARPAnet was demonstrated to a specialist public in Washington in 1972. However, it met with little interest on the part of politicians or the telephone companies.

Only a year later, it was found that three quarters of the traffic on the net were messages, electronic mail, a use that had not been foreseen at all in the original design. Personal contact between scientists by means of the written word was more important to them than the ability to coordinate their work activities.

The invention of the Ethernet, by Bob Metcalfe at PARC in 1973, was a further milestone in the evolution of computer networks. Starting with the basic idea that there could be a computer on every academic's desk in the not-too-distant future, he designed special-purpose circuit boards and communications protocols that allowed up to 256 computers to be connected together via co-ax cables. Soon there were about a hundred Alto computers linked together at PARC; each scientist could make use of the resources of the network, for example the astronomically expensive laser printer that had also recently been developed in the PARC laboratories.

Quite soon, the two networks were talking to each other, when the PARC scientists linked their ARPAnet connection to their own Ethernet. From then on, every work station had access to the new "Internet", though it was still strictly closed to the general public.

In his book, *Computer Lib – you can and must understand computers now*, which he published himself in 1974, Ted Nelson described a new concept of reading and writing which he called hypertext: "By hypertext I mean nonsequential writing. Ordinary writing is sequential for two reasons. First, it grew out of speech and speech-making, which have to be sequential; and second, because books are not convenient to read, except in sequence. But the structures of ideas are not sequential. They tie together every which way. And the pity is that [...] we've been speaking hypertext all our lives and never known it."

Although Vannevar Bush's article *As we may think* (which seems to have had a lasting effect on Nelson) contained an initial approach to this non-sequential idea, Nelson came to a different conclusion: a global network he called Xanadu. His words read like a flowery description of the present-day Internet: "Now the idea is this: to give you a screen in your home from which you can see into the world's hypertext libraries. (The fact that the world doesn't have any hypertext libraries – yet – is a minor point.) To give you a screen system that will offer high-performance graphics and text services at a price anyone can afford. To allow you to send and receive written messages at the Engelbart level. To allow you to explore diagrams. To eliminate the absurd distinction between 'teacher' and 'pupil'. To make you a part of a new electronic literature and art, where you can get all your questions answered and nobody will put you down."

The idea of Nelson's hypertext formed the conceptual basis of the page description language HTML (HyperText Markup Language), programmed by the British information scientist Tim Berners-Lee at the CERN nuclear research centre (Centre Européen pour la Recherche Nucléaire) in Geneva in 1989. In view of the many local Ethernet networks, which had grown up all over the world within the various scientific institutions and companies, Berners-Lee formulated the idea of joining them all together with the aid of a hypertext system. In 1990 he named it the World Wide Web, or WWW for short.

5.7 THE WWW

Like the ARPAnet, the WWW was first intended as a scientific tool for physicists all over the world, so that they could carry out joint research, sharing and comparing their results quickly and easily. A new feature was the idea of a universal resource locator, URL for short, to identify each internet server. Three standards, URL, HTML, and HTTP (hypertext transfer protocol), made up the entire technical basis of the World Wide Web. It was HTTP which ensured that text and graphics would always appear in the same format, regardless of the type of computer at the receiving end. Probably Berners-Lee's greatest contribution was making different computer systems compatible with one another by creating a universal interface, the World Wide Web.

The World Wide Web began to consolidate in 1991 when CERN decided to place the software in the public domain, available free on the Internet. At that time, about 160,000 computers around the world were organised in over 800 different networks with internet access. In 1992 the US Government then decided to deregulate the Internet, allowing trade and other business use. The growing commercialisation contributed greatly to the number of users, as an increasing number of providers discovered the possibilities.

The Internet and the World Wide Web were now open to all. But in spite of all the remarkable achievements and developments, the ease of operation suffered from a serious anachronism. The command-line interface was hopelessly old-fashioned compared to the graphics interface that was by now more or less standard for PCs. To use the internet one required an elementary knowledge of the programming language UNIX, in which the individual steps were entered when prompted by the system, and also a detailed knowledge of the various protocols in order to reach a particular server and the information it held.

Then the early graphics browsers came along, such as Lynx, Cello, Samba, Midas, Viola, and the most popular variant, Mosaic, written by Marc Andreesen and others at a small university in Illinois, which made use of the brilliant interaction options of a graphics interface. For the first time, the Internet and the WWW took on an outward and visible form, and thus made sense; previously they had been no more than a technical invention, an extremely well-matched conglomerate of different communications protocols. Collecting these into a graphics interface led, via the means of display in an easy-to-visualise form, to completely new options for using the net – and as a by-product to a completely new kind of medium.

In view of the success and potential of the new graphics web browsers, Jim Clark, the founder and former president of Silicon Graphics, decided to join forces with Andreesen and create a new generation of browsers. As Bob Metcalfe remarked, they have the potential of becoming the new operating system for PCs; events may yet prove him right. Netscape Navigator was ready for marketing in 1994 after a very short development time. Its functionalism and clear layout were unmatched by anything else, and in addition it was available free on the Internet for scientific and private users; it thus quickly became the most popular browser, installed on very many computers.

The no-cost Navigator attracted attention, and rapidly became the model for other browsers, in effect setting the standard. Netscape's motives in giving it away for free were not entirely altruistic, but it was a pioneering step which changed the users' expectations – that not only information but also software should cost nothing – and thus the character of the Internet as a whole.

Soon afterwards Microsoft brought out its Internet Explorer, a serious competitor that was to lead to the 'browser wars': Microsoft and Netscape repeatedly outdid each other with better and better software, each product incorporating the advantages of the other and attempting to go a step further.

1995 saw the final breakthrough of the Internet: the number of users now exceeded 45 million, and browsers were everyday items. From then on they acted as portals providing access to information, communications, and transactions – the graphics user interface plus browser had become the gateway to the world.

The Java programming language, developed at Sun Microsystems by James Gossling and others in 1995, was the beginning of the end of the era of local desktop computers, both technologically and conceptually. Java allowed the user of a computer connected to the Internet (the 'client') to execute programs that were held not on his own computer but on a selected server (the 'host'). The tiny 'interpreter' that was the sole prerequisite for using Java soon became so widespread that Netscape and Microsoft incorporated it in their browsers; soon Java became the software standard for the Web.

Java also represented a break with the classic von Neumann concept, by which a program must be stored in the computer. For the first time in the history of computers, users of a Java program did not need to bother with either installation and configuration, or maintenance and updating, of the software; they simply received a service from the host.

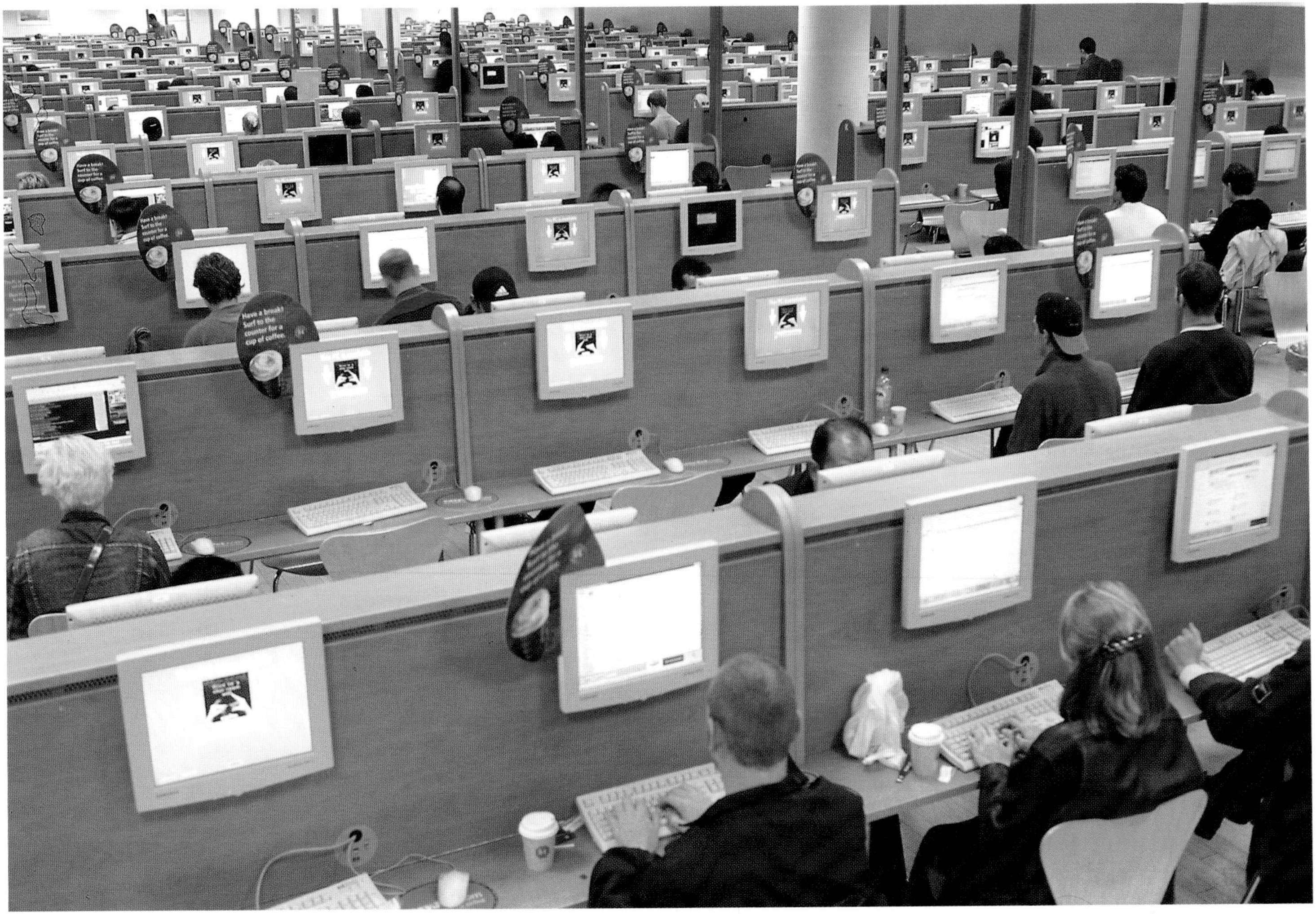

THE WORLD'S LARGEST INTERNET CAFÉ, WITH 850 COMPUTER TERMINALS: THE EASY INTERNET CAFÉ IN AMSTERDAM. **2000**

The Flash animations that grew up as a result offered computer users dynamic interfaces for communication and interaction, enriched by speed and motion. Until now the Web interfaces had been very static, laid out in the form of tables containing text and images; now the Web acquired characteristic new aesthetics with plenty of movement and in which everything was based on pointing and clicking.

Java's main virtue is the fact that it is independent of the platform on which it runs, since it is based solely on standard Internet protocols. So a programming language again took on the role of an operating system, because only applications using Java can run (via the Internet) on any conceivable computer. The Internet, the only superordinate standard, thus effectively became a computer itself, as Sun was claiming by the late 1990s: "The network is the computer."

Sun took this to its logical conclusion by offering a network computer with no operating system or hard disk of its own, intended to replace the PC. However, this strategy failed in the early 1990s, partly because the Internet was still in its infancy, but probably also because users resented no longer being in physical possession of their own personal data and programs. Since the mid-1990s the Internet has developed faster than even its greatest proponents could have predicted a few years earlier. The hysteria over the 'new markets', and their collapse a short time later, are without a doubt an indication that people's expectations were simply too high. Yet the possibilities of the Web would appear to be far from exhausted.

The number of users around the world with Internet access, roughly 300 million at the time of writing, should not be allowed to hide the fact that at least 5.7 billion people, 95% of the world's population, are non-users. The consequences of global networking are far-reaching. The Internet has not only dramatically changed the traditional ways in which information and also goods are distributed; it would even appear to be capable of influencing and altering the entire structure of business, world-wide.

The graphical user interface acquires a central role in the networked computer, since in the form of the browser it is able to 'urbanise' the network and thus combine the numerous new options. At first sight, the browser is just one of many windows in the desktop interface, but in effect it becomes a window on the world that seems to ride the network from server to server.

Furthermore, the browser, as the new standard interface, really appears to be becoming a kind of new operating system for a world-wide network which itself can fulfil the classic criterion of a computer: an electronic tool that can process data in any desired way in accordance with a given set of instructions.

The growing extent and importance of the Internet have led to a boom in information technology in general and thus to a world-wide renaissance of telecommunications. The large national telephone companies such as NTT in Japan, Nokia in Finland, Deutsche Telekom in Germany, AT&T in the USA, and others have become some of the most important and wealthiest organisations in the world. The renaissance of information technology also led to a renaissance of information design, since a well-designed interface, matched to the tasks and target groups – and with its accessibility and operability – is an important criterion for the success of any network and what it offers. This makes the user interface the most important element of a task, a service, or a set of data on the Internet.

Networking also indicates that the role of the computer as a tool of mankind is losing its importance, and the computer is starting to slip into a new role. It is in the process of becoming an all-integrating and all-embracing information and communications medium; it would then fulfil one of the most far-reaching utopias of the history of computing, becoming an amplifier of human intelligence. As Vannevar Bush's article concluded: "Presumably man's spirit should be elevated if he can better review his shady past and analyze more completely and objectively his present problems. He has built a civilisation so complex that he needs to mechanise his records more fully if he is to push his experiment to its logical conclusion and not merely become bogged down part way there by overtaxing his limited memory."

However, networking, and also the form and function of the Internet as a kind of self-evolving hypertext document of unlimited size, raise the question whether the computer is perhaps also in the process of becoming a medium. That would redefine not only its basic role as a tool but also the functions, tasks, and forms of its interfaces.

5.9 THE COMPUTER AS A MEDIUM

The underlying question, whether the computer could possibly be a medium, now seems somewhat out-dated in the face of technological realities in the fields of computers, communications, and entertainment electronics, and the blurred dividing lines between them. The very existence of electronic books, computers with built-in TV tuners, television sets containing microprocessors, digital video recorders and TV servers, telephones and mobile phones with Internet ability – some of them with integrated pocket calculators, engagement diaries, and dictating machines – proves without a doubt the *fait accompli* of the 'medialisation' of the computer and the computerisation of the media.

Approaches to the media tradition of the computer can even be found in two of its most important precursors: Babbage's Difference Engine for printing tables of values, and Hollerith's punched-card equipment. In each case, letters and numerals were calculated and then made visible in a process akin to letterpress printing. We must also bear in mind that media productions have long-since been largely digital; that applies particularly to the classic (analogue) media such as books, sound recordings, and films.

Since the rise of the Internet, at the latest, the computer has indubitably been both a media technology and a medium in the sense that it is a device for conveying perceptions. The microchip in the medium we call the computer allows both its integration in all electronic media technologies and also the integration of any imaginable medium in the computer, simply because it is freely programmable. Turing's universal machine has developed into a new kind of universal medium, so versatile that its technical format and content would appear to be limited only by human imagination.

Seen from its current state of development, the computer stands in astonishing logical consistency with the media tradition, a tradition that exhibits a clear historical trend from techniques of information storage – story-telling, painting, manuscript books, printing – to techniques of transmission – radio and television, for example – and enriches this chain by adding the techniques of calculation and simulation.

A further consequence of the digital information, communications, and entertainment media, namely the supposed absolute superiority of the digital media compared to their analog predecessors, with constant availability, is however still far removed from consumer reality and an endlessly repeated marketing trick by the producers of electronic digital media technologies. The imaging and transmission quality of analog media such as the gramophone record, the photograph and the film still greatly exceed those of their successors the compact disc or digital photos and films, thanks to their enormous depth of information and fine resolution. Paradoxically, digital media are just as subject to aging as their analog equivalents, with the difference that the older media remain usable in degraded form, in contrast to a crashed hard disk, a corrupt diskette, or unplayable CDs.

Together with the accompanying medialisation of the computer and computerisation of the media, the interface of the networked computer becomes, in the true meaning of the word, a universal interface and a universal medium, capable of transactions and communication just as much as access to information, services, and computing tasks.

WINDOWS 'DESKTOP' (ABOVE). **MICROSOFT** USA **1997** AND MAC OSX OPERATING SYSTEM (BELOW). **APPLE** USA **2001**

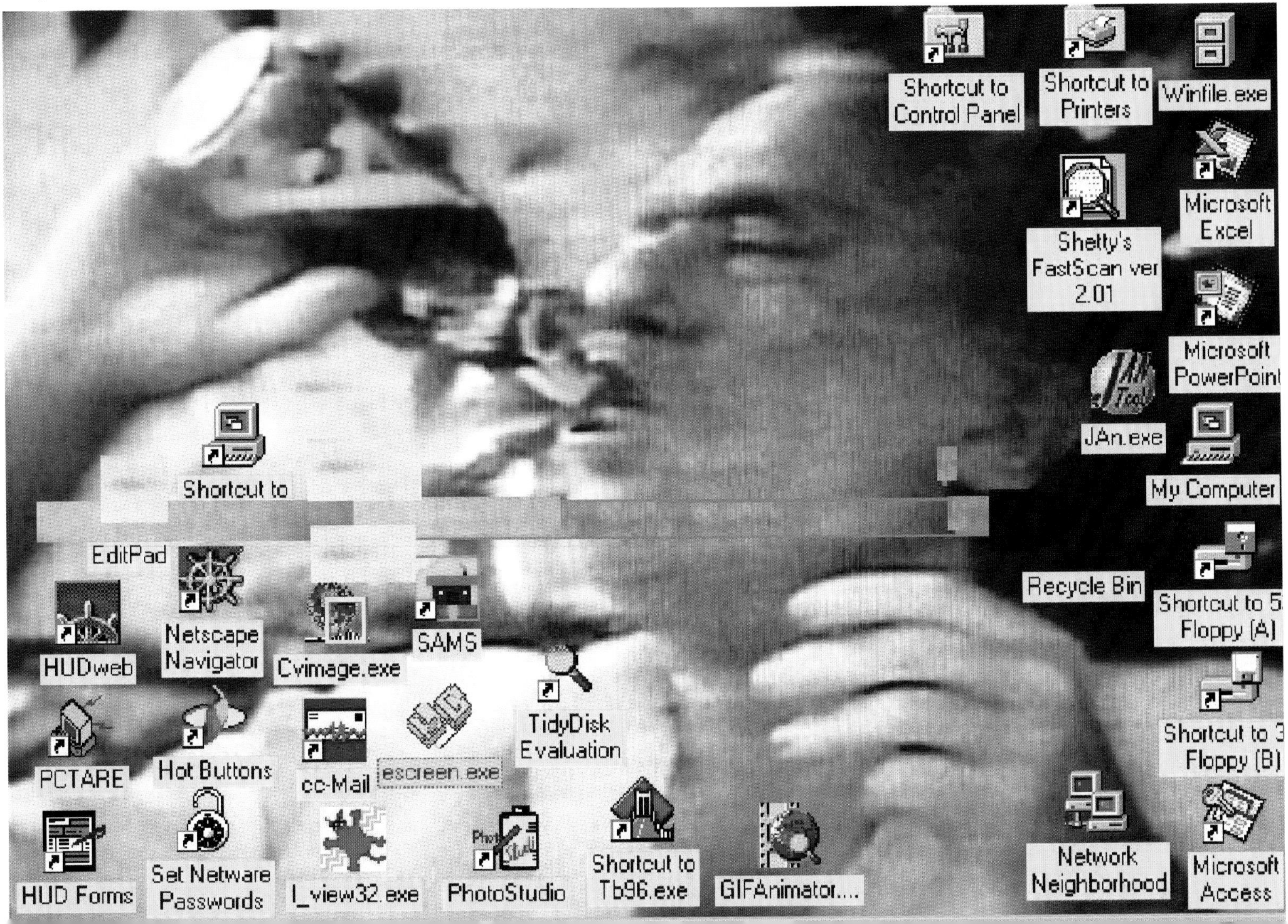

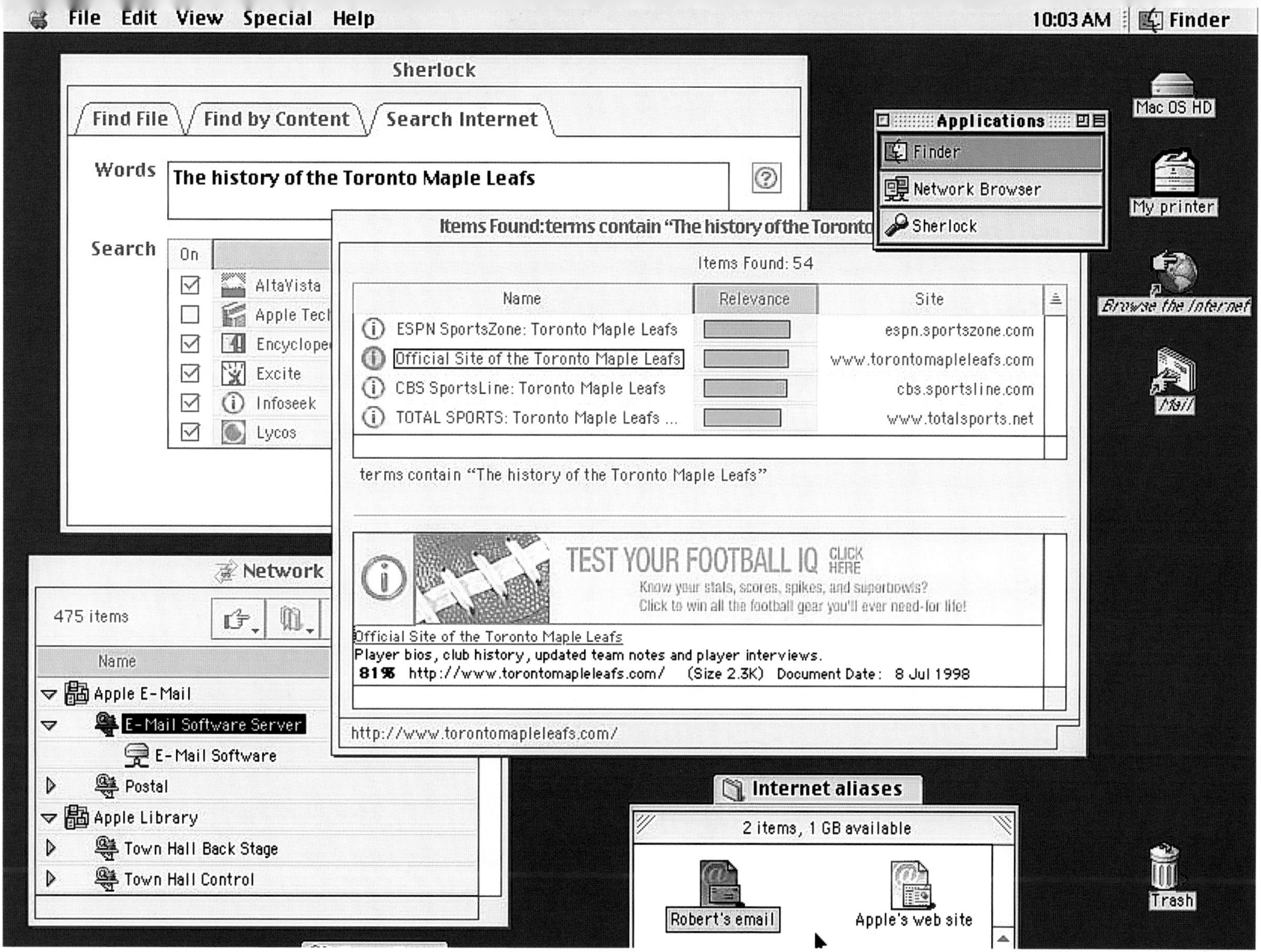
File Edit View Special Help
10:03 AM
Finder
Sherlock
Find File
Find by Content
Search Internet
Words
The history of the Toronto Maple Leafs
Search
On
AltaVista
Apple Tech
Encyclope
Excite
Infoseek
Lycos
Items Found: terms contain "The history of the Toronto
Items Found: 54
Name
Relevance
Site
ESPN SportsZone: Toronto Maple Leafs
espn.sportszone.com
Official Site of the Toronto Maple Leafs
www.torontomapleleafs.com
CBS SportsLine: Toronto Maple Leafs
cbs.sportsline.com
TOTAL SPORTS: Toronto Maple Leafs ...
www.totalsports.net
terms contain "The history of the Toronto Maple Leafs"
TEST YOUR FOOTBALL IQ
CLICK HERE
Know your stats, scores, spikes, and superbowls?
Click to win all the football gear you'll ever need-for life!
Official Site of the Toronto Maple Leafs
Player bios, club history, updated team notes and player interviews.
81% http://www.torontomapleleafs.com/ (Size 2.3K) Document Date: 8 Jul 1998
http://www.torontomapleleafs.com/
Applications
Finder
Network Browser
Sherlock
Mac OS HD
My printer
Browse the Internet
Mail
Network
475 items
Name
Apple E-Mail
E-Mail Software Server
E-Mail Software
Postal
Apple Library
Town Hall Back Stage
Town Hall Control
Internet aliases
2 items, 1 GB available
Robert's email
Apple's web site
Trash

A VIEW INSIDE THE POWERMACINTOSH G3, YOSEMITE MODEL. **APPLE** USA **1999**

SELDOM HAS A COMPUTER LOOKED SO LITTLE LIKE A COMPUTER. THE POWERMAC G4 CUBE WITH A CORDLESS KEYBOARD AND A MOUSE WITHOUT KEYS – THE WHOLE MOUSE IS PRESSED TO CLICK – LOOKS MORE LIKE A DESIGNER OBJECT THAN A PIECE OF TECHNICAL EQUIPMENT – MAYBE ANOTHER REASON WHY THE PRODUCTION WAS STOPPED AFTER A FEW MONTHS, DUE TO A LACK OF DEMAND. **APPLE** USA **2001**

adidas

6.0 CONVERGENCE AND VOLATILISATION

"COMPUTING BELONGS IN FURNITURE AND FOOTWARE MUCH MORE THAN IT DOES ON THE DESKTOP."

MIT MEDIA LAB (THINGS THAT THINK CONSORTIUM) 1995

<< MICROPACER: A TRAINING SHOE WITH BUILT-IN PEDOMETER COMPUTER THAT CALCULATES THE DISTANCE COVERED AND AVERAGE SPEED.
ADIDAS GERMANY **1984** AND **1999**

THE GLASSTRON DATA AND VIDEO GOGGLES LIBERATE USERS FROM THEIR SURROUNDINGS: IN FRONT OF THE EYES APPEARS A VIRTUAL 30" SCREEN.
SONY JAPAN **1999**

6.1 THE LIMITS OF THE DESKTOP INTERFACE

In the course of its history, the man/machine interface has undergone an evolutionary development, bringing it from the inside of the computer to the outside, and even further away in the form of the terminal and the console. In the form of the graphical user interface it has become the computer's 'face' with which we interact visually. The possibility of networking computers together, either locally or via telephone lines, has turned the machine on our desk into a peripheral, and thus the interface into a kind of remote control by which we get other computers, 10,000 km away or more, to work for us.

The increasing user-friendliness of this interface automatically made the computer more accessible, with the consequence that using it moved away from programming towards operating and the application. In the meantime these two dimensions have come increasingly closer, so that almost universal tasks can be formulated and solved. As a programming, application, and operating tool for using the universal machine, the interface has not simply developed out of the computer's differing roles and tasks, but has also to a large extent shaped, extended, and redefined them.

Until the present time, this development has produced a rich palette of coexisting interfaces, ranging from the naked but highly efficient text and command-line interfaces for programming and operating certain terminals, all the way to the highly complex virtual-reality interfaces used in the automotive industry and in other fields of industrial design, which can achieve an extremely high level of representation and simulation.

In spite of new forms of interaction, such as images, sound, and video sequences, the development of the graphics user interface *per se*, as the state-of-the-art operating standard for present-day PCs, would appear to be marking time. In view of the enormous quantitative progress in computers in the past fifteen years – higher speeds, greater storage capacity, and better resolution of the output devices – qualitative progress in the interface has remained largely unfulfilled.

The criticism of the graphics interface is almost as old as the interface itself, which basically has hardly changed since 1984. Jeff Raskin, who played a significant part in developing the Apple Macintosh over a quarter of a century ago, even ventured the opinion that the graphics user interface is incompatible with humans, and that computers will remain frustrating, difficult, and taxing to work with so long as their interface remains unchanged.

Again and again, criticism is levied at the desktop metaphor. Its greatest strength – reducing reality to a few actions and objects – is at the same time its greatest weakness. The comparison with a real office environment is also not very convincing: few common features can be found, but many contradictions. The 'desktop' model, implemented for the first time in the Alto in 1974, was introduced to represent a limited quantity of data belonging to a single user. Personal computers were conceived as individual systems with just a few programs for calculating and editing. They and the associated 'folders' easily fitted on an imaginary desk. At that time, networks, with their vast pools of shared data, were unknown. As the number of files increases, so does the problem of keeping track of them. Organizing the data in nested folders necessarily leads to an unclear structure, and a significant proportion of the time spent working at the computer is inevitably wasted in finding and retrieving files. Search functions added to the operating systems to correct this evil still have the great disadvantage that they operate in a linear fashion, usually producing sensible results only if the user knows the precise name of the file (or can at least remember part of the name).

Continuous increases in computer performance have been accompanied by simultaneous inflation in the size of operating systems and applications programs, leading to problems of operation and maintenance, with frustrating results for the normal user. The average computer user probably wastes an hour a day in problems of one sort or another with the computer. One researcher at the MIT Media Lab estimates that 85% of all users lose their tempers with the computer, even to the extent of physical assault. It would seem that the feeling of not understanding the computer – or perhaps of being misunderstood by it – arises from the inadequacy of its interface as a means of interaction and communication.

However, it must be said that the graphical user interface, like any piece of industrial design, can remain valid only so long as the technical framework for which it was conceived and designed does not change. Its undisputed merit is a new quality of interaction with the computer that

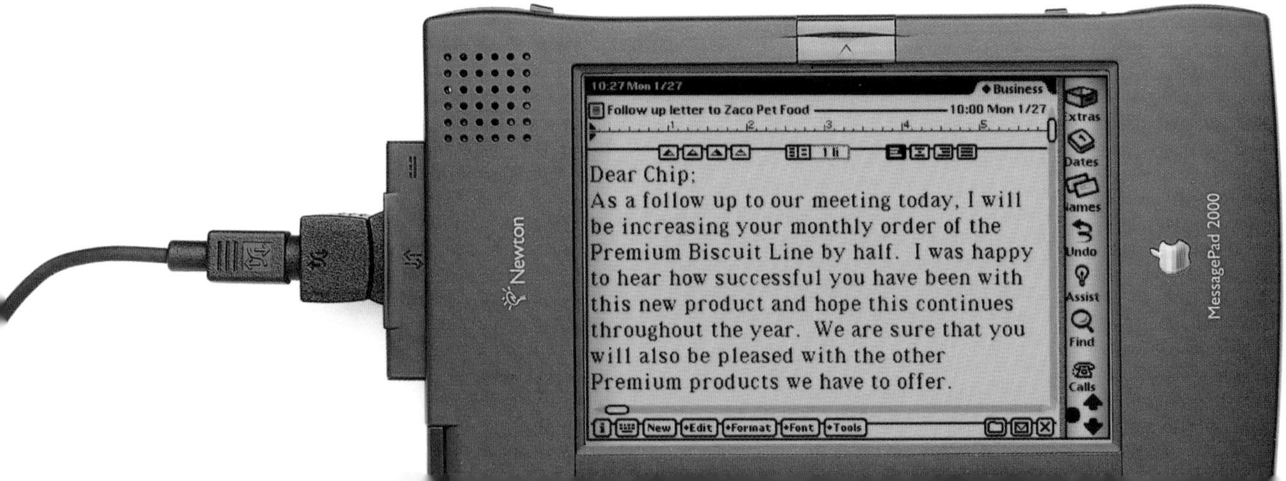

THE NEWTON MESSAGEPAD WAS AN EARLY (AND UNSUCCESSFUL) PRECURSOR OF THE NOW COMMON PERSONAL DIGITAL ASSISTANT. SHOWN HERE IS THE LATER MODEL 2000 WITH OPTIONAL KEYBOARD. **APPLE** USA **1993-97**

pushes the technical aspects to the background. In addition there is the standardisation of operation which makes it possible (at least in principle) to use any desired program so long as one knows something about what it does.

The restricted set of actions in the graphics interface is also a mixed blessing. Compared with the human senses and a person's differentiated means of expression, a computer's ability to absorb and impart information is hopelessly narrow and underdeveloped. A large potential for interaction and communication between people and their computers therefore remains untapped.

With a view to the computer of the future, two main lines of development can already be observed: convergence – the merging of the computer with other electronic technologies – and 'volatilisation' – as a consequence of its progressive miniaturisation. In any event, the new applications of the relevant technologies will shape the future interfaces at least as much as the interfaces shape the tasks and applications.

6.2 CONVERGENCE

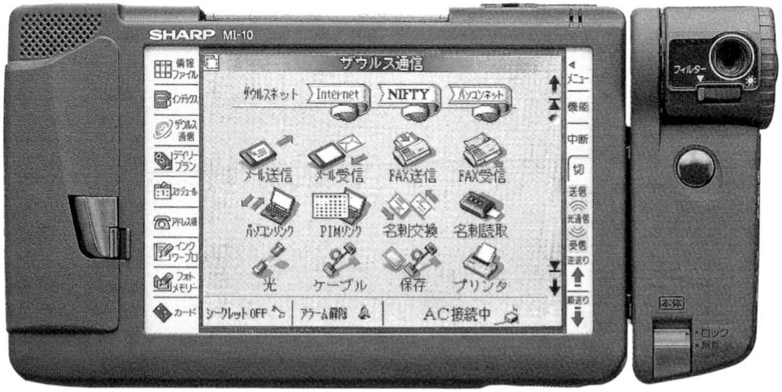

ZAURUS PI-7000 PERSONAL DIGITAL ASSISTANT WITH BUILT-IN CAMERA.
SHARP JAPAN **1996**

Convergence here means the current technological tendency of the computer to draw closer to other technologies, and vice versa. The first convergence phenomenon has already become manifest with the Internet as a combination of the computer and the telephone. From this point of view, using the Internet can be seen as interactive menu-controlled telephoning with data transfer.

Since the mid-1990s, digital TV and interactive TV have been the key words of a further major convergence, implying a cross between the computer and the television. Both sides are actively promoting it: the TV and advertising industry sees the computerisation of television as bring-

THE MI-10 WITH FOUR-COLOUR LCD DISPLAY CONTAINS THE NORMAL FUNCTIONS OF A PERSONAL DIGITAL ASSISTANT, BUT ALSO ALLOWS ONE TO DICTATE MESSAGES, SEND AND RECEIVE FAXES, EDIT AND SEND IMAGES AND SOUND FILES, AND HAS INTERNET ACCESS. **SHARP** JAPAN **1996**

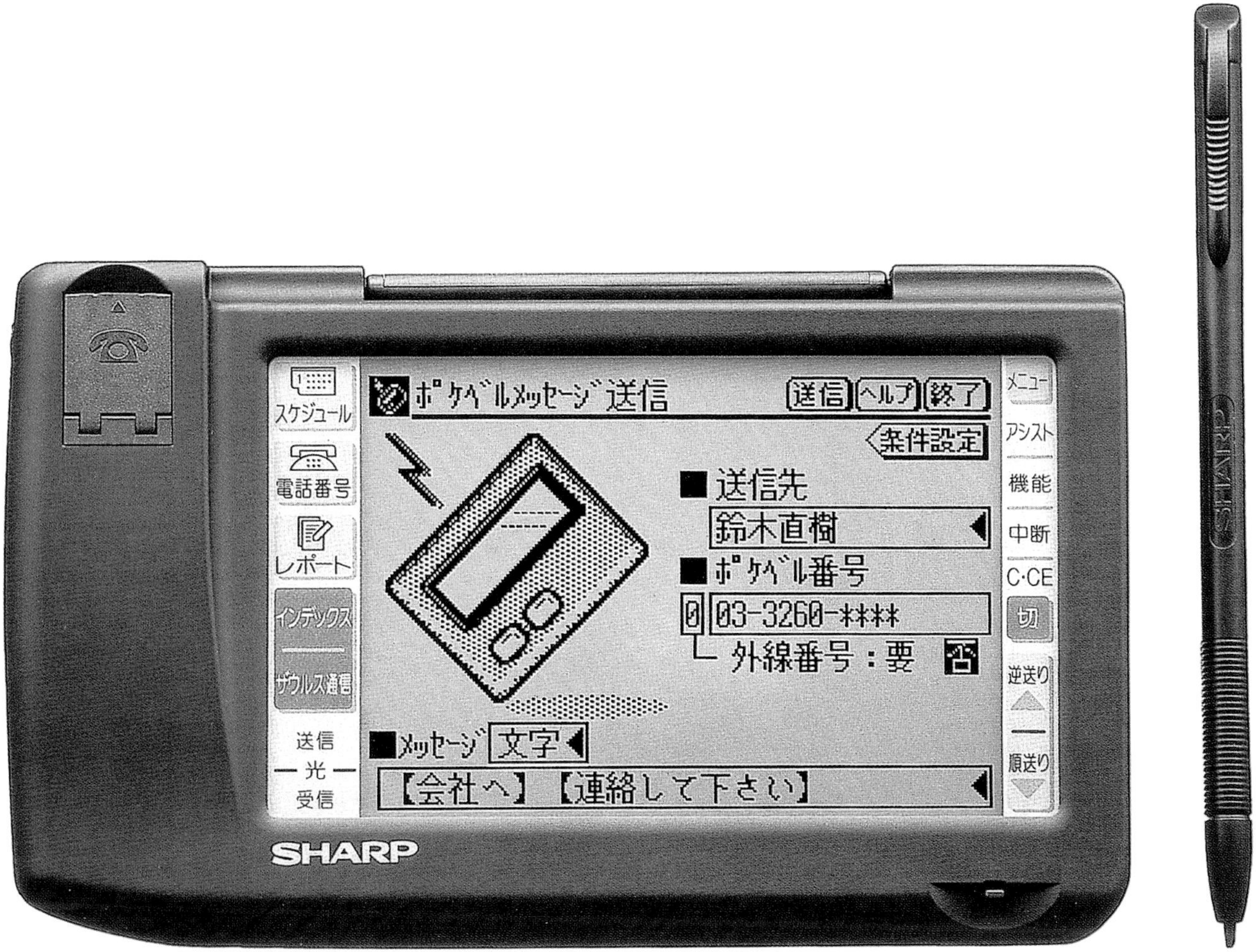

"THE AVERAGE USER LOSES AT LEAST ONE HOUR A DAY TO COMPUTER PROBLEMS. A RESEARCHER FROM MIT'S MEDIA LAB ESTIMATES THAT 85% OF USERS TAKE OUT THEIR ANGER VERBALLY OR PHYSICALLY ON COMPUTERS."

ing about completely new means of marketing that will give the consumer a chance to react directly to what is on offer. At the same time, the computer industry sees a possibility of extending the group of PC users – which appears to be reaching saturation point – to embrace the group of TV owners, an order of magnitude larger. Both sides reckon that the new hybrid medium will be good business. Although the first interactive TV sets are already on the market, nobody yet knows what standards will apply in future; in the final analysis, the users will decide which of many approaches will assert itself and acquire the status of a technological standard. This convergence is currently taking place from both sides: starting with the television, for example in the form of set-top boxes, and also starting with the computer, in the form of Web-TV or television tuner boards.

The convergence technology favoured by the TV and advertising industry is the set-top box which not only receives TV channels but also comprises further functions such as e-mail or Internet access. But it is already faced with competition from various sides, with the effect that the entire structure of both industries could change fundamentally. Digital TV or video servers, for example made by TiVo and FAST, are already on sale for people who wish to digitise TV signals as they are received via cable or satellite and to save programmes on their hard disks – with a current capacity of up to 30 hours. The associated Electronic Programming Guide (EPG) is continuously and automatically updated with all the programme information; it can be programmed from anywhere in the world via the Internet.

The potential of this new equipment is enormous, and could become a nightmare for the TV and advertising industry in the not-too-distant future: programmes can be interrupted at any time while the viewer has a meal, goes for a walk, or answers the telephone, without missing anything. Commercial breaks can be skipped or filtered out automatically – the advertising industry's most powerful weapon would suddenly become worthless. Even the classic programme structure, dictated by prime viewing times, would lose its significance if people could watch and skip when it suited them. In the long run, the television companies would no longer be stations that hold a large audience captive at a certain times of day, but merely the providers of programme material.

A further thorn in the side of the TV industry is the technological approach of making digital television receivable and usable on the basis of an open computer standard rather than a standard defined and controlled by the industry. This has already been put into practice very successfully by the Berlin company Convergence using the open-source computer operating system Linux. The initial prototypes of this system, known as LinuxTV, can be received on over 1,500 TV channels; consumers are now able to control what they see and when.

The freely programmable television/computer in combination with the fundamental nature of digital media formats – freely manipulable, copiable without loss of detail, distributable without restriction – would appear to mean (for the television and advertising industries) an inevitable loss of control over the viewers and thus an undermining of their long-established position of power.

At first, the variety of the computerised media and the medialised computer will lead to a confused mass of different interfaces. Whether the media machine of the future will resemble more a television or a computer is something that will be decided above all by its operability: the operating and programming interfaces that will lie somewhere between the conventional buttons on a television and the icon-clicking of the graphics user interface. In the final analysis, public acceptance will decide which type of equipment and which interface methodologies become established.

REFRIGERATOR WITH INTERNET CONNECTION: DESIGN STUDY FOR THE NETWORKED HOUSE IN THE USA. **INTEL** USA **1998**

6.3 VOLATILISATION

By 'volatilisation' we are to understand the tendency towards miniaturisation, projected forward to the extent that computers disappear entirely from the user's field of view. Approaches can already be detected in the form of ever-smaller computers such as palmtops, personal digital assistants, or mobile telephones with Internet ability. However, the continued miniaturisation of future computers will also make completely new means and principles of interaction necessary, since keyboards, mice, and similar input devices will presumably no longer be feasible. A possi-

TWO DESIGN STUDIES FOR WEARABLE COMPUTERS IN THE USA AND THE NETHERLANDS. **1998** AND **2000**

ble approach is control by the spoken word, describing items on a miniature screen, as evidenced by current developments in mobile phones. The interfaces of the future will have to function in a very unobtrusive way, since the user's concentration in a mobile situation is very dependent on the immediate environment. A person's remaining concentration (after filtering out ambient disturbances) should be taken up not with operating the machine but with interacting with the task in hand.

The volatilisation tendency can be seen, too, in the rise of 'embedded systems' – electronic equipment with built-in processors that enable it to carry out certain computer functions. Wireless networking systems will allow these devices to communicate with other equipment and be freely controlled by their owners.

The so-called wearables – computers integrated into articles of clothing – are designed to disappear from the conscious awareness of the wearer, and in future will wait in the background ready to help with a few specific functions. As a kind of hardware interface to the network or to a larger computer at home, they will act as a remote control for information and services when their owner requires it; this is a logical consequence of the historic tradition in which the interface has moved further and further from the computer itself.

According to preliminary data published by Intel, some 8 billion microprocessors would be manufactured during the year 2000. In the same year, the number of installed processors would exceed the number of people on earth, which the Intel researcher David Tennenhouse described as the "man/machine turning point".

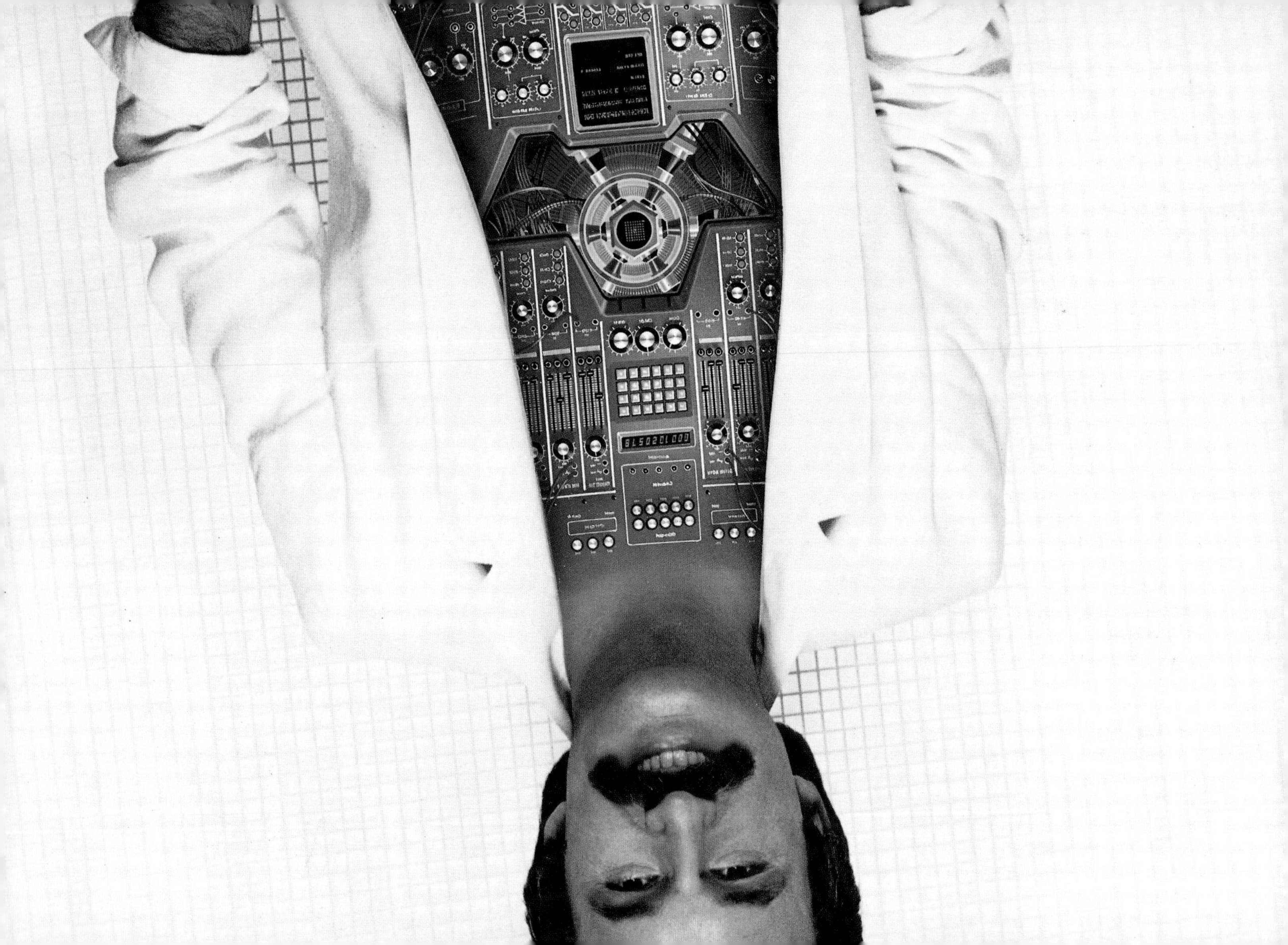

COMPUTERS". THIS DETAIL FROM GIORGIO MORODER'S ALBUM "E=MC²" ILLUSTRATES A VARIANT OF THIS UTOPIA. **1979**

The extent to which volatilisation and convergence are already industrial reality can seen in the uses the 8 billion processors were destined for: only 2% (160 million chips) would be built into computers, 6% in robots, 12% in vehicles. The remaining 80% of all microprocessors were intended for what Intel called miscellaneous electronic technologies.

In a future in which computers are so tiny that they are not only part of man's immediate and subconscious environment, but could even be integrated into it (as has already taken place in the surgical context), then the distance between people and their tools would shrink to zero, making interfaces superfluous: brain and computer would interact and communicate with one another, in an intuitive and automated way.

This form of man/computer convergence as a consequence of miniaturisation would bring about what is perhaps the most radical utopia in the entire history of computing – the symbiosis dreamed up by James Licklider: "Man-computer symbiosis is an expected development in cooperative interaction between men and electronic computers. It will involve very close coupling between the human and the electronic members of the partnership. The main aims are 1) to let computers facilitate formulative thinking as they now facilitate the solution of formulated problems, and 2) to enable men and computers to cooperate in making decisions and controlling complex situations without inflexible dependence on predetermined programs. In the anticipated symbiotic partnership, men will set the goals, formulate the hypotheses, determine the criteria, and perform the evaluations. Computing machines will do the routinizable work that must be done to prepare the way for insights and decisions in technical and scientific thinking. Preliminary analyses indicate that the symbiotic partnership will perform intellectual operations much more effectively than man alone can perform them. Prerequisites for the achievement of the effective cooperative association include developments in computer time sharing, in memory components, in memory organisation, in programming languages, and in input and output equipment."

WEARABLE PERSONAL COMPUTERS: THE RUPUTER WRIST COMPUTER PROVIDES THE BASIC COMMUNICATIONS FUNCTIONS OF A PDA WHILE OCCUPYING A MINIMUM OF SPACE. **SEIKO** JAPAN **1998** >>

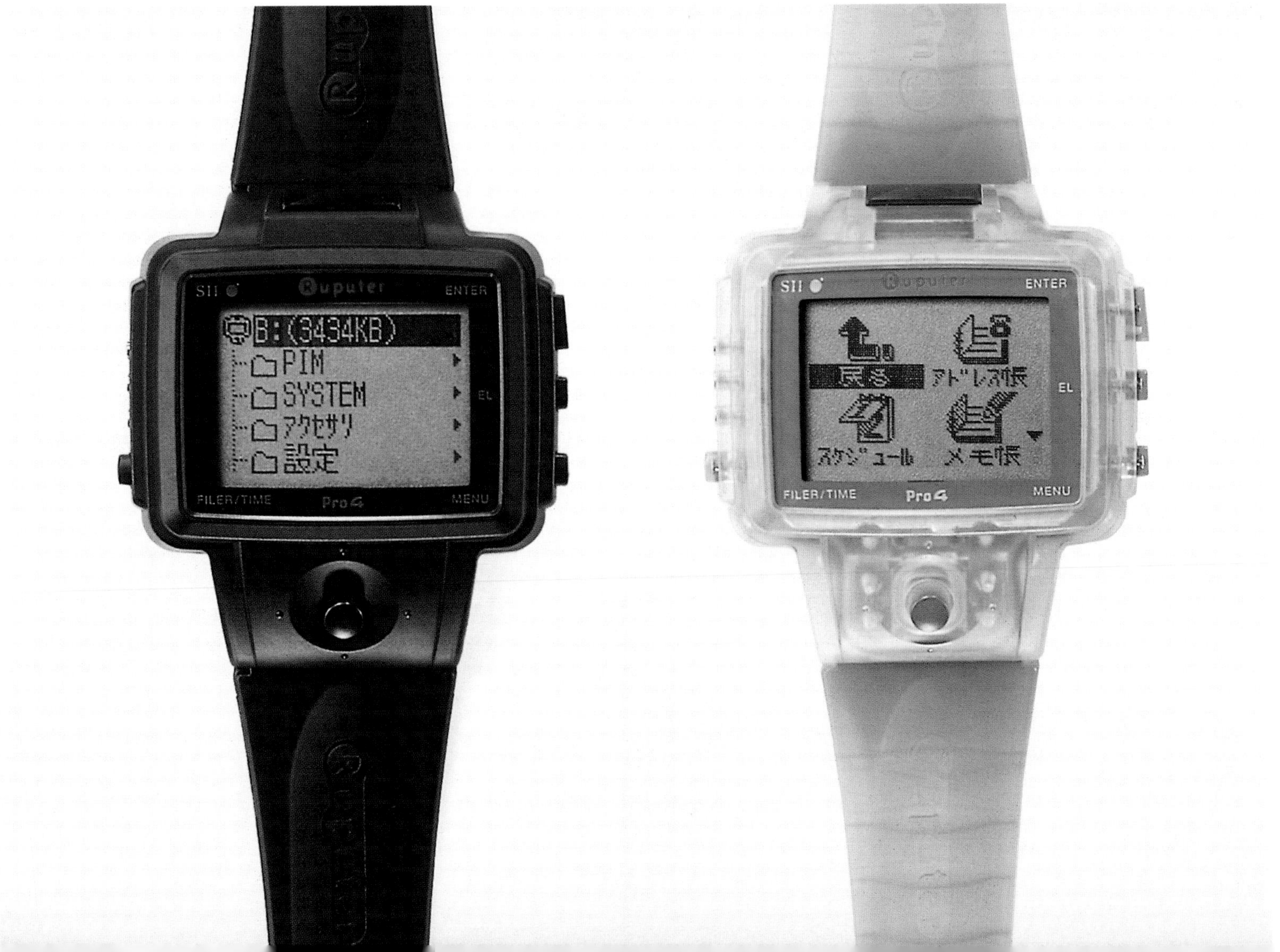
SII
Ruputer
ENTER
B:(3434KB)
PIM
SYSTEM
アクセサリ
設定
EL
FILER/TIME
Pro4
MENU
SII
Ruputer
ENTER
戻る
アドレス帳
スケジュール
メモ帳
EL
FILER/TIME
Pro4
MENU

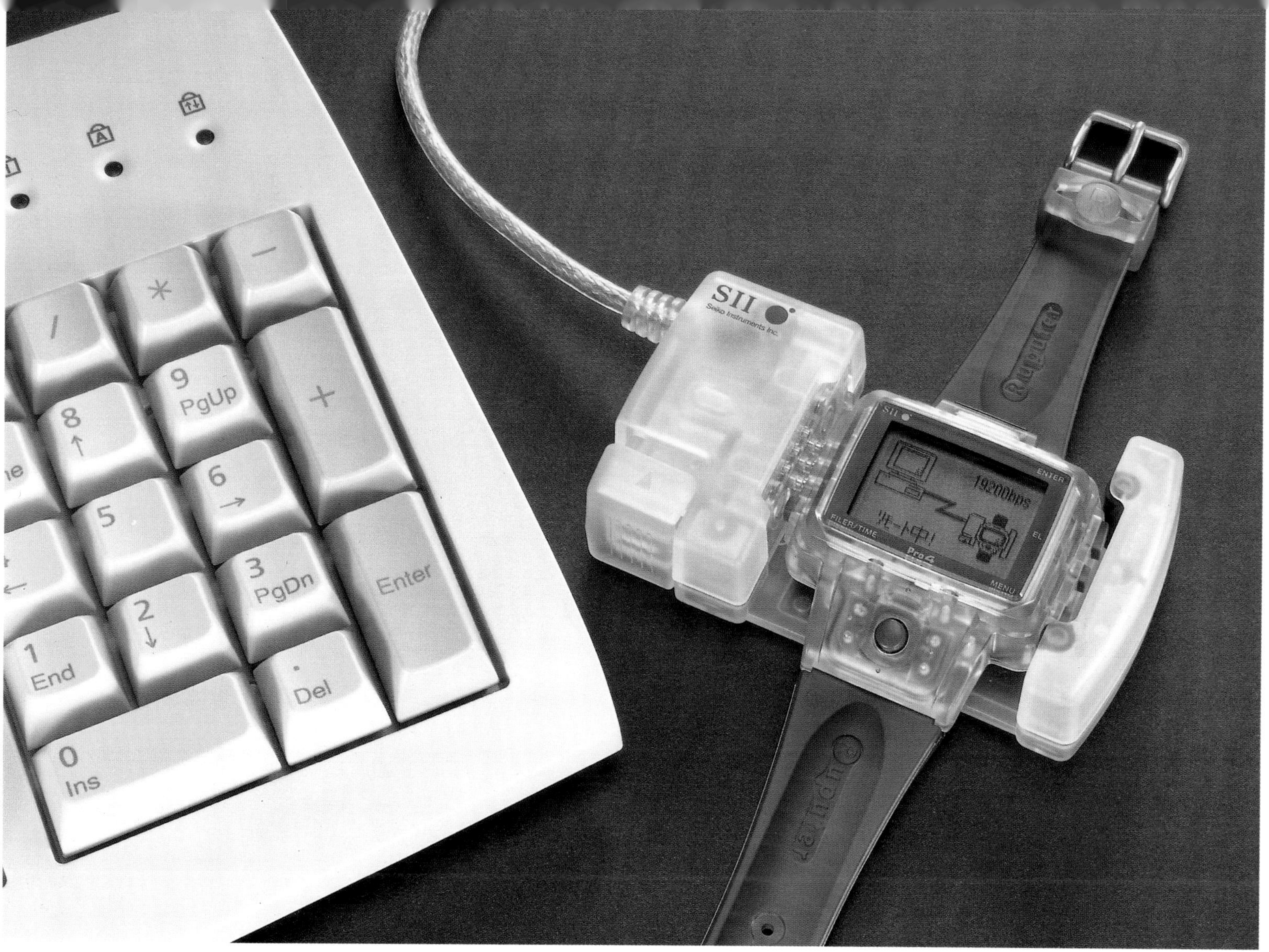
SII
Seiko Instruments Inc.
19200bps
ENTER
FILER/TIME
EL
MENU
Pro4
9
PgUp
8
6
5
3
PgDn
2
1
End
0
Ins
Del
Enter

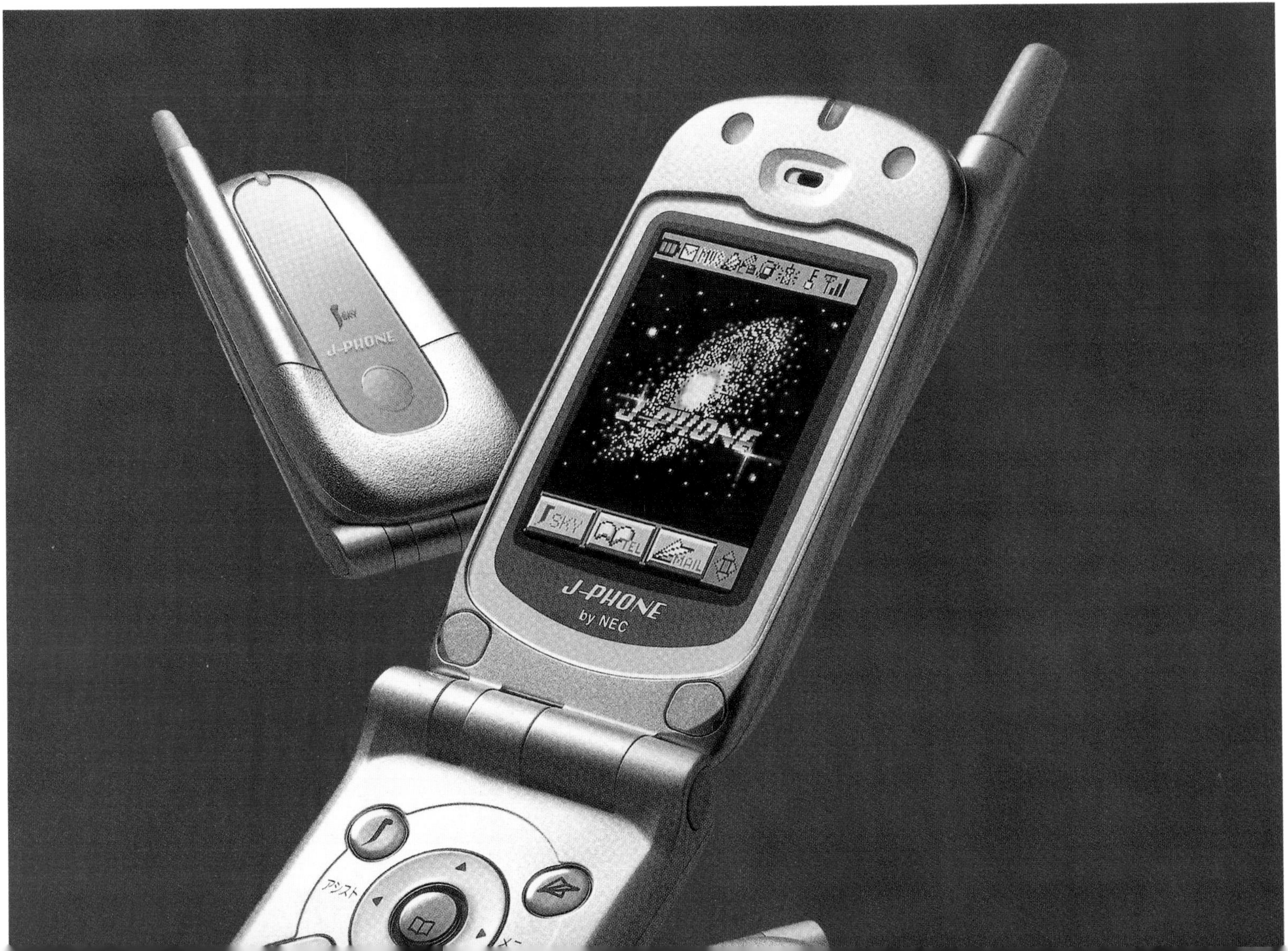
J-PHONE
by NEC
SKY
TEL
MAIL
J-PHONE

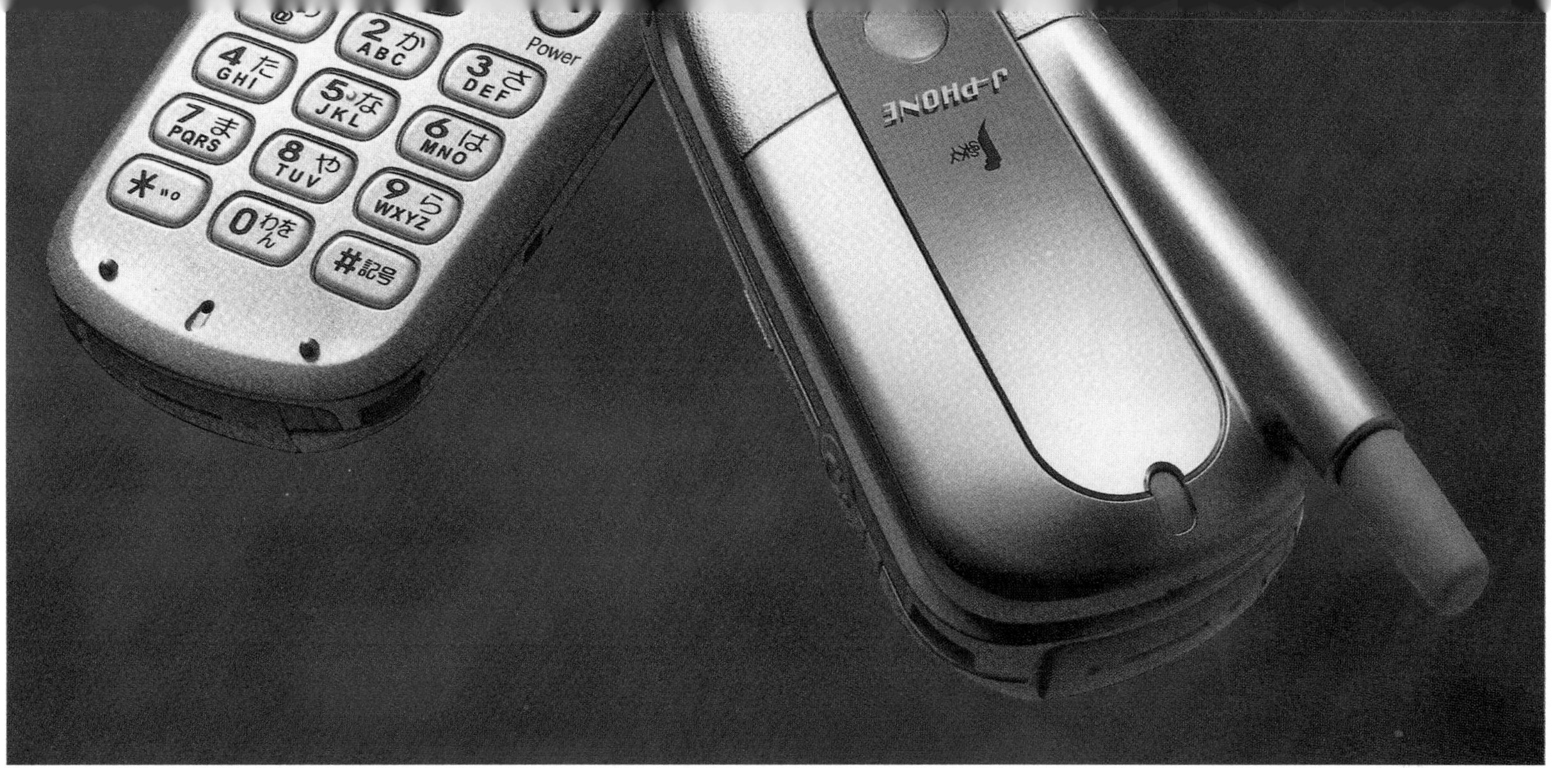

THE DISPLAY OF THIS TELEPHONE FOR THE JAPANESE I-MODE NETWORK IS A GREAT IMPROVEMENT ON THOSE OF EUROPEAN AND AMERICAN MANUFACTURERS IN TERMS OF SIZE, RESOLUTION, AND COLOUR RENDERING. IT IS EFFECTIVELY A SMALL COMPUTER SCREEN. **J-PHONE** JAPAN **2001**

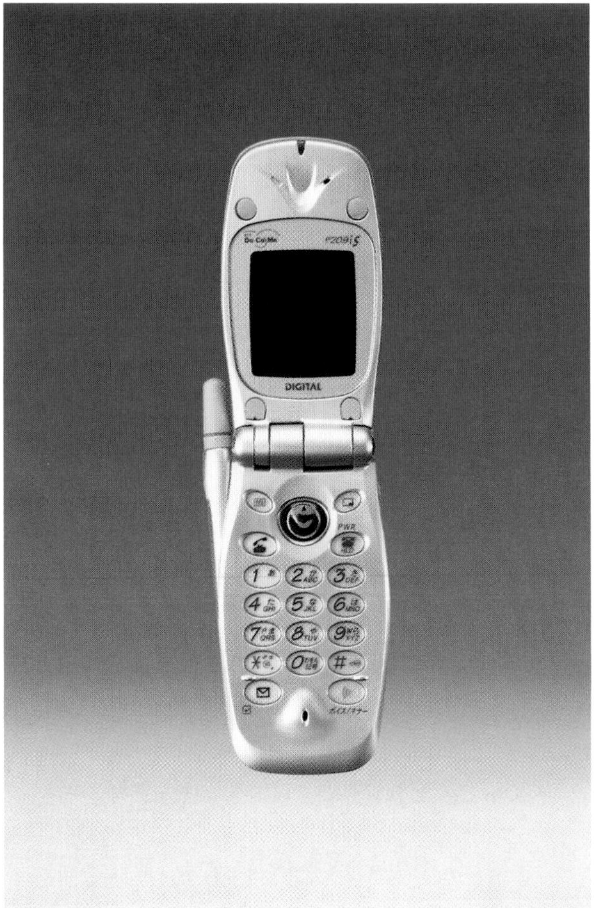

P209IS MOBILE TELEPHONE. **NTT DOCOMO** JAPAN **2000**

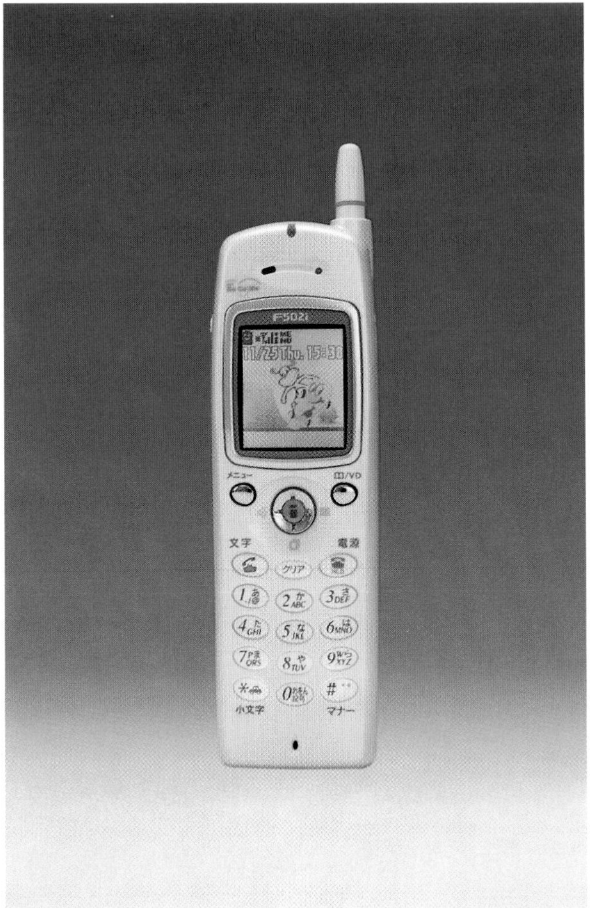

F502I MOBILE TELEPHONE. **NTT DOCOMO** JAPAN **2000**

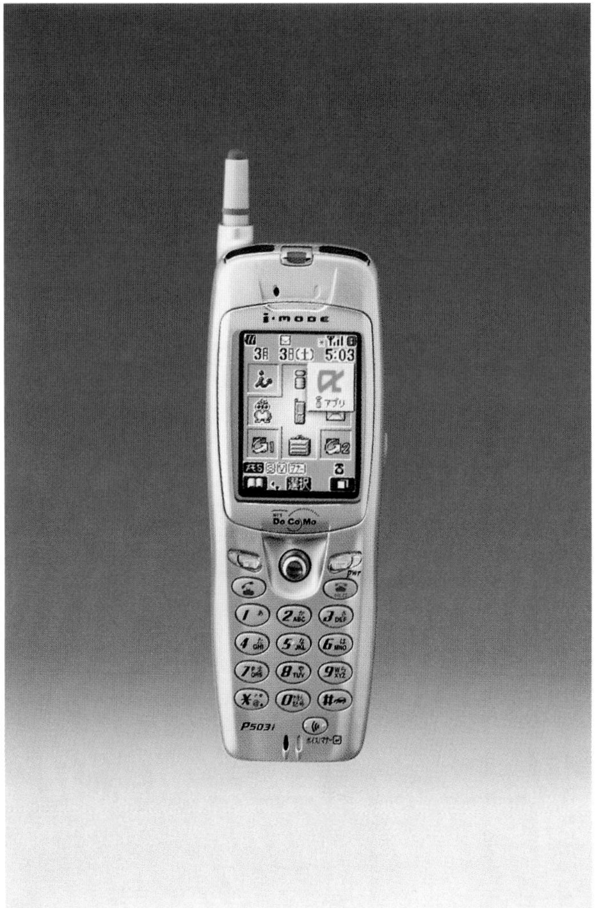

P503I MOBILE TELEPHONE. **NTT DOCOMO** JAPAN **2000**

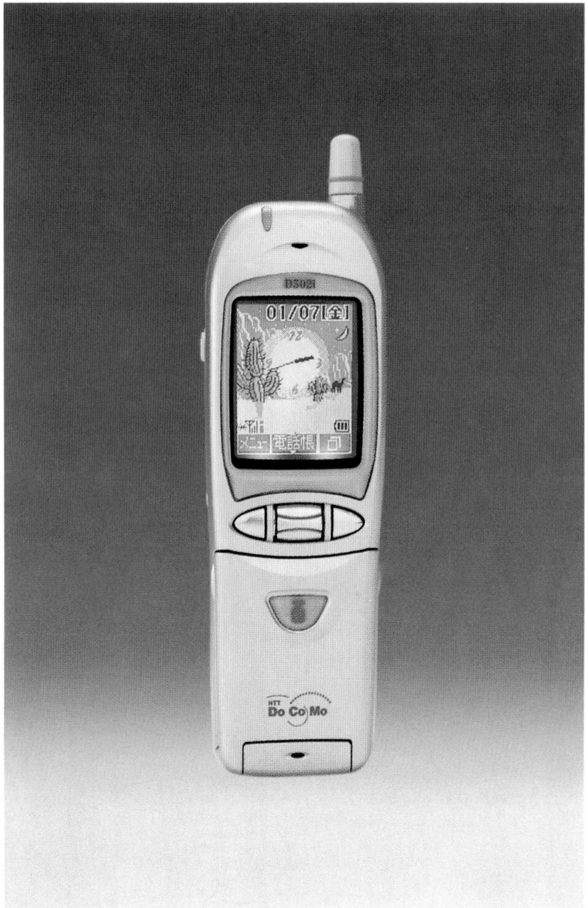

D502I MOBILE TELEPHONE. **NTT DOCOMO** JAPAN **2000**

αPPLI
おはよう
めざまし天気
きょうの北海道札幌市中

αPPLI
ekitan Navi
京浜東北線 普通
川崎
21:12発車
21:10にお知らせ
発車まで約2分
中止
音♪

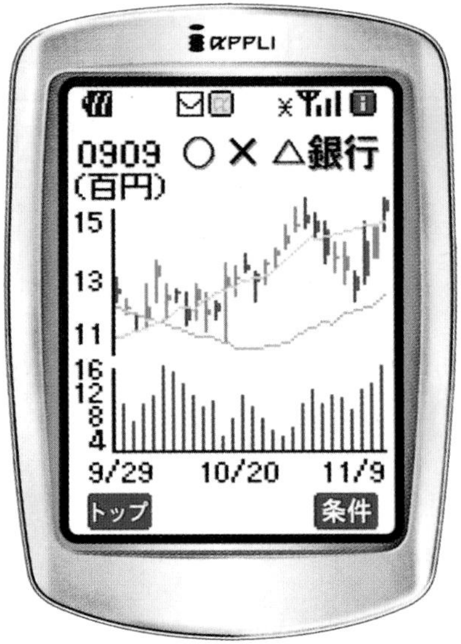
αPPLI
0909 ○×△銀行
(百円)
15
13
11
16
12
8
4
9/29
10/20
11/9
トップ
条件

αPPLI
1UP
0
READY!
終了
停止

αPPLI
Woo・・・
歌ってごらんよ
停止
保存

αPPLI
XII
IX
III
VI
2000年12月05日(火)
サブメニュー
戻る

STUDY IN FORM, FUNCTION, AND OPERATION OF FUTURE MOBILE PHONES. **NOKIA** FINLAND **2000**

SONY
SONY
4MB
MEMORY STICK

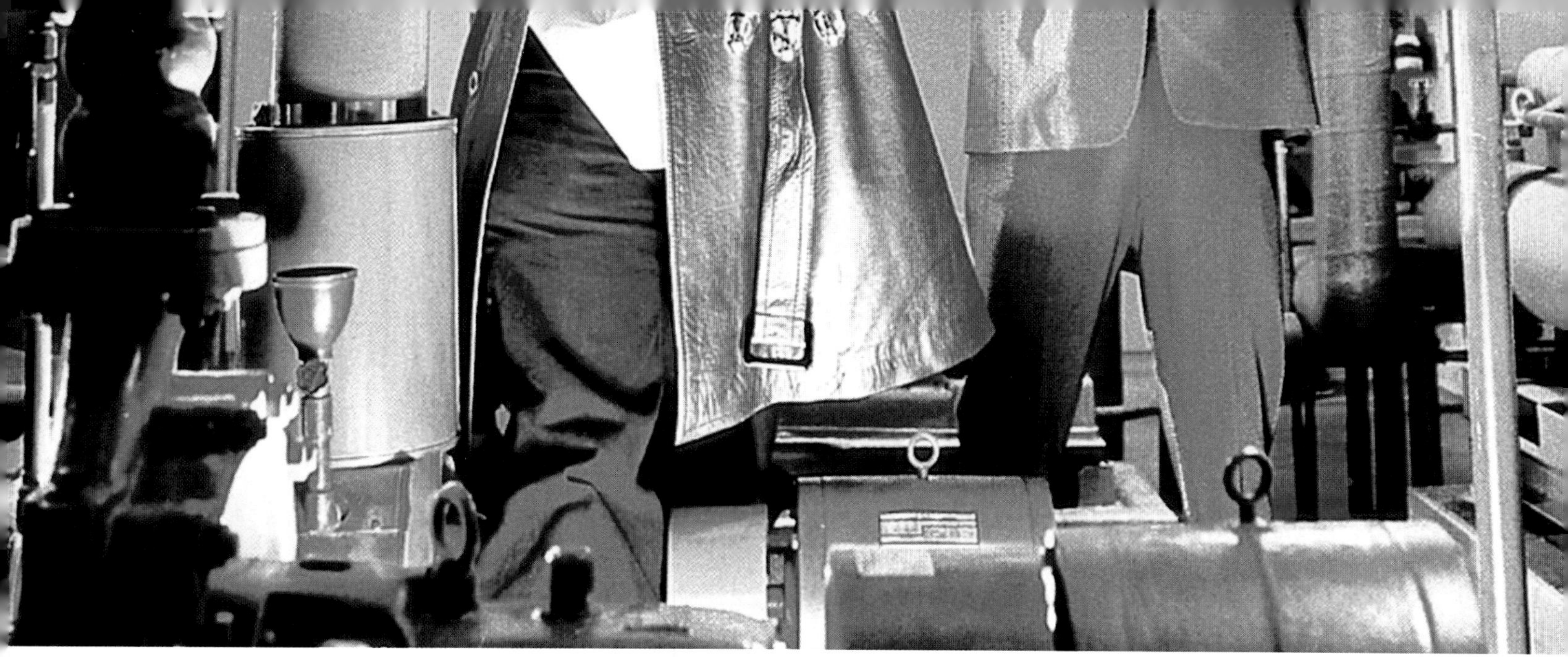

VISION OF THE FUTURE? MAN/COMPUTER OUTFIT IN A TRADITION SOMEWHERE BETWEEN STANLEY KUBRIK AND KRAFTWERK. THE MUSIC DUO **DAFT PUNK** FRANCE **2001**

<<< AIBO MODEL ERS-201 ROBOT DOGS. **SONY** JAPAN **2000**

<< THE MEMORY STICK ALLOWS EXCHANGE OF DATA BETWEEN A WIDE VARIETY OF ELECTRONIC EQUIPMENT, FOR EXAMPLE DISPLAYING STORED IMAGES IN A DIGITAL PICTURE FRAME. **SONY** JAPAN **1998**

A

APPLE I. 1976

APPLE COMPUTER INC. Founded in 1976 by Steven Jobs and Steven Wozniak in Cupertino, California

The Apple story began when Steven Wozniak – then programming >ATARI games – designed a simple computer whose main circuit board was mounted on a piece of plywood and enclosed in a wooden case. This Apple I >141, one of the first microcomputers, had to be connected to a television set. The Byte Shop in Mountain View, California, the pioneer among computer shops, ordered 50 computers at a price of $500 each. A total of 200 were sold.

The little company became known all over the world when the Apple II >169 was announced a year later. With the keyboard built into a plastic case, it looked much more like a proper computer. The price of $1,300 made it of interest to self-employed people and small businesses; it possessed colour graphics and sound, so was also popular for games.

million units of this model had been sold by the end of 1984.

In late 1979 Jobs and Wozniak began developing a more powerful computer, which they named the LISA. It soon became clear that it would take years before it was ready for the market, so as a stopgap they designed the Apple III, which was quite different from the previous model; it appeared in 1980. In parallel they produced improved versions of the Apple II with names such as IIe, IIc >250, and IIgs.

In 1982 the company's sales reached 1 billion dollars. The following year the LISA >231 came on the market as the first commercially available computer incorporating the graphical user interface originally developed at the Xerox PARC laboratory >228. Its high price of $9,995 was probably the reason it did not sell well. The improved LISA II, at only half the price, was not able to rescue the product line which now had to reckon with competition

STEVE JOBS AND JOHN SCULLEY DURING THE PRESENTATION OF THE MAC AND LISA COMPUTERS. **1984**

The Apple Macintosh >232, named after a Scottish variety of apple, came out in 1984. 50,000 of them were sold within 74 days; three months later the figure had doubled, and within a year there were half a million Macintoshes in use around the world. The Mac II was announced in 1987 and sold even better: 50,000 a month.

The Macintosh marked a breakpoint in the history of the computer, the point when the graphical interface and its new method of operation began to take over. It was for this model that Apple created the new field of desktop publishing, which revolutionised the field of graphic art in the early 1990s.

Apple's first portable computer, the PowerBook 100 (advertised as "the book of love"), appeared in late 1991 at a price of $2,500. Improved models followed.

NEWTON MESSAGEPAD 120. **1994**

Apple was also active in the field of hand-held computers with the Newton >276, produced in several versions from 1993. With its very compact size and touch screen, it was a forerunner of the principle later popularised by Palm, but its recognition of handwritten input was not sufficiently advanced to make it a success.

Later Apple computers, all based on the Macintosh, were the Quadras in 1991, the Power Macintoshes announced in 1994, models G3 and G4 >268, the iMac (1998), the portable iBook (1999), and the iCube >269 (2001) that soon became a cult object.

Although the company went through several crises in the 80s and 90s, and its share of the world market fell to between 5% and 10%, Apple has probably been the most creative and influential of all computer manufacturers. It certainly gave a decisive impetus to the personal computing market.

///

ATARI INC. Founded in 1972 by Nolan Bushnell and Ted Dabney in Sunnyvale, California

In 1961, students at the MIT programmed what was probably the world's first computer game, Space War, on a PDP-1 (>DIGITAL EQUIPMENT CORPORATION). This inspired Nolan Bushnell to design the Computer Space video gaming machine, which he completed in 1969. His company, Nutting Associates, set up the coin-operated machines in gaming halls in Silicon Valley; Computer Space was a great success.

A

Bushnell's new company, Atari – the word is the equivalent of "check!" in the Japanese board game Go – suddenly became famous when the video game Pong came on the market in 1972. Pong is frequently (but incorrectly) stated to have been the first video game. The idea – a kind of electronic table tennis >136 – was so simple that it was immediately imitated: Atari had neglected to patent it.

In 1974 the company announced a variant of Pong for the home. Unlike its main competitor, the Magnavox company's Odyssey, it could display colour graphics on a suitable television set.

A new project named Stella made no progress because Atari was not able to invest enough money in it. In 1976 the competitor Fairchild marketed the Channel F, which could play several video games stored on cartridges; this was a serious threat to Atari. Bushnell had wanted to produce a similar device, but soon ran out of money and the same year sold the company to Warner Communications for $28 million.

With Warner capital, the Stella appeared in 1977 under the name Video Computer System (VCS), with nine games on cartridges. A year later the Japanese company Taito set up its Space Invaders machines in gaming halls; Atari acquired the rights and modified the game for the VCS console. Space Invaders was a great hit, so there was much demand for the home version and thus for the VCS.

However, Nolan Bushnell was infuriated by the Warner management methods and left his company in 1978 to join the Pizza Time Theatre chain which combined fast food and video games under one roof.

In 1981 Atari brought out a successor to the VCS console, the Atari 2600 >136. The number referred to the data transmission speed of the acoustic coupler, a forerunner of the modem. The 2600 soon became the most popular computer games system in the world, with a vast library of games that are still offered for sale or swap. Particularly successful was Pacman, which is played to this day in every

GAME CARTRIDGES FOR THE ATARI VCS

GAME CONSOLE FOR THE ATARI 2600. **1981**

ATARI 800 HOME COMPUTER. **1978**

imaginable form – on the Gameboy or the mobile phone as well as the computer.

By 1982 Atari was an 2 billion-dollar company employing over 10,000 people around the world. Its video games dominated the market in the gaming halls and in the home. The following year it introduced the 5200, a less popular successor to the 2600, and also Atari's first home computer, the 1200XL. Like its successors, the 600XL and 800XL, this machine possessed unusually good colour graphics.

1984 marked the climax of the home computers – most of which could also be used for games – and thus the end of the boom in video games. Warner sold its Games Consoles division to Jack Tramiel, the founder of >COMMODORE COMPUTERS. That year Atari marketed the 7800, a cross between the 800 and the VCS, which it was compatible with; buyers could thus continue to play the many games designed for the VCS. In the long term, however, Atari could not compete with the home computers made by Apple and Commodore.

In 1985 Tramiel introduced the 520ST, a $600 computer which could hold its own against the Apple Macintosh costing three times as much. Like the Mac, it used the graphical user interface originally devised by Xerox for the Alto, but the use of colour made it even better. The ST also had a Midi interface, making it immediately popular with musicians and producers of music, and it has remained so to this day. A year later, in 1986, it was replaced by the improved 1040ST, the first microcomputer with a main store of 1 megabyte.

In the meantime, Tramiel had enticed many Commodore managers and engineers to Atari, and in the years to come had a neck-and-neck race with his former company.

Atari's first PCs appeared in 1988. However, since the company produced the main components itself, as opposed to importing from Asian producers, they were considerably more expensive than the models made in the Far East, and did not sell well. The production line closed down the following year. The games consoles named Panther (1988) and Jaguar (1993) were also not very successful. Later computers, none of which could repeat the success of the ST models, included the Lynx portable video games system (1989), the Mega STE (1991), and the multimedia Falcon series (1992).

C

In 1998 the company, on the brink of ruin, was sold for five million dollars to the American games manufacturer Hasbro, which froze all technical developments and simply made use of the licensing rights for games and merchandise. In the spring of 2001 Atari was acquired by the French games manufacturer Infogrames.

///

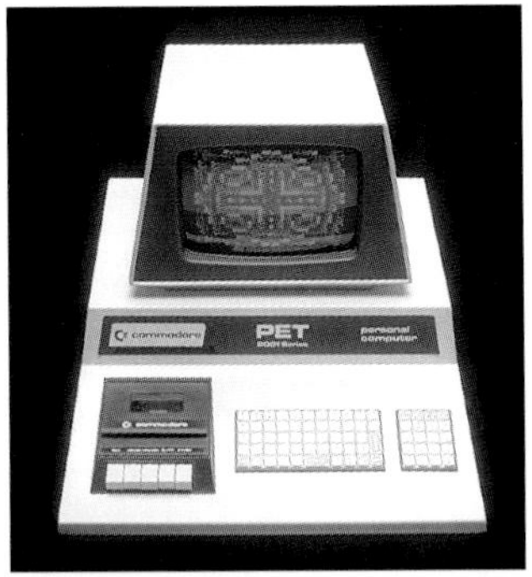

COMMODORE COMPUTERS Founded in the mid-1950s as a chain of typewriter repair shops; in 1962 Jack Tramiel reformed the company as Commodore Business Machines, Canada

Commodore started by producing adding machines. After acquiring a typewriter manufacturer and a large office furniture company, it soon became the market leader in North America.

On a trip to Japan in the late 1960s, Tramiel came across the first electronic pocket calculators containing microprocessors made by Fairchild Semiconductors. He recognised the potential, and in 1971 marketed the C110, the first American pocket calculator, made by the Bowmar company. This rapidly became a sales hit – before other companies like >TEXAS INSTRUMENTS and >SINCLAIR entered the market.

In 1977 the company brought out one of the first microcomputers, the Personal Electronic Transactor, or PET for short >155. This computer consisted of a roughly cubical case containing the monitor and the keyboard, an unusual design. Owing to technical problems that were never fully solved, the PET and its rather less angular successor the CBM never achieved quite the popularity of its main competitor the >APPLE II which came on the market at about the same time.

Commodore's next computer, the VC 20 (sold in Japan as the VC 1001), was a bombshell for the new market in home computers. However, its available

COMMODORE VC 20. **1981**

COMMODORE C64. **1982**

store – not counting the BASIC in ROM – was a meagre 5 kilobytes, and in 1982 it was followed by the more powerful C64 >177 with 38 kilobytes of useful store. Even so, half a million of the VC 20 had been sold by 1985.

The C64, like the VC 20, could be connected to a colour TV and so produce sound and fast graphics. The sound chip, with three channels and offering some of the functions of a much more expensive synthesizer, was in a class of its own at that time.

The C64 soon became the epitome of a home computer. Thousands of games programs were written for it. An interesting variant was the portable SX64 with a built-in colour monitor and diskette drive; at 17 kg it weighed even more than the >OSBORNE 1. After only two years, four million of the C64 had been sold world-wide. By the time production ceased in the late 80s, the number had risen to an estimated 17 to 22 million. The C64 was thus the best-selling computer of an entire decade.

Following internal disputes, Jack Tramiel left his company in 1984 and bought the ailing >ATARI from Warner Communications. Commodore lost a far-sighted strategist and one of the most experienced managers in the computer business.

Now that the C64 and its successor the C128 were technically no longer up to date, Commodore badly needed a new model using the more powerful 16-bit technology. In 1985 it announced the Amiga 1000; this machine was not compatible with any of the former models, being based (like the Apple Macintosh and Atari ST) on the new Motorola chips. Although the Amiga had many adherents, thanks to its outstanding graphics ability, it was never able to match the sales figures of the earlier Commodore computers.

The company's losses increased. It brought out a few more Amiga models, the A2000, A500, A3000, and A400; also the CD32 for the video-games market. But these could not halt the slide, and in 1994 Commodore ceased trading and sold the licence for all Commodore and Amiga products to the German computer chain Escom. This company in turn went bankrupt a year later. Various attempts to revive the Amiga finally failed in 1998.

COMMODORE C264, ALSO: PLUS-4. **1984**

C

COMPAQ Founded in 1982 by Rod Canion, Jim Harris, and Bill Muerto in Houston, Texas

In its first year Compaq brought out a portable computer whose compact dimensions were the reason for the company's name. The machine was elected 'computer of the year'. It was not the first portable computer, as Compaq claimed, though it was considerably lighter than the >OSBORNE I since it used an innovative LCD screen. In 1986 Compaq introduced a computer based on the Intel 80386 processor; this successful model made it one of the leading manufacturers of IBM-compatible computers. Ten years later, Compaq was a world leader in both desktop PCs and notebook computers.

In 1998, after months of negotiations, Compaq took over the ailing >DIGITAL EQUIPMENT CORPORATION and Tandem Computer, becoming the world's second largest computer

Compaq's history took a less spectacular course than that of other major manufacturers, and its products were marked by reliability rather than revolutionary features. Nevertheless – or perhaps for that reason – Compaq always had a 'nose' for the trends, which quickly put it on the road to the top.

///

CONTROL DATA CORPORATION Founded in 1957 by William Norris in Cambridge, Massachusetts

When William Norris set up Control Data he was able to draw on the expertise of Seymour Cray, already a well-known hardware designer, and other brilliant engineers from Engineering Research Associates (ERA); he had been a cofounder of ERA in 1946 (it was bought by >REMINGTON RAND in 1952).

In 1960 the company announced the CDC 1604,

CONTROL DATA 8600 (INCOMPLETE). **1972**

CONTROL DATA 7600. **1969**

tors. It was designed for scientific applications and was very powerful. Shortly afterwards, Cray designed the CDC 160A, intended as an input/output unit for the 1604. It was soon available separately and was a kind of early minicomputer.

As chief designer at Control Data in the 1960s and early 1970s, Cray was responsible for the equally successful models CDC 6600 >83 and 7600 >88, at first described as high-performance computers, later as supercomputers. It was at CDC that he developed the famous C shape, allowing extremely short internal cable paths.

The CDC 6600 represented the technical maximum when it came on the market in 1964, and for a long time remained the fastest and most powerful computer available – with considerably more performance than the equivalent >IBM machines. Only a few were sold, to the National Security Agency amongst others, but they were always in the headlines in the trade literature, which reinforced the reputation of this legendary supercomputer.

Control Data never really recovered after Cray left in 1972. From the start, the computers produced by his own company >CRAY RESEARCH were far superior to the CDC. In spite of Norris' proven business acumen, Control Data lost its core business; sales plummeted, and Norris resigned from the management in 1986. The company survived as a small supplier of high-tech products and services to the American forces.

///

CRAY RESEARCH Founded in 1972 by Seymour Cray in Chippewa Falls, Wisconsin

While at Engineering Research Associates and >CONTROL DATA CORPORATION, Seymour Cray had learned everything there was to learn about the design of high-performance computers and the market for them. On founding his own company he set about building even better computers that made no compromises.

His first computer, the Cray 1, was installed in 1976 at the Los Alamos National Laboratory. A total of 17 of them were produced over the next three years; they were twice as fast as the CDC 7600.

Cray made use of his proven C-shaped layout which allowed the integrated circuits to be placed closer

C

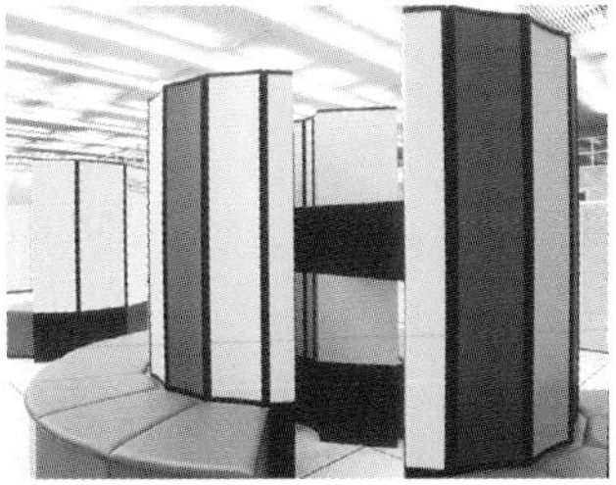

CRAY-1 SUPERCOMPUTER, **1976**,

together. No connecting cable in this supercomputer was longer than 1 foot (30 cm). The Cray 1 was surrounded by a leather-upholstered bench, under which the power cables ran: Cray took the view that programmers and scientists should feel at home with his computers. Subsequent models were available in a choice of colours.

Above all, Cray Research computers were unmatched in speed and performance. They were built in small numbers but used for the most demanding of applications: prototype design and simulations in the automotive and avionics industries; difficult problems in chemistry, biology, and medicine; and the most computation-intensive tasks of all, weather forecasting and climate research.

The world's first multiprocessor computer, the Cray X-MP, was announced in 1982, followed by the Cray 2 >91 with a performance ten times that of the Cray 1. Six years later the company released its Y-MP, using

of up to 4 gigaflops – that is to say, 4 billion floating-point operations per second.

Spurred on by revolutionary technical visions, Seymour Cray then experimented with gallium arsenide, which promised faster semiconductors than the normal silicon. His inconclusive trials brought the company to the brink of insolvency, making it hard to develop follow-on models.

Cray therefore decided to split off the Cray 3 project, and so founded the Cray Computer Corporation in Colorado Springs in 1989; there he continued his experiments with gallium arsenide chips. But the company went bankrupt in 1995 after his failure to build a working computer system. Cray died in 1996 following a car accident.

In the last years of his life, Seymour Cray attracted attention with his massively parallel supercomputers (>THINKING MACHINES CORPORATI-

D

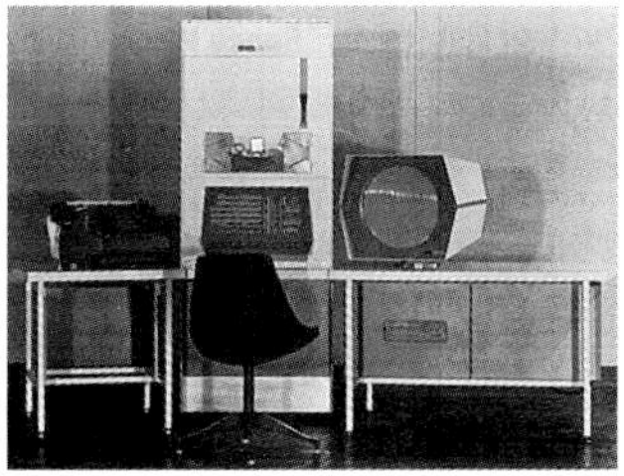

PDP-1 – WITH THE FIRST MONITOR. **1959**

THE FIRST MINICOMUTER: THE PDP-8i. **1965**

raising the performance of the whole to as much as 16 gigaflops. This concept was used in 1993 by his old company Cray Research, for which he continued working, to implement the T3D based on commercially available silicon chips. The later T3E-1200E model was used in a joint experiment involving several research establishments in 1998 to achieve a speed of 1 teraflop (a trillion operations per second). This figure has not been exceeded since.

Cray Research continued on its successful course with the C90 and J90 series. In 1996 it was sold to >SILICON GRAPHICS and four years later to the Tera Computer Company which was then renamed Cray Inc.

///

DIGITAL EQUIPMENT CORPORATION (DEC) Founded in 1957 by Kenneth Olsen and Harlan Anderson in Maynard, Massachusetts

Olsen had come into contact with the Whirlwind computer >23 as a student in Cambridge, Massachusetts, when working at the Lincoln Laboratory in the early 1950s. There he was later largely responsible for its successor, the TX-0, which was then one of the most advanced computers – both technologically and from the point of view of its operating concept.

So it was that the first DEC computer, the PDP-1 (Programmed Data Processor) developed in 1960, bore a remarkable similarity to the TX-0 and, like it, was based on transistors rather than vacuum tubes >107. The PDP-1 also became famous as the computer on which the world's first computer game (Space War) was programmed and played. The PDP-1 cost $120,000, and roughly 50 were sold.

Right from the start, all the technical details of DEC computers were published in small-format manuals that were given away to buyers and potential buyers. DEC specifically encouraged its customers to learn how the computers worked, and even to modify or extend them in accordance with their own ideas. This was very different from the business methods of >IBM, whose considerably more expensive computers were only leased and the customer was not allowed to touch anything inside.

The PDP-8, announced in 1965, then created a new generation: that of the minicomputer. This transistorised computer was so compact that it could be set

H

PDP-8E MINICOMPUTER. **1972**

HEWLETT PACKARD'S FIRST HEADQUARTERS:

up wherever it was needed. The basic price was $18,000 including the teletypewriter, and it was capable of executing roughly 35,000 instructions per second. Its low price stood in great contrast to its high performance and was to prove a serious threat to IBM. Over the years, more than 50,000 PDP-8s were sold.

Larger models such as the PDP-6, PDP-10, and PDP-11 were popular in universities and other research establishments.

Digital Equipment Corporation was bought by >COMPAQ in 1998.

///

HEWLETT-PACKARD Founded in 1939 by Bill Hewlett and Dave Packard in a garage in Palo Alto, California; fifty years later the state of California officially declared this garage as the 'birthplace'

One reason for the importance of the valley was the immediate proximity of Stanford University and the fact that a number of engineers and scientists who had graduated there remained close to the campus when they set up business. The two founders of Hewlett-Packard, for example, had met at electronics lectures; one of their friends was Barney Oliver, who worked for them from the start.

One of Hewlett-Packard's major contracts was to produce several sound generators for Walt Disney Studios. During the Second World War, the young company made a name for itself with high-precision measurement and control equipment used by military establishments and armaments suppliers. As a result, Hewlett-Packard grew rapidly to over 200 employees and an annual turnover of a million dollars. In the post-war years the range of products included various instruments for measuring and testing electronic equipment, including an electronic voltmeter. By 1959 the number of employees

HP 35 CALCULATOR. **1972**

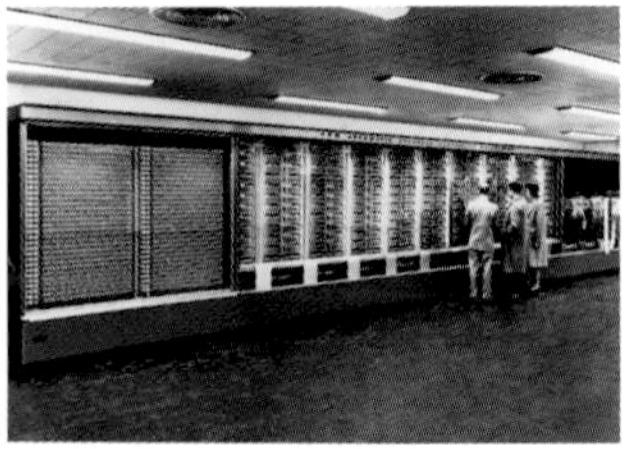

IBM ASCC. **1944**

In 1966 Hewlett-Packard made an entry into the rapidly growing computer business with its model 2116A. That year the German subsidiary became a pioneer of a new management style when it did away with time clocks and introduced flexitime. It was some eight years before the American parent company followed suit.

In 1972 the company announced the HP 35, the world's first scientific pocket calculator. The HP 3000 minicomputer for scientific and research applications appeared at about the same time.

In 1982 Hewlett-Packard brought out a series of IBM-compatible PCs and also its first laser printer, the size of refrigerator and costing $100,000. Only two years later this was followed by the first LaserJet printer at a price of $3,500; almost overnight, a new market was created. The competitors, mainly Asian companies, were concentrating on daisy-wheel and matrix printers. The LaserJet was fast, compact, and robust; it needed neither continuous paper nor special coated paper.

The first ink-jet printer, the DeskJet 500, came on the market in 1988, and printed only in black. In the meantime, colour ink-jet printers had attained such a high image standard when used with special paper that they were in serious competition to photographic prints.

IBM (INTERNATIONAL BUSINESS MACHINES) Founded in 1911 as the Computing-Tabulating-Recording Company in New York

In the 1890s the US Census Bureau ran a competition to find new techniques for evaluating data >12. Hermann Hollerith, of German extraction, was awarded the contract to supply his new punched-card machines for the next census. He founded the Tabulating Machine Company in 1896 and sold it five years later to the Computing Scale Company; this became the technological foundation for the later International Business Machines which came into existence in 1924 as a result of various mergers and acquisitions.

In the years to come, Thomas Watson, the first chief executive of IBM, developed the typical IBM virtues of employee motivation, customer-orientation, and a strong sales team. For decades, his slogan "Think"

I

ILLUSTRATION FROM AN IBM ADVERTISEMENT. **1951**

was written up like a mantra in every IBM office and factory. IBM rapidly expanded into South America, Europe, Asia, and Australasia.

The electric typewriter division was set up in 1933, and within a few years IBM had become the world leader in this field. After years of joint development with Harvard University, the Automatic Sequence-Controlled Calculator (ASCC) >19 (alias Harvard Mark I) was unveiled in 1944 and hailed in America as the world's first computer. >KONRAD ZUSE's pioneering work was of course unknown until after the war.

In 1952 IBM announced its first commercial vacuum-tube computer, the Model 701 >46, which was used mainly by government departments and major research establishments.

The company again caused a revolution in data processing in 1956 when it introduced RAMAC,

became a standard technology for data storage, so that programs no longer needed to be read from punched cards or magnetic tape each time they were run.

In the same year IBM introduced the FORTRAN programming language (formula translator), which soon supplanted machine code for many applications, becoming the most commonly used language in the scientific and engineering fields.

In 1964 IBM announced its System/360, the first-ever family of intercompatible computers, which was to become the first de-facto standard in electronic data processing >49. System/360 laid the foundation stone for IBM's dominance of the world market in the second half of the 1960s, with its strategy of unbundling: software, hardware, maintenance and other services were now charged for separately rather than as a package deal. This caused the turnover in all three fields to grow in leaps and bounds, so un-

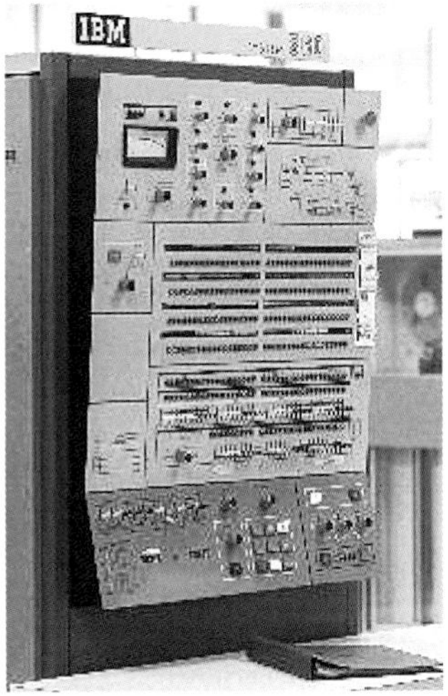

SYSTEM/360 MAINFRAME. **1964**

IBM PERSONAL COMPUTER. **1984**

M

In 1971 IBM announced the 8" diskette as a new type of storage medium for data.

In the 1970s, computers, which had come to be taken for granted in scientific research, now started to penetrate various fields of business and public life. Computer tills and terminals in banks became familiar to everyone; many of them were developed by IBM.

IBM had neglected the rapidly growing microcomputer market, but in 1981 it brought out its first PC. The company now acquired a completely new circle of customers such as private individuals, small companies, and schools. The original IBM PC had 18 kilobytes of store, one or two diskette drives, and could be equipped with a monochrome or colour monitor >208. As a break with IBM tradition, neither the processor nor the operating system (DOS) were developed in house but were bought in from outside. As is well known, DOS was written by the young company >MICROSOFT.

Though IBM set a long-term standard with this computer, its prices were very soon undercut by other companies producing successful copies. The IBM corporate structure was also ill prepared for consumer business, which led to a net loss of over 8 billion dollars in 1993. Louis Gerstner, who was called in from American Express that year, undertook some drastic measures to cut costs. When the Internet age dawned soon afterwards, IBM was better prepared: the client-server architecture again became relevant, and the company's strong focus in this field paid off.

In order to acquire a better market position, in 1995 IBM acquired Lotus, one of the largest software houses. Two years later, the IBM RS/6000 computer (known as Deep Blue with reference to the Deep Thought chess program and IBM's nickname Big Blue) beat the Russian grand master Gary Kasparov. The computer's ability to analyse a chessboard configuration in a fraction of a second proved superior to human intelligence in this historic duel.

///

MICROSOFT Founded in 1975 by William Gates and Paul Allen in Albuquerque, New Mexico

The company name was originally spelled Micro-Soft, then Micro Soft, and finally (from 1976)

M

Microsoft. Its first activity was writing a BASIC interpreter for the >MITS company.

Shortly afterwards, Bill Gates wrote an "open letter to hobbyists", published in a computer magazine, in which he condemned the piracy of software that was undermining the survival of small software companies.

PAUL ALLEN AND BILL GATES. **1968**

In 1979 the young company moved from New Mexico to Bellevue in the state of Washington. In that year 28 employees accounted for a turnover of almost 2.5 million dollars. By the time the >IBM PC was announced two years later, with MS-DOS as its operating system, both figures had grown sixfold. Gates' stroke of genius was to retain all marketing rights for MS-DOS; this clever move ensured that Microsoft rose to become the market leader, its stock shares soared in value and its founders grew rich. The fact that IBM accepted the condition implies that the traditionally minded company underestimated the strategic importance of the PC market.

In 1983 Microsoft announced Windows, its own version of the graphical user interface of the Alto computer, but two years were to elapse before it was finally available. This tactic – early announcement followed by late delivery of a working product – was later copied by many software and hardware companies. In the meantime, in 1986, the company had moved to Redmond, Washington.

However, it was not until version 3.0, announced in 1990, that Windows became a serious competitor to >APPLE's graphical interface, the Finder. The successor, Windows 95, reached the shops in 1995 after an elaborate marketing campaign; in the first four days it sold a million copies.

In the same year Microsoft produced its Internet Explorer, in competition to the Netscape Navigator, until then the undisputed market leader in Internet browsers. Microsoft had taken surprisingly long to discover this field, but exploited it by linking the Explorer to the operating system. Such methods and

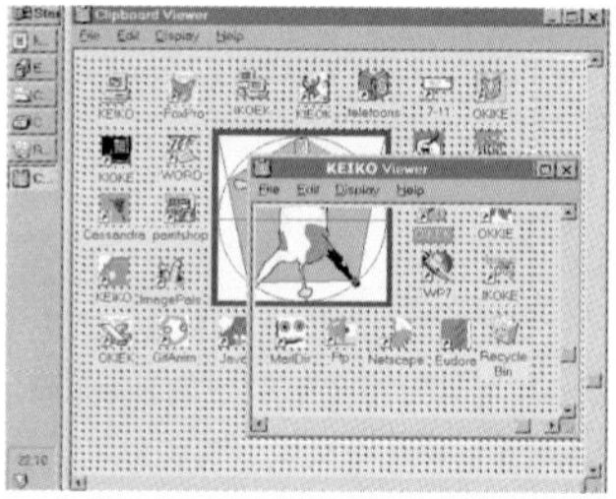

WINDOWS 3.1 OPERATING SYSTEM. **1992**

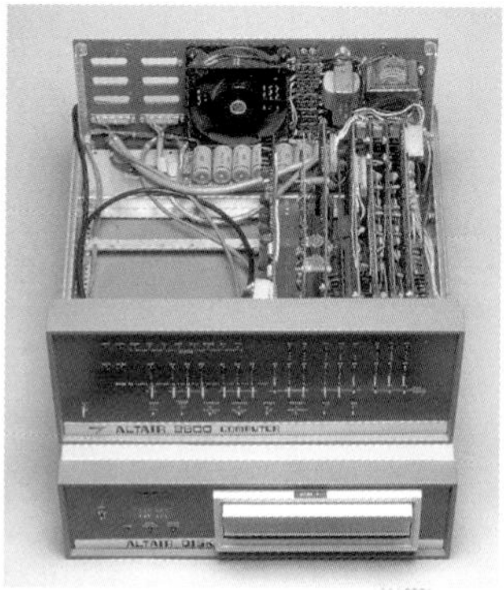
THE MITS ALTAIR 8800. **1974**

the fact that Microsoft's quasi-monopoly in operating systems was considered to stifle innovation, caused the US Justice Dept. to intervene in the late nineties. By then roughly 90% of the world's single-workstation computers were running under a Microsoft operating system.

///

MITS (MICRO INSTRUMENTATION TELEMETRY SYSTEMS) Founded in 1968 by Ed Roberts in Albuquerque, New Mexico

In the early years the company was a successful producer of electronic calculators. Business took a sudden downturn in 1972 when >TEXAS INSTRUMENTS released a chip combining all the functions of a calculator.

At just the same time, Roberts' friend, Les Solomon, technical editor of the magazine *Popular Electronics*, suggested developing a computer kit, something he felt do-it-yourself enthusiasts all over the USA were waiting for. So it came about that the December 1974 issue of the magazine bore a cover picture of the Altair 8800 >133, the first computer based on the new 8080 microprocessor >133. The kit could be ordered from MITS for $395.

The Altair was the first freely programmable computer at a price everyone could afford. MITS was overwhelmed by the sudden demand. Some intrepid fans even went so far as to camp in front of the company headquarters to be sure of getting a kit. The company grew so fast that its turnover reached 13 million dollars by the time Roberts sold out in 1977.

The Altair possessed very little store and no operating system – let alone software to run on it – so anyone who had successfully assembled the computer had to enter machine-code programs by means of switches. The output appeared on a row of LEDs. Acting on Roberts' initiative, the recently founded Micro-Soft company (>MICROSOFT) rewrote the popular BASIC >133 programming language to run on the Altair. Roberts sold it to purchasers of the Altair for $150, though separately it cost $500.

When the Pertec Computer Corporation took over MITS in 1977, the new owners were under the impression they had acquired the exclusive rights to

O

Microsoft BASIC. However, the ensuing court case awarded Microsoft the right to continue marketing its product. Pertec developed the Altair and sold a whole series of microcomputers, but the company was badly managed and soon disappeared from the market.

After selling out, Ed Roberts returned to his home state of Georgia where he completed his medical studies, and afterwards going into general practice.

///

OSBORNE COMPUTERS Founded in 1972 as Osborne and Associates by Adam Osborne in California; renamed Osborne Computer Corporation in 1979

Adam Osborne's entry into the computer market was publishing manuals for microcomputers based on the new Intel processors, for example *The Value of*

After selling his publishing business he met the engineer Lee Felsenstein in March 1980. Together, they forged plans to produce the first-ever portable computer. Felsenstein designed the Osborne 1 based on an Intel processor. It weighed about 15 kg and included a comprehensive set of professional software for writing, calculating, and programming – all for $1,795. It came out in 1981, and sold well, achieving a turnover of 70 million dollars in the following year.

Later improved models were the Vixen in 1982 and the Osborne Executive a year later. But other companies had entered the lucrative new market for portables; the company was not able to repeat its earlier success and was wound up in 1983.

Adam Osborne returned to the publishing world in 1984 when he founded Paperback Software International Ltd, a company specializing in inexpensive programs. After a series of legal dis-

THE FIRST PORTABLE PC: THE OSBORNE-1

R

THE UNIVAC 1 MAINFRAME. **1951**

ADVERTISEMENT FOR THE UNIVAC 120. **1953**

company in 1990 and returned to India, the land of his birth, where he again invested in computer technology.

///

REMINGTON RAND INC. Founded in 1927 by a merger of the Remington Typewriter Company and the Rand Kardex Corporation in Ilion, New York

E. Remington & Sons, a precursor of Remington Typewriter, marketed the first commercially successful typewriter in 1873. Further innovations followed, such as North America's first electric typewriter in 1925. Two years later the company merged with Rand Kardex, a family-run business making filing and index systems. The resulting Remington Rand Company specialised in office equipment, including calculators.

In 1949 Remington Rand brought out the 409, a computer whose successors were later sold under the names UNIVAC 60 and 120. The following year the company acquired the Eckert-Mauchly Computer Corporation, whose founders had played a major part in developing the pioneering ENIAC and BINAC computers. In 1951 Presper Eckert and John Mauchly completed the first commercial mainframe computer in the USA, the UNIVAC (Universal Automatic Computer). The US Census Bureau was the first customer for this vacuum-tube computer. The following year it achieved fame when it forecast Eisenhower's victory in the presidential election, based on a small sample of votes cast. A total of 46 of the UNIVAC I were built.

The UNIVAC 1103 Scientific, launched in 1953, was the first commercial computer using 'random-access memory'.

In 1955 Remington Rand merged with the Sperry Corporation to become Sperry Rand, which until 1983 sold various computers under the name UNIVAC. Particularly noteworthy was the System 1108, the first multiprocessor computer system, which came out in 1965. The historic name UNIVAC lives on in the company name Unisys, chosen when Sperry Rand's computer division merged with the data processing company Burroughs in 1986.

///

S

SILICON GRAPHICS INC. Founded in 1982 by Jim Clark and others in Mountain View, California

Silicon Graphics caused a furore in 1984 when it announced its powerful work stations using a separate processor, the '3D chip', for calculating and displaying graphics images.

At an early date the company thus discovered a market in office computers for professional applications involving graphics, simulation, and virtual reality. It soon became the market leader in this segment for customers who could not afford a supercomputer.

Since 1989 Silicon Graphics co-operated with Seymour Cray whose company >CRAY RESEARCH it acquired after Cray's death in 1996.

In 1993 Silicon Graphics developed the Graphics Engine, based on its own 3D chip, for the Japanese company Nintendo. This allowed computer games to operate at an unprecedented speed.

In 1996 the O2 visual workstation and the Onyx display supercomputer were announced, followed by the Octane visual workstation.

In 1999 Silicon Graphics completely changed its processor architecture, using chips made by the market leader Intel, in order to remain competitive. The company name was abbreviated to SGI.

///

SINCLAIR RESEARCH LTD Founded in 1961 by Clive Sinclair in Cambridge under the name Sinclair Radionics

Sinclair Radionics brought out its first product, the micro-amplifier, in 1962, and four years later a pocket TV known as the Microvision. But the early years were a struggle, and Clive Sinclair kept his

THE SINCLAIR ZX 80 HOMECOMPUTER, **1980**,

... AND ITS FOLLOW-UP MODEL, THE ZX 81. **1981**

head above water by writing articles and selling transistors he had tested. After a matchbox-sized radio, sold by mail order, in mid-1972 he announced one of the smallest pocket calculators of its day, the Executive, with an 8-digit display. Improved models with a wider scope were the Cambridge, the Oxford, and the Scientific Programmable which could execute simple sequences of instructions.

In 1976 Sinclair produced the first digital watch, known as the Black Watch, whose red LEDs showed the time when a button was pressed. Two years later there followed a pocket TV. Sinclair also produced radios and hi-fi components.

In mid-1979 Sinclair's company Science of Cambridge Ltd brought out a microcomputer kit under the name MK14, an inexpensive model for the rapidly growing circle of electronics hobbyists. It was so successful that he decided to produce a more complex computer. In 1980, his company, now known as Sinclair Computers Ltd, announced the ZX80 >158, the world's smallest and cheapest computer. With 1 kilobyte of store, its price was £80 for the kit or £100 for a ready-assembled computer. The ZX used a cheap membrane keyboard – soon nicknamed the Mickey Mouse keyboard – and was connected to a normal TV set. Data and programs could be saved to and read from a standard cassette recorder. The computer was popular, even in the USA; over 20,000 had been sold by the middle of the year.

In the spring of 1981 it was followed by the ZX81 in a matt black case; thanks to the use of a cheaper new chip the price fell to £70 and later only £50 >161. The storage capacity had also risen to 8 kilobytes, and floating-point arithmetic was now possible. The ZX81 was more popular than its predecessor, selling 50,000 within a year. The US watch company Timex produced it under licence and sold it in America as the Timex 1000. Shortly afterwards a tiny printer became available, which burned 32 characters per line into a narrow roll of silvery thermally sensitive paper; this was seen as little more than a toy.

The ZX Spectrum, with 16 or 48 kilobytes of store, was even more successful than the ZX81 >159. With 200,000 sold by early 1983 it represented a genuine threat to the >COMMODORE C64, the market leader among home computers. However, the Spectrum's Microdrive magnetic tape drive did not catch on and soon disappeared from the market.

MICRODRIVE FOR THE SPECTRUM. **1984**

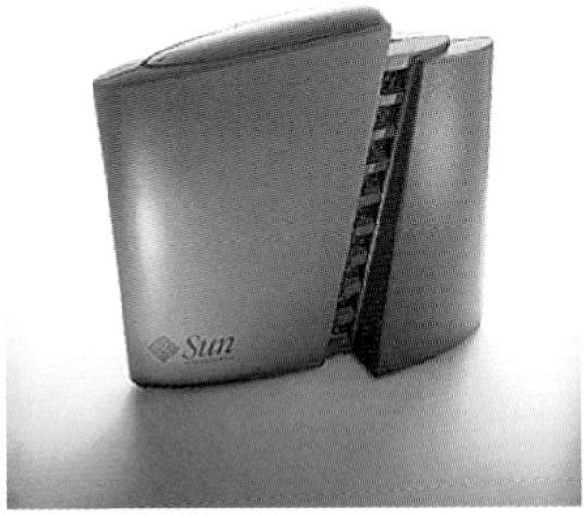

In 1984 the company brought out the improved Spectrum +, the Spectrum 128, and finally the QL (Quantum Leap). With its multi-tasking operating system and graphics interface with windows, the name was justified, but production difficulties meant that it was not a market success.

In 1985 Sinclair surprised the British public with a very compact and elegant electric tricycle available from computer shops. Driven by a car battery – with pedal assistance when necessary – the C5 had a top speed of 21 km/h but a range of only about 15 km before the battery needed recharging. Production ceased after 17,000 had been sold and the company had lost 7 million pounds.

The Sinclair company was taken over by Amstrad in 1986, and Sir Clive (as he now was) founded a new company by the name of Cambridge Computers. Its first product was the now legendary Z88 >219, an unusually lightweight but robust laptop

few seconds to 'boot up', since the entire software was held in ROM, allowing rapid work over long periods.

///

SUN MICROSYSTEMS Founded in 1982 by Andreas von Bechtolsheim in Palo Alto, California

From the start, the company philosophy was based on network computing, for which Sun was to provide some decisive impetus. The first product, released that same year, was a work station equipped with the TCP/IP network protocol long before it became a general standard. In 1984 Sun introduced its file-sharing system, with which several users in a network could have access to the same files.

In 1987 Sun became market leader for work stations, whose importance as network servers increased over the years. In 1989 the company succeeded in using

THE FIRST PC FROM TANDY RADIO-SHACK ...

... THE TRS-80. **1977**

T

that it fitted in a case only 10 cm high, nicknamed the pizza box. A year later Sun announced the first work station costing under $5,000.

In subsequent years Sun further extended its market leadership in single-processor and multi-processor servers, basing them on the UNIX operating system which was to become an absolute standard in this market segment.

In 1995 Sun defined a technological standard for the Internet with the Java programming language. Network applications can run on any computer where the compact Java interpreter is installed, making the Internet a kind of universal operating system.

///

TANDY / RADIOSHACK Founded in 1919 by Dave Tandy and Norton Hinckley in Dallas, Texas

The Tandy story began with the manufacture of shoes and other leather goods. By the end of the Second World War, the Hinckley-Tandy Leather Company had an annual turnover of more than 8 million dollars.

In 1963, by which time it had been renamed Tandy Corporation, it acquired a small chain of electronics shops knows as RadioShack, which was threatened with insolvency after four years of producing a cheap transistor radio – too cheap, in fact. From now on, Tandy's main field of business switched to developing, producing, and marketing electronic equipment. In 1972 RadioShack announced its first electronic pocket calculator, the EC-100, at a price of $130. In the mid-seventies the market for CB radio, which had formed RadioShack's main business, collapsed in the USA, and Tandy was forced to look for a new product.

The example of >MITS Altair 8800, announced in late 1974, inspired Tandy to develop its own microcomputer, but unlike the Altair kit, it was to be sold ready assembled, with a keyboard and monitor and adequate storage and also its own programming language. The TRS-80 Model I appeared in August 1977, based on the Zilog Z80 processor >137. The idea of a complete solution was enthusiastically received. It sold 55,000 in the first year, and Tandy was hardly able to meet the demand.

The Model II, available in 1979, was a proper Personal Computer, intended for the office market.

T

It had a faster processor, an 8" diskette drive, interfaces for printers and other peripherals, and many options for extending the scope. The TRS-80 Model III came out in 1980, followed by the Model IV in 1983 and the Tandy Color Computer that could display 16 colours on a normal colour TV.

The company brought out its first IBM-compatible PC in 1984 under the name Tandy 1000. It sold more than any other Tandy model, since it followed the de-facto standard but at a more affordable price.

The Tandy Corporation is now one of the largest manufacturers and sellers of micro-electronics and entertainment electronics.

///

TEXAS INSTRUMENTS Founded in 1930 by Clarence Karcher and Eugene McDermott in Texas

Until the early 1940s the company was known as Geophysical Services and concerned itself with prospecting for petroleum in Texas, Saudi Arabia, and the Persian Gulf. Then came the first contracts for the US armed forces, producing electronic equipment and even complete radar installations.

In 1952 the company, by now known as Texas Instruments, began producing the new transistors, and two years later announced the world's first transistor radio. Until the late 1950s TI remained the major manufacturer of transistors.

In 1958 the TI engineer Jack Kilby invented the integrated circuit almost simultaneously with Robert Noyce of Fairchild Semiconductors. This allowed a large number of tiny transistors to be incorporated in a single piece of semiconductor material. The first commercial use of the IC was a hearing aid, produced in 1964.

FROM AN ADVERTISEMENT FOR THE TI 99/A

In the year 2000 Kilby was awarded the Nobel Prize in physics for his achievement.

In 1967 TI introduced an electronic desk calculator, weighing over a kilogram in spite of its aluminium case. It operated on numbers of up to six digits, printing the results on a thermal printer, another TI invention. 1972 saw the introduction of the DataMath, the world's first scientific pocket calculator, at a price of $120. Although this was in no way a programmable computer, the roots of 'computing for all' lie partially in this device.

In 1974 TI announced a further innovation, the first microcontroller. Unlike the Intel 8008 that followed a year later, it was not freely programmable but was designed for a specific task, controlling a microwave oven.

In 1980 the company entered the home-computer market with the TI 99/4, soon to be followed by the TI 99/4A >144. This was able to display 32 x 24 characters in text mode, or up to 256 x 182 pixels in graphics mode, both in 16 colours, but was hampered by its phlegmatic BASIC as an operating system. There followed accessories such as a speech synthesizer and a cabinet containing a diskette drive and extension slots.

In 1983 TI announced two further home computers, the 99/2 and the 99/8; however they were not a match for the competition by >COMMODORE, >SINCLAIR, >APPLE, and others, and were a commercial failure. The Compact Computer of the same year was a precursor of the notebook computer and had a single-line display of 31 characters. It was also relatively unsuccessful, and Texas Instruments soon withdrew from the computer market.

TI remains one of the leading suppliers of microprocessors, storage chips, and other semiconductor devices.

///

THINKING MACHINES CORPORATION

Founded in 1983 by Danny Hillis and others in Mountain View, California

Even in his youth, Hillis acquired a reputation as an eccentric genius, when on a bet, he crossed the lake in front of the campus at the Massachusetts Institute

Z

of Technology on home-made hovercraft shoes. He studied under Marvin Minsky at the Artificial Intelligence Lab at MIT, and was awarded a degree for his parallel-processor design.

His company's first computer was the Connection Machine 1 in 1986 >99, with visual design by the Japanese artist Tamiko Thiel. It was the first massively parallel supercomputer, with 65,636 single-bit-processors all working simultaneously on the same problem. The rows of flickering red lights under the glass covers on the cabinets indicated that the machine was 'thinking'.

This CM-1, like its successor the CM-2, was a cube eight smaller cubes. The processors were mounted at the corners, with the connections between them running along the edges of the cubes. This network structure, based on the neurons in the brain, was the reason for the unsurpassed performance of these machines in which the connections were at

In 1991 Hillis brought out the CM-5 with a maximum performance of 64 gigaflops. It was thus more powerful than the supercomputers made by >CRAY RESEARCH. It was also considerably larger than the CM-1 and the CM-2 >100.

In the course of its short history, the Thinking Machines Corporation has installed roughly 70 Connection Machines. One of them found its way into the Museum of Modern Art in New York.

///

ZUSE KG Founded in 1949 by Konrad Zuse in Bad Hersfeld, Germany

Zuse began developing a program-controlled calculator in 1934. He built the first experimental models two years later, while still living with his parents in Berlin. The Z1, a hand-made mechanical calculating device, was completed in 1938, and

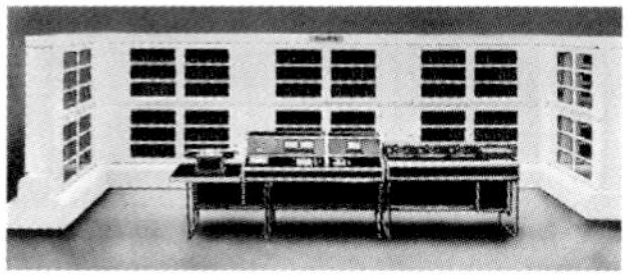

ZUSE Z5. **1950**

ZUSE Z23. **1961**

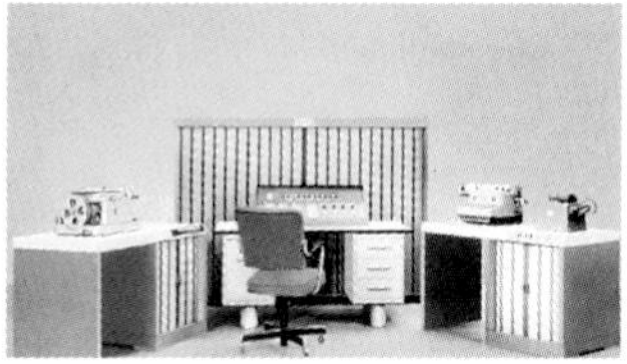

ZUSE Z31. **1963**

first programmable computer using electromechanical components. It was the size of three large refrigerators, and used the binary system; it could add, subtract, multiply, divide, and take square roots. Its storage capacity was 64 words of 22 bits.

After these early models had been destroyed by bombs in the war, Zuse founded his company in 1949 and installed the Z4 in the faculty of applied mathematics at the Swiss Polytechnic in Zurich. The company's other business activities in the early years included development contracts with the American company >REMINGTON RAND, whose UNIVAC was the first commercial computer.

Zuse also developed his last relay-based computer, the Z5, for the optics company Ernst Leitz in Wetzlar. The subsequent electronic models Z11, Z22, and Z23 were soon being used by a number of optics companies in central Europe for the complicated calculations involved in lens design.

In the mid-1950s Zuse's company equipped several German universities with digital computers, including Darmstadt, Hanover, Stuttgart, Berlin, and Freiburg.

The transition from vacuum-tube to transistor technology meant a considerable investment in capital and qualified staff, for which the German banks were not prepared to lend money as they saw no market for Zuse computers. As a result, the company was acquired by Brown Boverie & Cie of Mannheim, partially at first and fully in 1964. In the late sixties it was taken over by the electronics giant Siemens. Production of Zuse computers finally ceased in 1970, after a total of 250 had been built.

Konrad Zuse, who had left his company in 1964, died in 1995 at the age of 85. In the course of his life he had registered 50 patents. In the meantime he is recognised, even outside of Germany, as the original inventor of the computer.

Apple Computer Inc. (ed.) *"Macintosh Human Interface Guidelines"*, Cambridge/Massachusetts 1992 | **Augarten, Stan** *"Bit by Bit-An Illustrated History of Computers"*, New York 1984 | **Bolz, Norbert; Kittler, Friedrich u.a. (ed.)** *"Computer als Medium"*, Munich 1999 | **Bush, Vannevar** *"As we may think"*, in: *The Atlantic Monthly*, July 1945 | **Ceruzzi, Paul E.** *"A History of Modern Computing"*, Cambridge/Massachusetts 2000 | **Dick, Philip K.** *"Do Androids Dream Of Electric Sheep?"*, New York 1968 | **Engelbart, Douglas C.** *"Augmenting Human Intellect: A Conceptual Framework"*, Bericht an das *SRI*, Menlo Park/California 1962 | **Engelbart, Douglas C.** *"Special Considerations of the Individual as a User, Generator, and Retriever of Information"*, in: *American Documentation*, April 1961 | **Engelbart, Douglas C.; English, William u.a.** *"Display-Selection Techniques for Text Manipulation"* in: *IEEE Transactions on Human Factors in Electronics*, March 1967 | **Fallows, James** *"Navigating the Galaxies"*, in: *The Atlantic Monthly*, April 1996 | **Fallows, James** *"The Java Theory"*, in: *The Atlantic Monthly*, March 1996 | **Friedrich, Otto** *"Computer - Man of the Year"*, in: *Time Magazine*, 3. January 1983 | Gibson, William: *"Neuromancer"*, New York 1984 | **Gilder, George** *"The Coming Software Shift"*, in: *Forbes Magazine*, August 1995 | **Gilder, George** *"Telecosm"*, New York 1996 | **Grassmuck, Volker** *"Into the Muddy Waters of the Turing Galaxy – Death and Metaphoric Rebirth of the World in Media and of Media in the Universal Medium"*, Tokyo 1998 | **Grau, Oliver** *"Into the Belly of the Image"*, Berlin and Hamburg 1999 | **Greenberger, Martin** *"The Computers of Tomorrow"*, in: *The Atlantic Monthly*, May 1964 | **Heidenreich, Stefan** *"Icons"*, Berlin 1997 | Johnson, Steven: *"Interface Culture"*, Stuttgart 1999 | **Jungk, Robert; Mundt, Hans Josef (ed.)** *"Maschinen wie Menschen"*, Frankfurt am Main 1973 | **Laurel, Brenda (ed.)** *"The Art of Human-Computer Interaction"*, Cambridge/Massachusetts 1998 | **Levy, Steven** *"Artificial Life"*, New York 1992 | **Levy, Steven** *"Hackers – Heroes of the Digital Revolution"*, New York 1984 | **Licklider, James R.** *"Man-Computer Symbiosis"*, in: *IRE Transactions on Human Factors in Electronics*, March 1960 | **Licklider, James R.** *"The Computer as a Communication Device"*, in: *Science and Technology*, April 1968 | **Linzmeyer, Owen W.** *"Apple Confidential"*, San Francisco 1999 | **Martin, James** *"Telecommunications and the Computer"*, New York 1976 | **McLuhan, Marshall** *"Understanding Media – The Extensions of Man"*, London 1995 | **Negroponte, Nicholas** *"Being Digital"*, London 1999 | **Nelson, Theodor H.** *"Computer Lib – You Can and Must Understand Computers Now!"*, San Francisco 1974, Seattle 1987 | **Neumann, John von** *"The Computer and the Brain"*, New Haven and London 1986 | **Nielsen, Jacob** *"Designing Web Usability"*, Indianapolis 2000 | **Roch, Axel** *"Die Maus. Von der elektrischen zur taktischen Feuerleitung."*, in: *LAB. Jahrbuch der Kunsthochschule für Medien*, Cologne 1995 | **Rohrer, Tim** *"Feelings Stuck in a GUI Web: Metaphors, Image-Schemata, and Designing the Human Computer Interface"*, June 1995 | **Schneider, Birgit** *"Textile Processing. Punkte, Zeilen, Spalten – Vorläufer elektronischer Bildtechniken"*, Berlin 1999 | **Segaller, Stephen** *"Nerds 2.0.1 – A Brief History of the Internet"*, New York 1998 | **Shneiderman, Ben** *"Codex, memex, genex: The pursuit of transformational technologies"*, in: *Intl. Journal of Human-Computer Interaction*, 10, 1998 | **Shneiderman, Ben** *"Designing the User Interface"*, Cambridge/Massachusetts 1998 | **Simon, Herbert A.** *"Verändert der Computer unser Leben"*, in: *Bild der Wissenschaft*, June 1982 | **Springer, Martin**

"On Convergence", Berlin 1999 (not yet published) | **Steinberg, Steve G.** *"Lifestreams"*, in: Wired, Februar 1997 | **Stephenson, Neal** *"Snow Crash"*, New York 1993 | **Stephenson, Neal** *"Diamond Age"*, New York 1995 | **Stephenson, Neal** *"In the Beginning was the Command Line"*, New York 1999 | **Sterling, Bruce** *"The Hacker Crackdown"*, New York 1993 | **Sterling, Bruce** *"The Life and Death of Media"* (Vortrag), Montreal 1955 | **Weinberger, David** *"In Your Interface"*, in: *Wired*, September 1995 | **Weizenbaum, Joseph** *"Die Macht der Computer and die Ohnmacht der Vernunft"*, Frankfurt am Main 1977 | **Williams, Michael R.** *"A History of Computing Technology"*, Englewood Cliffs/New Jersey 1985 | **Wolf, Gary** *"Steve Jobs: The Next Insanely Great Thing"*, in: *Wired*, February 1996 | **Wolf, Stefan; Zimmerli, Walther C. (ed.)** *"Künstliche Intelligenz – Philosophische Probleme"*, Stuttgart 1994 | **Young, Jeffrey S.** *"Steve Jobs – The Journey is the Reward"*, Glenview/Illinois 1988 | **Zuse, Dr. Horst** *"Die Entwicklung der Programmiersprachen"*, Berlin 1999 | **Zuse, Konrad** *"Der Computer mein Lebenswerk"*, Berlin 1984 | **Zuse, Konrad** *"Die Rechenmaschine des Ingenieurs"*, Berlin 1936

APPENDIX III PHOTO CREDITS

Despite intensive research it has not always been possible to establish copyright ownership. Where this is the case we would appreciate notification.

www.adidas.com 272 | **Apple Computer Inc.** 165, 167, 222, 230, 234, 246, 247, 248, 249, 265, 266, 268, 269, 270, 276, 298, 299 | **BASF Corporate Archives, Ludwigshafen am Rhein** 076, 077, 078 | **Bilderdienst Süddeutscher Verlag** 047 | **Heiner Blum Fotoarchiv** 018, 038 | **Compaq Computer GmbH** 122, 123, 304. 307 | **Computer Museum History Center** 014, 016, 022, 024, 034, 035, 036, 046, 051, 057, 058, 084, 085, 086, 088, 089, 091, 092, 104, 106, 108, 109, 110, 111, 114, 118, 119, 120, 121, 124, 126, 127, 128, 129, 130, 137, 142, 144, 168, 172, 173, 202, 210, 228, 236, 302, 304, 307, 308, 313, 314, 317, 319, 320 | **Cray Inc./Tera Computers** 091, 306 | **Daft Life Ltd/Yosuke Komatsu** 296 | **defd-movies** 059, 060, 061, 064, 065, 190, 191, 192, 254, 255 | **dpa** 299 | **Deutsches Museum, Munich** 018, 038, 044, 079, 315 | **DJ Hype** 194 | **Filmbild Fundus Robert Fischer** 004, 193 | **Focus/Los Alamos National Labaratory/Science Photo Library** 027 | **Focus/David Parker/Science Photo Library** 090, 306 | **Focus/James King-Holmes/Science Photo Library** 283 | **Das Fotoarchiv/Philipp Hympendahl** 282 | **Das Fotoarchiv/Jochen Tack** 260 | **Das Fotoarchiv/SVT** 020, 030, 031, 032, 033 | **Frogdesign Germany GmbH** 253 | **Fujitsu Limited** 095, 096, 097, 103 | **Markus Gaab** 182, 184, 186, 194, 195, 272 | **Hewlett-Packard Germany GmbH** 148, 308, 309 | **Hitachi Japan** 102 | **IBM Germany GmbH** 006, 012, 013, 026, 042, 046, 047, 048, 054, 056, 062, 063, 066, 070, 071, 072, 073, 080, 081, 082, 083, 087, 094, 206, 208, 209, 212, 213, 217, 251, 252, 309, 311 | **Imagine Fotoagentur/Corbis/Westligh** 003 | **Infogrames Germany GmbH** 139, 141, 189, 300, 301 | **Intel Germany GmbH** 132 | **J-phone** 288 | **Stefan Landrock** 218 | **Nokia Germany GmbH** 293 | **NTT DoCoMo** 280, 290, 291, 292 | **Paturi Bildarchiv** 008, 010, 021 | **Philips Electronics** 283 | **Seiko Instruments Inc.** 286, 287 | **Sharp Electronics Corp.** 278, 279 | **Smithsonian Institution/National Museum of American History** 166 | **Sony Germany** 274 | **Sony Japan** 294, 295 | **Stanford University, Department of Special Collections** 237, 238, 239, 241 | **Vogel Medien Würzburg** 127, 136, 137, 144, 146, 149, 154, 158, 159, 160, 174, 175, 196, 198, 199, 200, 211, 214, 215, 216, 217, 224, 242, 250, 303, 304, 314, 317, 318, 320 | **Dr. Horst Zuse** 322

A

ABC Electronics
- ABC 26 *199*
Adidas
- Micropacer *273*
ALGOL *133*
Allen, Paul *133*
Amdahl
- 470 V/6 *086*
Amdahl, Gene *086*
Andreesen, Marc *258*
Apple Computer Inc. *298*
- Apple I *140, 164*
- Apple II *141, 145, 155, 169, 170, 171, 231*
- Apple IIc *250*
- Apple IIe *165, 171*
- Apple III *165*
- Desktop Mouse 1 *238*
- LISA *230, 231, 232, 246*
- Mac OS *232*
- Mac OS 8.5 *265*
- Macintosh *232, 233, 234, 246, 275*
- Macintosh LC III *171*
- Macintosh Se *243*
- Macintosh System 1.0 *243*
- Macpaint *248*
- Newton MessagePad 2000 *276*
- PowerMac G3 Model Yosemite *267*
- PowerMac G4 Cube *268, 269*
- Titanium PowerBook G4 *271*
ARPAnet *256, 258*
ASCII *049, 112*
Assembler *116, 177, 225*
Atari Inc. *299*
- "Pole Position" *175*
- "Pong" *136, 139*
- 400 *189*
- 800 *189*
- 800 XL *144, 174*
- VCS 2600 *136, 141, 184*
Atkinson, Bill *233*

B

Babbage, Charles *008, 009, 010, 013, 262*
BASF *076, 077, 078*
BASIC *133, 136, 137, 138, 140, 146, 147, 162, 177, 203, 204*
Berners-Lee, Tim *257, 258*
Bradley, Milton *194, 195*
Bricklin, Dan *141*
Browne, Sir Thomas *008*
Burroughs *074, 075*
Bush, Vannevar *020, 055, 226, 262*
Bushnell, Nolan *142*

C

Clark, Jim *259*
Colossus Computer *028, 029*
Commodore Computer *302*
- CBM *144*
- CBM 2001 *203*
- PET 2001 *144, 155, 156*
- VC 20 *144*
Compaq *304*
- Desktop Pro PC *214*
- Portable PC *214*
Control Data Corporation *305*
- CDC 6600 *068, 083*
- CDC 7600 *088, 089*
- HR 70 *085*
Convergence *278*
CP/M-Operating System *138, 147, 204*
Cray Research *306*
- Cray X-MP *090*
- Cray-2 *91, 092*
Cray, Seymour *083, 092, 100*

D

Difference Engine *008, 010, 262*
Digital Equipment Corporation *307*
- PDP-1 *107, 109, 112, 118, 119*
- PDP-8 *108, 109, 116*
- PDP-8e *120, 121, 122, 123*
- PDP-8i *115*
- PDP-10 *126*
- PDP-11 *127, 128, 129*
DOS-Operating System

E

Eckert, J. Presper *021, 045*
EDVAC *020, 023*
Eisenhower, Dwight D. *045, 051*
Engelbart, Douglas *226, 227, 228, 229, 236, 257*
ENIAC *020, 021, 023, 026, 027*
Ethernet *256, 257*

F

Fairchild Semiconductors *108*
FORTRAN *047, 133, 225*
Fujitsu
- Facom M-320 *096*
- Facom M-340 *096, 097*
- Facom M-380 *097*
- Facom V-870 *096*
- Facom VP-100 *095*

G

Gates, Bill *133, 224*
Gossling, James *259*
Greenberger, Martin *055, 107*

H

Harvard Mark I > IBM
Hewlett-Packard *308*
- HP 35 *148*
Hillis, Danny *099, 101*
Hitachi
- GS 8900 *103*
- MP 6000 *102*
Hoff, Ted *117*
Hollerith, Hermann *012, 263*
Honeywell
- H-316 *124, 125*
- Kitchen Computer *104*
HTML *257, 258*
http *258*
HyperCard *233*

I

IBM *309*
- 3031 *082*
- 4341 *087*
- 701 *046, 047*
- 702 *047*
- 704 *047*
- 705 *048*
- AP *217*
- Floppy disk *138*
- Harvard Mark I (ASCC) *019, 020, 021, 023, 045, 046*
- Magnetic tape system 3422 *094*
- Monitors:
3278 *210*
3279 *208*
4878 *206*
5292 *209*
- PC AT *213*
- PC XT *212*
- PS/2 Model 65 SX/80 *216*

- Stretch *056*
- System/360 *049, 054, 067, 068, 069, 070, 071*
  Model 30 *067*
  Model 75 *062, 067*
  Model 91 *063*
- System/370 *069*
  Model 115 *080*
  Model 135 *072*
  Model 148 *072*
  Model 168 *081*
- Thinkpad 701 *251*
Imsai
- 8080 *133, 150*
Intel *108, 112, 117, 282, 283*
- 4004 *132*
- 8080 *133*
Intertec
- SuperBrain *198*

J

Jacquard, Joseph-Marie *011, 012*
Java *259, 261*
Jobs, Steve *141, 167, 170, 231, 244, 253*
Joystick *136, 182*

K

Kare, Susan *240, 241*
Kay, Alan *231*
Kilby, Jack *108*
Kildall, Gary *138*

L

Leibniz, Gottfried Wilhelm von *009, 011*
Licklider, James *256, 287*
LINUX *281*
Lisberger, Steven *190*
Logo-Programming language *231, 233*

M

Magnavox
- "Odyssey" *136*
Mauchly, John W. *021, 045*
Metcalfe, Bob *256, 259*
Micropro *145*
Microsoft *069, 133, 137, 312*
- DOS-Operating System *138, 146, 147, 204, 243*
- Excel *235*
- Explorer *259*
- Windows *178, 233, 264,*
- Windows 1.0 *232*
- Word for Windows *235*
MITS *313*
- Altair 8800 *130, 133, 134*
Moore, Gordon *112*
Mouse *226, 227, 229, 236, 237*
Mouse House
- Hawley X063X-Mouse *239*

N

Nelson, Ted *257*
Netscape Navigator *259*
Neumann, John von *009, 020, 023, 047, 259*
Next
- Next Cube *253*
Nokia *262, 293*
Noyce, Robert *108*
NTT DoCoMo *262, 280, 292*
- D 502 I *291*
- F 502 I *290*
- P 503 I *291*
- P 209 IS *290*

O

Olivetti
- M 20 *146*
- PCS M 21 *217*
Olsen, Kenneth H. *115, 132*
OS/2-Operating System *069*
OS/360-Operating System *069*
Osborne, Adam *147, 204*
Osborne Computers *314*
- Osborne-1 *147, 203, 205*

P/Q

Papert, Seymour *231, 233*
Pascal-Programming language *225*
PhotoShop *249*
Processor Technology
- Sol Terminal Computer *152*
QuarkXpress *233*

R

Raskin, Jeff *275*
Remington Rand *315*
- UNIVAC 1 *014, 044, 046, 051*
- UNIVAC 1110 *084*
- UNIVAC 490 *058*
- UNIVAC III *058*
- UNIVAC-LARC *057*
Robotron
- EC 2640 *079*
Russell, Ken *059*

S

SAGE-Programm *023, 025, 034, 035, 036*
Schickard, Wilhelm *008, 011*
Scott, Ridley *232*
Seagate *145*
Seiko
- Ruputer wrist computer *286, 287*
Sharp
- MI-10 *279*
- Zaurus PI-7 000 *278*
Shockley, William *107*
Sholes, Christopher *112*
Signetics
- Instructor 50 *200*
Silicon Graphics *259*
Sinclair, Clive *162, 219*
Sinclair Research Ltd. *317*
- Spectrum QL *159*
- Z 88 *219, 220, 221*
- ZX 80 *158, 163*
- ZX 81 *136, 137, 161, 162, 163*
Sketchpad *225*
Smalltalk-Programming language *231*
Sony
- AIBO-Robot dogs Model ERS-210 *294*
- Glasstron Goggles *274*
- Memory Stick 211 *295*
Sun Microsystems *259, 261, 319*
Supercalc *204*
Sutherland, Ivan *225, 226, 228*

T

Tandy RadioShack *319*
- TRS-80 *137, 141, 155, 172, 173*
Tarkovsky, Andrej *061*
Teletype 33 ASR *109, 110, 111, 112*
Televideo
- Portable IC *215*
- TS 804 *215*
Tennenhouse, David *283*
Texas Instruments *108, 320*
- TI 59 *149*
- TI 99/4A *144*
Thinking Machines Corporation *322*
- Connection Machine-1 *099*
- Connection Machine-2 *098*
- Connection Machine-5 *100*
TiVo *281*
Tulip Computers
- System One *196*
Turing, Alan Mathison *009, 014, 263*

U/V

UNIX *258*
URL (Universal Ressource Locator) *258*
Vaucanson, Jacques de *009, 011, 012*
Ventura Publisher *233*
VisiCalc *141, 145, 170*
Volatilisation *277, 282, 285*

W

Watson, Thomas *044, 068*
Whirlwind-Computer *022, 023, 024, 025, 107, 225*
WordStar *145, 204*
World Wide Web *257, 258, 260, 261*
Wozniak, Steven *141, 167, 169, 244*

X/Y/Z

Xerox PARC
- 8010 Star *229*
- Alto *228, 231, 256, 276*
Zilog
- Z 80 *133, 163*
- Z 81 *133*
Zuse KG *323*
- V 1 *019*
- Z 1 *019, 039, 040*
- Z 3 *018, 019, 039, 040*
- Z 4 *039, 040, 041*
Zuse, Konrad *009, 018, 039, 040, 041*

ACKNOWLEDGEMENTS

Martin Springer and Bernd Curanz (Convergence, Berlin), Barbara Koch and Klaus Efler (IBM Germany), Uschi Maucher and Karl-Heinz Panse (Factory 7 IBM Bildarchiv, Stuttgart), Daniela Bartolic (Hewlett-Packard Germany), Bianca Meyer (Frogdesign Germany), Maike Fuhlrott (Nokia Germany), York Seewald and Lothar Schmidt (Vogel Verlag, Würzburg), Birgit Weislmaier (Intel Germany), Tamiko Thiel (Munich), Dr. Horst Zuse (Berlin), Celine Klötzer (Häberlein & Mauerer, Berlin), Miriam Hoffmann (Sony Germany), Christiane Hennet (Deutsches Museum, Munich), Felix Krause (Infogrames Germany), Kirsten Sommer (Infogrames Germany), Marion Moja (Silicon Graphics Germany), Karen Kriesel (Compaq Germany), Anette Wolpert (BASF Germany), Dietmar Henneka (Stuttgart), Sabine Mende (Wacom Europe), Karyn Mathews, Dag Spicer and Chris Garcia (The Computer Museum History Center, California), Alex Soojung-Kim Pang (Stanford University, Palo Alto), Herbie Pfeifer (Montgomery & Pfeifer, San Francisco), Tim Streeter (Cray America, San Francisco), Birthe Walter and John Randolphs (San Francisco), Aki Shimazu (Sony Japan), Nancy Ikehara and Toshiaki Koike (Fujitsu Japan), Norihiro Watanabe (Casio Japan), Norio Hasegawa (NTT DoCoMo Japan), Yasuo Satomi and Asuka Shibata (TASCHEN Japan) and Simone Philippi, Anja Lenze, Katrin Becker (TASCHEN Cologne).

Dorothea Mertes, Felix Nowack and Anki Weiner, Jah Fish, Alex Geh, Frederik Knothe and Maren Beuscher, Hartmut Beuscher, Stefan Landrock, Kerstin Braun, Oliver Helbig, Ruth Wurster and Gerd Hatje, Markus Gaab, Stephanie Wurster and Jesko Fezer, Henrik Wurster, Elisabeth and Dieter Wurster. To Okko Müller.

IMPRINT

Hohenzollernring 53, D-50672 Köln

www.taschen.com

COORDINATION: Simone Philippi, Katrin Becker, Cologne

ENGLISH TRANSLATION: Hugh Casement, Wörth

DESIGN: Christian Wurster, Felix Nowack, Berlin

PRODUCTION: Ute Wachendorf, Cologne

Printed in France

ISBN 3-8228-1293-5

EXIT
Happy Hospital!
Why are so many older hospitals grim, colorless places? Tradition, or inertia, or whatever it was that caused this unhappy situation is fast being overcome by architectural designers who recognize the actual therapeutic value of color and beauty to the sick . . . and to those who serve the sick.
Today, architects the world over are using Formica* to prove that a cheerful material can be more sanitary and less costly to maintain than the drab, uninteresting interiors of the past.
For instance, here in the Good Samaritan in Cincinnati, Formica is on walls and window stools in training wards, corridors and nurses' dormitory rooms. Formica's smooth, tough, long-wearing surface actually repels dirt . . . what dirt might adhere to its non-porous surface wipes clean with the swish of a damp cloth.
Formica is unharmed by alcohol, mild acids, alkalies and boiling water.
Beauty Bonded
FORMICA
at Home with People
at Work in Industry

Cadillac
... First Choice - Where Choice is Unrestricted
The great majority of motorists, if left entirely free to select the car they would most like to own, would undoubtedly choose a Cadillac. For forty-four years, the knowledge has grown that Cadillac is never built to meet a price—or to harmonize with any particular economic situation. It is built to provide the finest personal transportation it is practical to produce—and there is no further restriction on those who design and manufacture it. It is only natural that such strict adherence to such a high purpose, over such a long period of time, should have placed Cadillac in a class apart—that it should long since have become the world's most desirable motor car.
CADILLAC MOTOR CAR DIVISION • GENERAL MOTORS CORPORATION

A HIGH HONOR FOR YOUR DAUGHTER
AMERICAN
LOCOMOTIVE

"LOOK MOMMY!
We left some for you"
Peanut Crunch Peanut Butter is a great thrill for kiddies . . . a great treat for mom and pop! With meals — or in-between, everybody likes Peanut Crunch Peanut Butter, the blended combination of crispy, toasted peanut bits and smooth, delicious peanut butter. Contains essential vitamins that help build strong bodies. Look for Peanut Crunch Peanut Butter on your grocer's shelves.
HOLSUM
Peanut Crunch
PEANUT BUTTER

USA-1958
A BOLD NEW CAR FOR A BOLD NEW GENERATION
BOLD PONTIAC

What's cooking?
A completely different holiday recipe—glorious sunshine, ever-changing scenery, amazing contrasts in breath-taking, adventurous South Africa! Make South Africa your travel adventure of a lifetime . . . see your Travel Agent or SATOUR for free and friendly information.
SOUTH AFRICA
SOUTH AFRICAN TOURIST CORPORATION
475 Fifth Avenue, New York 17, N.Y.
I would like to know more about a South African holiday.
NAME
STREET
CITY
ZONE
STATE

She's touching bottom . . . in efficiency
Now everybody's on top
with Moore Speediset . . . 1 typing
instead of 4 systems . . . 4 typings
A diver's helmet wouldn't hamper her any more than the slipshod system the whole office had to live with. Efficiency was lacking, work was delayed, deliveries fell behind. This showed up in Company earnings because the cost of doing business was kept high.
Things improved after a Moore man looked at 4 separate forms that slowed operations. In their place he designed a 4-part Moore Continuous Speediset form that combines—in one typing—invoice, shipping memo, packing slip, label and delivery receipt. It saves 3 typings, speeds work, keeps cost down.
Want top efficiency? Call in the Moore man. He offers you the widest range of forms. He knows how to design the right business form for every form of business.
MOORE
BUSINESS FORMS, INC.

There's always something going on in LAS VEGAS!
HOTEL
The Fabulous Resort Hotel Strip
Hotel LAST FRONTIER · FLAMINGO · EL RANCHO
THUNDERBIRD · DESERT INN · SAHARA

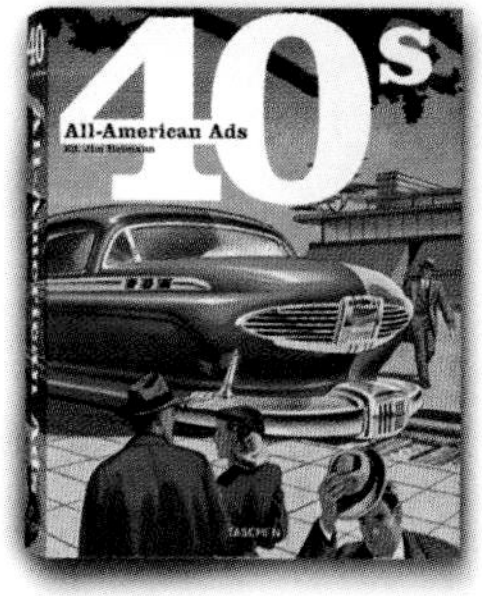

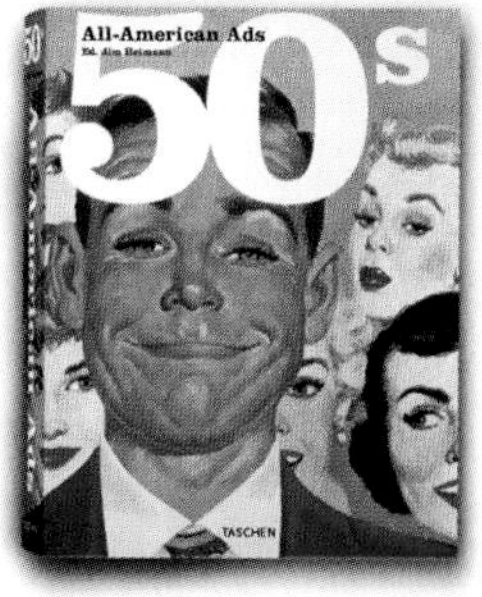

All-American Ads of the 40s Jim Heimann / English/German/French / Flexi-cover, 768 pp., 1,000 ills. / US$ 40 / € 32 / £ 20 / DM 49,95 / PES 4.995 / ¥ 4,500

All-American Ads of the 50s Jim Heimann / English/German/French / Flexi-cover, 928 pp., 1,400 ills. / US$ 40 / € 32 / £ 20 / DM 49,95 / PES 4.995 / ¥ 4,500

Zoom back in time to mid-century America.
For our new series covering the entire century, we've collected thousands of ads for cars, travel, technology, liquor, cigarettes, movies, appliances, furniture, war bonds, toothpaste, you name it—the full spectrum of products and services available to the eager American consumer. Wonderfully illustrated, these ads in our first two installments portray an accurate picture of the colorful capitalism that dominated the spirit of the 40s and 50s. Surprisingly, not too many of these ads would make it past today's censors: politically incorrect more often than not, these advertisements touting the glories of the all-American, squeaky-clean persona and the white, nuclear family often hint at the sexist and racist mentality of the time. Bursting with fresh, crisp colors, these ads have been digitally retouched to look as bright and new as the day they first hit the newsstands.

The 40s
World War II brought unprecedented pride and prosperity to the American people and nothing better mirrors the new wave of consumerism and progress than the ads of the time. From Western Electric communication tools (for "the modern battlefield") to Matsom sea liners ("Toward a Richer Tomorrow") to Seagram's whiskey (for "Men Who Plan Beyond Tomorrow") to the Hoover vacuum ("For every woman who is proud of her home"), the flood of products and services for every occasion or whim was practically endless. It's hard to believe that the company who made your ultra-compact mobile phone was once advertising portable radios with "Motorola: *More* radio pleasure for *less* money," or that Electrolux didn't have any qualms about using Mandy, the portly black maid, to promote their new silent refrigerators: "Lor-dy, it sure *is* quiet!" You'll also find some familiar products that, amazingly, haven't changed at all over the years, such as juicy Dole pineapples and wholesome Campbell's soup. Yumm.

The 50s
As McCarthyism swept across the United States and capitalism was king, white America enjoyed a feeling of pride and security that was reflected in advertising. Carelessly flooding society with dangerous misinformation, companies in the 50s promoted everything from vacations in Las Vegas, where guests could watch atomic bombs detonate, to cigarettes as healthy mood-enhancers, promoted by a baby who claims his mother feels better after she smokes a Marlboro. From "The World's Finest Automatic Washer" to the Cadillac which "Gives a Man a New Outlook," you'll find a colorful plethora of ads for just about anything the dollar could buy. Oh, and "Have you noticed how many of your neighbors are using Herman Miller furniture these days?" If only you could really travel back in time and pick up a few chairs for your collection …

Almost real
Building women out of bits and bytes

TASCHEN goes digital!

The first book in our groundbreaking new series on digital culture focuses on beauty and cutting-edge computer-generated female characters. Whereas most books on digital creation concentrate on technique and include detailed "how-tos," *Digital Beauties* is all about exploring the artistic achievements of today's best designers without a lot of complicated technical jargon. Here you'll discover a host of digital beauties from all around the world and a dizzying array of styles and techniques—moody black-and-white nudes, surreal portraits, Lara Croft-style adventure chicks, sleek ultra-futuristic babes, etc. Both 2D and 3D design are covered, with an emphasis on the latter; some images are so stunningly lifelike it's hard to believe they're 100% computer generated. In an age in which virtual characters are being copyrighted left and right, it's about time you got to know some of the "people" you'll be coming across in the future on TV and even in film; one such example is Steven Stahlberg's lovely Webbie Tookay, the first virtual model to sign with Elite Digital Models. Some of these digital creations have even been included in "sexiest women" lists—along with real humans, of course!

- Almost 100 artists from all around the world, with biographical and contact information and samples of their best work
- Inspirational approach with stylistic advice for amateur creators
- Stunning graphics

Digital Beauties Julius Wiedemann / English/German/French and English/French/Japanese editions / Flexi-cover, 576 pp., 800 ills.
US$ 40 / € 32 / £ 20 / DM 49,95 / PES 4.995 / ¥ 4,500

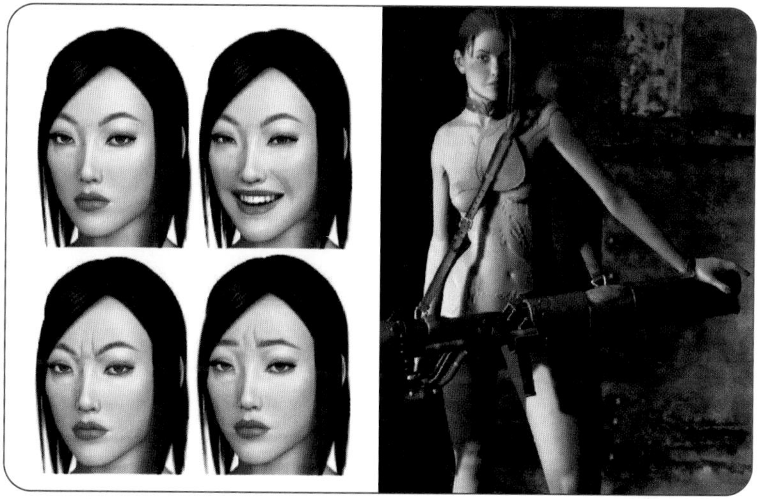

Future tense

Designers ahead of time

How do today's brightest and best designers see the future of design? What are the defining elements of form, function, and aesthetics at the turn of the millennium? In response to these burning questions, we've put together *the* definitive book on cutting-edge product design, furniture, ceramics, glassware, and textiles. Including a cross section of the world's most influential designers, from superstars to newcomers, and stunning images of their most progressive work, *Designing the 21st Century* is like no other book of its kind. Making it especially unique are the contributions from all designers featured: each sent us his or her answer to the question, "What is your vision for the future of design?" Crack the book to see how their revolutionary ways of thinking take shape. The experimental concepts and predictions featured here will serve as an important reference for generations to come—when researchers in 2101 want to see what was going on in design a century earlier, this is the book they'll turn to.

The authors:
Charlotte J. Fiell studied at the British Institute, Florence and at Camberwell School of Arts & Crafts, London, where she received a BA (Hons) in the History of Drawing and Printmaking with Material Science. She later trained with Sotheby's Educational Studies, also in London. **Peter M. Fiell** trained with Sotheby's Educational Studies in London and later received an MA in Design Studies from Central St Martin's College of Art & Design, London.
Together, the Fiells run a design consultancy in London specializing in the sale, acquisition, study and promotion of design artifacts. They have lectured widely, curated a number of exhibitions and written numerous articles and books on design and designers, including TASCHEN's *Charles Rennie Mackintosh, William Morris, 1000 Chairs, Design of the 20th Century* and *Industrial Design A–Z*. They also edited the six-volume Decorative Art series published by TASCHEN.